Investment Illusions

A Savvy Wall Street Pro Explodes Popular Misconceptions About the Markets

Martin S. Fridson

JOHN WILEY & SONS, INC.

New York · Chichester · Brisbane · Toronto · Singapore

To my mother, Mariann Moore, who
started me out with one share of Lear
Siegler common as a gift for my 14th
birthday and never doubted I would turn
it into something.

In recognition of the importance of preserving what has been written, it is a
policy of John Wiley & Sons, Inc., to have books of enduring value printed on
acid-free paper, and we exert our best efforts to that end.

This publication is designed to provide accurate and authoritative information
in regard to the subject matter covered. It is sold with the understanding that
the publisher is not engaged in rendering legal, accounting, or other
professional service. If legal advice or other expert assistance is required, the
services of a competent professional person should be sought.

Library of Congress Cataloging-in-Publication Data

Fridson, Martin S.
    Investment illusions: a savvy Wall Street pro explodes popular
misconceptions about the markets / Martin S. Fridson.
        p. cm.
    Includes bibliographical references and index.
    ISBN 0-471-56950-X (cloth)   ISBN 0-471-15551-9 (paper)
    1. Investment analysis.   2. Stocks.   3. Bonds.   4. Securities.
    I. Title.
    HG4529.F75   1993
    332.63 2—dc20   92-38939

Printed in the United States of America

10 9 8 7 6 5 4 3 2 1

Preface

Many books about stocks and bonds appear every year. Almost nobody gets rich by following their so-called "proven methods" for beating the market. Still, the stream of investment advice continues unabated.

Surely, the readers of these volumes must notice that they're failing to become independently wealthy, but somehow they never abandon hope of discovering the magic formula. Their disenchantment applies only to the latest messiah whose "amazingly simple system" has failed to work miracles.

Thanks to this perennial optimism, a comparatively easy method exists for writing a well-received investment book. First, promise spectacular results to those who follow your rules. Then, be purposefully vague about what the rules are. This simple device will prevent anybody from proving whether your system works or not.

Readers won't feel cheated, provided your prose is sufficiently witty. And if wit isn't your strong suit, you can indulge in denunciations of the two-bit politicians who are destroying the economy. Be sure, as well, to throw in some psychobabble and a few self-help nostrums. Finally, promote your book through television appearances in which you establish yourself as an unforgettable character (irrepressible punster, condescending oracle, unkempt genius, etc.).

Alternatively, you might write an investment book that actually imparts useful information. This is doing it the hard way. You can't rely on an established, cookie-cutter approach. Still, there are a few dependable ways of helping readers to invest their money intelligently.

For one thing, you can take a critical look at "sure-fire" investment strategies that aren't all they're cracked up to be. Misuse and misinterpretation of financial numbers is another rich vein. Additionally, you can provide an immense service by detailing classic scams and explaining how to avoid them. You might also devote some space to shortcomings of the information sources commonly available to investors. To wrap it up, you could discuss the relative attractiveness and efficiency of various sectors of the financial markets.

Investment Illusions is the second, less conventional sort of book. It denies the possibility of making easy money. You'll find in it no claims of fabulous bargains that others have unaccountably overlooked. Instead, I've undertaken laborious research to produce conclusions that are often unglamorous. My experience tells me that this approach will be more profitable for you in the long run.

Don't imagine for a moment that I've written this book for purely altruistic reasons. There's a practical, commercial motive for creating a book that debunks get-rich-quick schemes instead of extolling them: The competition isn't nearly as intense.

Why haven't more authors found out about this opportunity? I suspect it's because of a self-selection process in the investment field. Most of the people who go into this line of work are True Believers. They seek jobs as stockbrokers, securities analysts, or financial reporters because they love the market. Price charts, esoteric hedging strategies, frenetic trading, and the romance of fortunes being won and lost—investment professionals love everything about the securities business. Above all, they love the game of trying to make a killing. Even many level-headed professors of finance, dedicated though they are to scientific analysis of the capital markets, pursue astonishingly harebrained speculations once they leave the classroom.

Mixed in with the sometimes credulous majority, however, are a few inveterate skeptics. They're wary of newfangled investments. They resist concepts that were discredited long ago but are now being dusted off again. When the press hails a market forecaster who happens to be on a hot streak, these veterans bide their time. They've seen countless geniuses come and go. And they've observed an even larger number of companies that have posted astounding rates of earnings growth, only to collapse amidst allegations of accounting trickery and fraud.

My Wall Street colleagues have a name for stick-in-the-mud money managers who never want to play the currently fashionable game. They call these fuddy-duddies "old women." (The nickname qualifies as a twofer of political incorrectness.)

To be fair about it, the personality quirks of some of these naysayers can be trying. Abrasiveness is not unknown among them. A few insist on bringing the conversation around to their hobbyhorses on the slightest pretext. On the other hand, hard-core skeptics don't tend to lose big piles of money for their clients. By rejecting a lot of bad investment ideas, they avoid the debacles that periodically engulf their less discriminating peers. Even if they also miss a few profitable trades, their stubbornness produces a net benefit.

Certainly, the "I'm-from-Missouri" types have taught me many more valuable lessons about investments than the enthusiasts have. One of my goals in this book has been to pass along the wisdom of those who demand solid evidence that an investment makes sense.

Happily, the securities markets generate excellent examples of folly and knavery on a steady basis. I've consequently been able to illustrate most of my points with real-life examples. As an additional stroke of good fortune, many of the incidents uncovered in my research combine colorful characters and amusing sidelights. The result, I hope, is a book that manages to entertain while delivering a serious message.

Through patient effort and self-control, you can enhance your net worth by sharing in worldwide economic growth. More aggressive methods might make you rich beyond dreaming, but they also carry the risk of wiping you out.

The True Believers wish it weren't so. At times, they manage to ensnare others, so infectious is their determination to earn something for nothing. That's when *Investment Illusions* will be most valuable. Pick it up and browse if you ever catch yourself thinking that investment success is the product of anything other than disciplined thought and intensive effort.

MARTIN S. FRIDSON

New York, New York
February 1993

Acknowledgments

I couldn't possibly have written this book without the help of Irving and Margot Sisman. They provided time, space, and sustenance, and invaluable commentary, as the book emerged chapter by chapter. Equally important, I have Dr. and Mrs. Sisman to thank for the availability of my most important adviser, Elaine Sisman Fridson. It was she who masterminded the physical production of the manuscript, while at the same time passing along numerous tidbits to enliven the text.

Much less would have come of our efforts if Karl Weber of John Wiley & Sons, Inc., hadn't proposed a format of short, highly focused chapters. If *Investment Illusions* succeeds in sustaining the interest of readers who are nonprofessionals in the stock market, it's largely thanks to him.

Having lined up family support, a concept, and a stylistic approach, I lacked just one element essential to completing the project. I didn't have an independent income that would afford me the time to do all of the necessary research. Jim Dignan proved to be the next best thing. For his long hours of poring over microfiche, I'm immensely grateful.

Many others contributed ideas, editorial suggestions, and encouragement. Some of the ideas and suggestions ended up on the cutting room floor, but the encouragement all found its way into the book. With apologies to anyone I've left out, I acknowledge my vast debt to Ed Altman, Jeff Bersh, Rich Byrne, Mike Cherry, Anne Christopulos, Mark DeBellis, the Honorable Conrad B. Duberstein, Dave Fitton, Howard and Cathy Fridson, Ken Goldberg, Marty Gruber, Glenn Haberfield, Evelyn Harris, David Hawkins, Tony Kao, Rebecca Keim, Joe Kim, Les Levi, Mao-chu Luo, Jeff Maitles, Amin Majidi, Bill Mastoris, Ann Marie Mullan, Rich Rolnick, Peter Spiro, Jeff Stambovsky, Sharyl Van Winkle, Dave Waill, Steve Weiss, and Mark Zand.

M.S.F.

Contents

Part One   *Why Bad Things Happen to Good Investment Strategies*

1	On the Contrary	3
2	Who's Hot, Who's Not	8
3	Sounds Fine in Concept	13
4	It's Lonely at the Top	19
5	Technical Difficulties	26
6	Take Me Out of the Ballgame	32
7	It's an Ill Wind	37
8	Gambler's Blues	44

Part Two   *Numbers Rackets*

9	Out of the Blue	51
10	Fundamental Assumptions	55
11	Droll Models	60
12	Improbable Though It Seems	65
13	Beware the Bond Rating Bashers	71
14	The Missing Link	79

Part Three   *Smoke and Mirrors*

15	How to Run a Boiler Room	85
16	Two-Timers and Second Chances	90
17	When Audits Win No Plaudits	95
18	Pass the Trash	102
19	Buzzwords and BOMFOG	107
20	Incentive-Debased Pay	112

CONTENTS

Part Four *For Your (Mis)Information*

21 All the News That's Fit—And Then Some 123
22 Missing Records 128
23 Everyone's a Winner 134
24 Going By the Book Can Be Hazardous 141
25 The Art of Plain Talk 147

Part Five *Deficient Market Hypotheses*

26 Is Perfection Relative? 157
27 Unlovely But Not Unloved 163
28 Slow But Not So Steady 168
29 Foreign Matter 174
30 Muni Madness 180
31 I've Got the Horse Right Here 185
32 Begin by Collecting Your Thoughts 190

Bibliography 197

Index 225

Part One

WHY BAD THINGS HAPPEN TO GOOD INVESTMENT STRATEGIES

_____

1

On the Contrary

It Doesn't Pay to Swim Against the Tide When the Majority Happens to Be Right

"**I** gave up being a contrarian when I discovered that everyone else was one, too."

If you'll forgive a bit of hyperbole in this quip, picked up from a trader friend, you'll gain a useful insight. Contrary to popular opinion, it's not clear that you can strike it rich by simply going counter to popular opinion. "Obviously" overbought or oversold markets are not really as obvious as you might think.

These assertions, I realize, contradict a number of beloved clichés. The secret of wealth, it's often said, is to acquire straw hats in the winter. To make a killing, buy when the blood is flowing in the streets. And when even the shoeshine man is boasting about his stock market profits, it's time to sell. Remember, too, that no tree grows to the sky.

These are wonderful principles to keep in mind, provided you always know when prices have overshot the fundamentals. Even if securities are cheap "by every objective standard," they may get cheaper before they get dearer. As another old saw has it, nobody rings a bell at the stock exchange to signal the end of a bear market.

Never mind, you may say. There's no need to pinpoint the tops and bottoms. All that really matters is avoiding speculative excesses. In other words, the critical task is to be in cash when tulipmania sets in.

The Dutch tulip bulb craze of 1634–1637 is the incident invariably cited to demonstrate how easy it is to tell when speculation has gotten out of control. As contrarian investors have recounted on innumerable occasions, a single bulb sold at the height of the mania for the modern-day equivalent of $50,000. Anyone with common sense would have foreseen the market's subsequent 90%-plus sell-off.

Curiously, though, a small quantity of lily bulbs sold in the Netherlands just a few years ago for nearly $500,000. High-sounding prices don't necessarily indicate that people have taken leave of their senses. The catch is that a single bulb can quickly propagate a vast number of descendants. These can be sold at modest prices, permitting the investor to recoup what might otherwise seem an exorbitant outlay. A tulip progenitor is particularly prized if it transmits to its offspring characteristics that produce especially beautiful flowers.

This is just one of the misunderstandings that economist Peter M. Garber addresses in his study, "Who Put the Mania in Tulipmania?" According to Garber's evidence, there was no unbridled speculation during the 1630s in the established bulb market—the trading in rare varieties by serious tulip fanciers. Prices appear to have gotten out of line only in the loosely regulated futures market for ordinary bulbs, which traded by the pound. Even at that, Garber finds, the excesses persisted for just two to three weeks. After the February, 1637, collapse in the market for "pound goods," the more exquisite varieties continued to command high prices.

In short, there's less than meets the eye in the contrarians' favorite historical incident. Garber emphasizes the structural flaws in the futures market for ordinary bulbs, which the established traders avoided. There were no required margin deposits to ensure that participants would make good on their trades. No exchange acted as a counter-party to the contracts, which greatly aggravated the problem of an individual's failure to meet commitments. Transferring the tulipmania experience to the more highly regulated markets of three centuries later seems a dubious proposition.

Nevertheless, contrarians contend that the forces of greed and fear are readily identifiable and exploitable. It's as simple as listening to the conversation at cocktail parties. When everyone you speak to is obsessed with the market, you can be sure a sell-off is around the corner.

Regrettably, it's tough to test the predictive value of "soft data" such as cocktail chatter. Perhaps impressionistic methods of reading the market really work, but confirmation is inherently elusive. Impediments to quantification work to the contrarians' advantage. If the validity of a highly subjective technique is difficult to prove, it's also impossible to disprove. Contrarians can therefore go on forever regaling their followers with anecdotal evidence.

The stories typically involve great investors who spotted market tops through "obvious" signs of excess. No one can measure the number of times that comparable insights caused equally gifted individuals to get out too early.

Bottoms, too, can be more difficult to spot than investment lore has it. The fallacy to avoid in this area is the notion that because prices go down, they must later go up. Confederate bonds, after all, paused at various points on the way down from par before finally becoming worthless.

Beware, too, the standard yet highly misleading pendulum metaphor. No law of physics dictates that a security, though it may swing high and low, must return to an intrinsic value somewhere in the middle. Fundamental changes in a company's earning power can mean that an all-time low in its stock will prove to be, in retrospect, the high-water mark for the next decade.

Few would dispute the logic of this argument, but logic sometimes takes a back seat to contrarian bromides. Several of these clichés predictably come back into circulation whenever a market or a market sector sells off sharply:

- "Investors have thrown out the baby with the bathwater."
- "Every name in the group, whether decent or a dog, has been tarred with the same brush."
- "When the police raid a brothel, they even arrest the piano player."

A classic exposition of the overreaction thesis appeared in the April 9, 1990, "Heard on the Street" column in *The Wall Street*

Journal. The headline read, "Indiscriminate Run on Bank Stocks Means Some Investing Bargains May Be Available." (Key words: "indiscriminate," "bargains.") As a result of recent "dumping" of bank shares, the author noted, dividends of some stocks in the group were around 7%. This was double the market's 3.5% average. "Now is the time," some analysts were reported as saying, "for bold bank investors to step forward."

The *Journal* article added, "Any bargain hunter's short list has to include Citicorp." Investors saw only the half-empty glass of troubled real estate and highly leveraged transaction loans. But Citicorp also had a global presence and leadership in credit cards, home mortgages, and foreign exchange. What's more, the institution possessed the previously unheralded property of "granularity." By this, Chairman John S. Reed meant broad diversification, by geography and customer type, in Citicorp's loan portfolio. "The icing on the cake," said the author, "is a 7.2% yield, with a dividend increase expected before long."

A change in Citicorp's dividend was indeed in the offing. It turned out to be a reduction, rather than an increase, however. In January 1991, the board of directors slashed the payout by 44%. Even before that climactic event, Citicorp's stock had traded below 11, down from $22\frac{7}{8}$ at the time of the *Journal* article.

Hindsight is a decided advantage in evaluating investment recommendations. Still, the contrarian story on Citicorp and its peer institutions contained some recognizable pitfalls. For one thing, buying a common stock on the basis of a high yield is a risky strategy. Too frequently, the market is simply indicating a large danger that the dividend will be chopped or eliminated. Similarly, it was no proof of a bargain that Citicorp's stock was trading at less than book value and "only" six times earnings, as "Heard on the Street" noted. Like dividends, book values and earnings can fall. In Citicorp's case, they both did, thanks largely to the loan problems that the contrarians had downplayed.

More generally, seeming signals of an overreaction often turn out to be confirmation that the market has correctly assimilated important new information. If prices make an exceptionally large move, it doesn't follow that the move is *too* large.

It's gratifying to the ego to believe that you can remain rational when the crowd is euphoric or despondent. Contrarians who peddle investment advice count on this psychological motivation. Financially speaking, though, humility may be the better prescription. There's no sure-fire system of making sure to zig when everyone else zags.

2

Who's Hot,
Who's Not

Securities Analysts Often Get More
Credit (and More Blame) Than
They Deserve

*T*o judge by the relative emphasis it receives in the financial press, finding undervalued stocks is the primary mission of all investors. The sole function of securities analysts, as portrayed by the media, is to identify the issues that will go up the soonest and by the largest percentages.

Even though stock picking is the dominant mode of money management in most people's minds, trillions of dollars are invested on altogether different principles. Many large financial institutions focus primarily on collecting and reinvesting interest and dividends. Their main concern with respect to price changes is to limit their vulnerability to losses. To them, large capital gains are windfalls, rather than a central objective.

There are plenty of wealthy individuals who manage their portfolios along similarly conservative lines. Understandably, though, financial editors tend to devote more space to the exploits of analysts who recommend stocks that proceed to double or triple.

Given the skewed picture of the investment process that the public receives, it's no surprise that securities analysts' recommendations are widely misinterpreted. Contributing to this misunderstanding is the shorthand in which brokerage firms necessarily communicate the recommendations. "Buy," "Sell," and "Hold" are crisper designations than formulations such as "likely to outperform the market index over a one-year horizon." The latter phrase may strike you as bureaucratic pussyfooting, but study it carefully if you want to understand what an analyst's opinion can realistically accomplish for you.

The finite value of stock recommendations becomes apparent when you consider the two methods by which they are generated. First, an analyst may base a "Buy" or a "Sell" recommendation on information that is not known to others in the marketplace. In practice, this is comparatively rare. Securities and Exchange Commission regulations generally require companies to disclose their financial matters evenhandedly, instead of favoring selected analysts.

From time to time, a recommendation is the product of intelligence gathered from out-of-the-way sources. One example would be documents related to an obscure but potentially explosive legal proceeding. More often, though, brokerage firms' analysts all work with essentially the same data.

These conditions give rise to the second and more common type of recommendation, in which the analyst argues that the security's price does not properly reflect the known facts. The task in formulating this kind of a recommendation is to identify potential future events that might affect the value of the stock. Then, by assigning probabilities to these events, the analyst can derive a price that balances the risks and rewards.

So-called "event-driven" changes in stock prices illustrate the concept most clearly. Consider, for example, what happened to the shares of McDonnell Douglas, a major defense contractor, when the Stealth bomber program was canceled in 1991. McDonnell Douglas opened at $39\frac{1}{4}$ on January 7, the day the Defense Department pulled the plug. By the market's close on January 9, the stock had fallen to 28.

The Stealth bomber's demise was not entirely unexpected. McDonnell Douglas's share price prior to January 7 reflected experts' estimates of the probability that the program would be canceled. Investors would have been willing to pay more for the stock if they had been certain that the company's Stealth-related revenues would materialize. Conversely, if there had been no doubt that the program would be canceled, the value of McDonnell Douglas's stock would have been lower. Up until the moment the

Defense Department announced its decision, the uncertainty made it appropriate to price McDonnell Douglas's shares somewhere in between.

Let's imagine an event-driven situation of this sort in which the best estimate of the probabilities is 50/50. That is, the favorable outcome is exactly as likely to occur as the unfavorable outcome. Let's further suppose that our hypothetical stock, which we'll name Dynamogetics, will be worth 40 if the news is good and 20 if the news is bad. How much should you pay for the stock under these assumptions? You might argue that you can potentially earn a profit if you pay anything less than 40. (Naturally, you'd want to take commissions into account.) Over the long run, though, you can't make money by paying a price of 30 or higher in comparable situations. If the odds are 50/50, then half the time you'll walk away with 40 and half the time with 20. On average, you'll receive (40 + 20)/2, or 30. Therefore, if you pay anything above 30, the odds are that you will lose money.

Perhaps you're thinking that this point is too obvious and trivial to discuss. If so, consider what happens when a probability-based decision actually arises in the marketplace.

Without changing our previous assumptions, let's now suppose that Dynamogetics is trading at 32. Analyst Rita Rational concludes that the stock is slightly overpriced. She acknowledges that the security has an upside potential of 40, but notes that the good-news scenario has only a 50% chance of coming to pass. In the equally likely bad-news scenario, the stock will go down to 20. Risk and reward don't seem properly balanced at 32. If analyst Rational doesn't put an outright "Sell" on Dynamogetics, she will code it a "Hold," a "market performer over the near term," or something of that nature.

Analyst Patrick Plunger, in sharp contrast, is bullish. How many stocks in today's frothy market, he asks, have 25% appreciation potential? Plunger is pounding the table on this one—it's a "Buy" all the way. In fairness, analyst Plunger may not be acting irrationally in recommending Dynamogetics at 32. Perhaps he is simply mistaken. For example, if he overestimates the probability of the favorable outcome at 70% then 32 will indeed appear to be a cheap price for the stock. Mathematically, risk and reward would then seem evenly balanced at $(0.7 \times 40) + (0.3 \times 20) = 34$. Whether Plunger is making an unsupported recommendation or an honest error is beside the point, however. Either way, you'll lose money over the long run by following his advice.

In the short run, however, you may end up loving his recommendation. There's an even chance that Dynamogetics will in fact rise to 40. If it does, you can expect to be reading comments such as the following before long:

> The hottest hand in the high-tech sector these days belongs to Pat Plunger of Shooting Star Securities. His latest coup was spotting Dynamogetics languishing at 32 just a month before it blasted off to 40.

> Rita Rational seems to have lost her golden touch. Cooley Analytical's usually astute technology maven completely missed the one big winner in her group last year—Dynamogetics. Overly pessimistic rational left the company on "hold" while it rang up a 25% gain. Cooley's salesforce is reportedly fuming about her oversight.

Plunger will undoubtedly get his comeuppance before long. If he continues to recommend stocks that are fully valued—or even overpriced—the odds will catch up with him eventually. Soon it will be his turn to be pilloried for giving bad advice to customers. When the press turns on him, though, it will be for the wrong reason. The journalists will hang Plunger for putting a "Buy" on a stock that goes down. His true offense will be a systematic error in dealing with probabilities, but that won't make scintillating copy.

For you, the presumably discriminating investor, the point is to avoid a common fallacy about analysts and their opinions. In the popular mind, there is a simple way to test the quality of an analyst's "Buy" recommendation: If the stock went up, it was a good recommendation. Among the stocks that have a 75% probability of going up, however, one out of four will, by definition, either go down or remain unchanged. Therefore, you cannot determine whether an analyst is smarter than the market at large on the basis of a single recommendation. Nonetheless, that's what the financial press purports to do every week.

Once you appreciate just how difficult it is to evaluate research opinions, you'll stop expecting analysts to perform miracles. This will put you ahead of the game, at least in the sense that you won't be disappointed.

There are many legitimate investment strategies that have nothing whatsoever to do with trying to pick hot stocks. However, if you still elect to aim for big capital gains through individual security selection, recognize analysts' opinions for what they truly are.

"Undervalued" does not mean, "This stock is almost certain to go higher." A more accurate translation would be, "I believe that of the numerous stocks that I'll put into this category over the next several years, a majority will perform better than the averages. If I'm right, then investors who follow all of my recommendations should earn a somewhat higher rate of return than the Standard & Poor's 500 over an extended period."

This scarcely sounds like the express lane to immense wealth. Perhaps that's why the sober side of stock selection gets such limited press coverage. Most investors would much rather read about the analyst who touted a 50/50 proposition and hit the jackpot . . . this time.

If you're truly interested in investing rationally, you must discard the illusion that analysts alternate between periods of superhuman insight and bouts of astonishing obtuseness. Even more important, you must abandon dreams of enriching yourself by divining which of the two phases an analyst is in at any given moment.

3

Sounds Fine
in Concept

If No Other Company Is Pursuing
That High-Flier's Strategy, Maybe
There's a Good Reason

*F*inancial statements don't generate much excitement in the average crowd of investors. Perhaps a handful of cerebral types enjoy poring over dry statistics, but most folks prefer a bit of sex appeal. People with capital to put at risk are generally looking for a concept to rival the great money makers of yesteryear—a car for the common man, instant photography, fast food.

Wall Street is delighted to oblige. Research departments crank out concepts concerning vast new markets in Eastern Europe (or is it China?). There are stories about the desperate need for private prisons and stories about the aluminum-intensive car. There's the conglomerate concept, the concept of dismantling inefficient conglomerates through leveraged buyouts, the concept of reverse leveraged buyouts. If you listen long enough, you'll hear about a steel shortage, a water shortage, and even, from time to time, a stock shortage. But there is never a shortage of concepts:

- "Recessions *help* this company."
- "It's the next Xerox."
- "This is the best way to play the infrastructure boom."
- "If only 10% of the potential customers buy this product . . . ."

A few of these concepts actually live up to their immense promise, but it's clearly no more than a few. After all, how many people do you know (or even know of) who have become independently wealthy by speculating in high-concept stocks?

On the other hand, you probably do know some individuals who have lost money on great-sounding concepts, but you may not be aware of it. The reason is that the self-styled visionaries who lost their shirts are less vocal than the fortunate few who got in on the ground floor at Wal Mart. In reality, great concepts are less often the road to riches than investment lore would have it.

The trouble with concept stocks is that too high a percentage of them sound terrific. That's a problem because the U.S. economy cannot possibly grow fast enough for all of them to achieve their astronomical rates of projected growth. If you were skillful enough to pick out the gems consistently, you could amass untold wealth. Unfortunately, there is no sure-fire technique—other than hindsight—for differentiating the diamonds from the lumps of coal.

An alluring concept stock can become particularly tantalizing when the press begins to describe it in glowing terms. Soon, the hot growth company has vaulted from the financial pages to the trends-and-lifestyles columns. The chairman ascends to celebrity status, lecturing on management theory and writing newspaper columns about the solution to U.S. economic woes. This is the time to start thinking about taking profits in the stock.

Deregulation of U.S. airlines in 1978 produced a classic example of a concept that captured a moment in time, dazzling the financial markets in the process. People Express was a startup carrier launched by five former executives of Texas International, all in their 30s. The tale featured the obligatory sacrifices involved in scraping together the initial equity. One of the entrepreneurs even talked his wife into contributing an insurance check she had received in payment for some stolen jewelry.

The People Express concept was all about a group of young people "having a blast," as its charismatic chairman Donald Burr gushed. Every employee was required to buy at least 100 shares. The company's egalitarian principles compelled all senior managers, including Burr, to work occasional shifts as baggage handlers or flight attendants.

For the media, the upstart airline had a deeper significance than its stock price. The David-among-Goliaths was bringing cheap air travel to the masses. To editorial writers, People Express demonstrated the vast potential that lay waiting to be unshackled in other, still-regulated industries. Harvard Business School profiled Donald Burr in a case study of entrepreneurship in the 1980s. His humanistic style won praise in management expert Tom Peters's book, *A Passion for Excellence.*

Even hard-nosed financiers were susceptible to the infectious enthusiasm. One investment bank ordinarily concentrated on raising money for high-technology ventures, but the firm's managers dealt more from their hearts than their heads when the People Express team approached them. "We knew we were taking a big risk," said one of the principals, "but their whole philosophy—the fact that employees would be required to buy stock and would share the profits—appealed to us." By the end of 1983, People's chief financial officer was able to report with satisfaction, "We've come full circle, from us knocking on doors to a never-ending stream of people wanting to finance us."

Investors who eagerly anted up had to take a share of the airline's less glamorous side, however. For many travelers, People Express meant frustration in trying to reach a reservation clerk, the consequence of an inadequate supply of telephone lines. To the less impressionable of the pilots at The Little Airline That Could, spellbinding CEO Burr was "Guyana Jones." (The allusion was to the dynamic but demented evangelist Jim Jones, who persuaded his followers to commit mass suicide by drinking poisoned Kool-Aid.)

Even more worrisome for some investors who bought the People Express concept was the fact that the concept kept mutating. The original idea had been to bypass the largest cities in favor of second-tier destinations such as Buffalo and Sarasota. Within a few years, however, People was competing head on with the major airlines in Atlanta, Chicago, and Los Angeles, as well as flying to Europe. Burr had initially emphasized to investors his company's freedom from labor unions, which he was once quoted as labeling "animalistic." It was therefore doubly ironic when, in 1985, People Express abandoned its no-acquisitions policy and chose to buy unionized Frontier Airlines.

By that time, the company had also departed from its earlier concept of using debt only sparingly. Next to be abandoned was the People Express hallmark—no-frills service. From its early days, People had been perceived as an airline for backpackers who were willing to forgo or pay extra for amenities such as baggage handling and meals. In 1986, People Express installed first-class cabins in a bid to attract more business travelers.

A final casualty of People's conceptual transformation was its celebrated participatory style of management. Word came down that the airline was inserting an additional level into its hierarchy. Soon, People Express had created a new class of employees known as "customer service representatives." These workers performed essentially the same duties as the existing "customer service managers," but earned about half as much in base salary. The stock-ownership requirement, which had so impressed People's bankers, did not apply to the service representatives.

As People changed its methods of handling employees, turnover rose. Chairman Burr accelerated the trend by firing a few of his co-founders, including People's president. The once-deferential press now printed former employees' descriptions of Burr as "a masterful manipulator" and "a total, absolute dictator."

Burr defended his repeated recasting of the People Express vision by saying that modifications had been necessitated by changing conditions. As competition from the big airlines intensified, People was obliged to broaden its geographical base. Adding major metropolitan routes and acquiring regional carriers were strategies for meeting that objective.

Sometimes, though, "adapting to changed conditions" is just another way of saying that the concept wasn't sound in the first place. Air transportation, like a lot of businesses, is ferociously competitive. If a simply defined strategy is not already being pursued by some existing carrier, maybe it's because there's no real niche for it.

The unromantic reality of the marketplace may be that a company aiming to grow as swiftly as People Express intended to must evolve along much the same lines as its competitors. By doing so, however, it may cease to offer anything distinctive to consumers. An undifferentiated newcomer is an excellent candidate for extinction as soon as a recession arrives and its better-established rivals slash their prices.

Alternatively, an innovative company can settle for a small but lucrative share of a big market. That approach, unfortunately, may afford very limited growth. Without eye-popping sales gains quarter after quarter, the company's stock will not be regarded as a hot concept.

A few companies manage to solve the riddle. Progressive Corp., for example, has parlayed unconventional strategies into a major role in an industry (insurance) with many well-entrenched competitors. McDonald's, Holiday Inn, and Service Merchandise have achieved considerable success by finding new ways to provide mundane services. In retrospect, these all sound like better concepts than a no-frills airline concentrating on off-the-beaten-path cities in a newly deregulated environment. Back in 1981, however, the superiority of insuring high-risk drivers and selling jewelry through catalogue showrooms may not have been so obvious.

As late as November 1985, Donald Burr saw the dawning of a new era for People Express. The Frontier Airlines acquisition, he said, showed that his brave little carrier was in a position to buy other properties. Purchases of commuter carriers Britt Airways and Provincetown-Boston Airlines in fact followed. Just seven months later, however, Burr was selling rather than buying. Competitors were escalating the battle by offering selected seats (frills included) at fares lower than People's lowest. Onto the block went People's Boeing 747s. United Airlines agreed to take money-losing Frontier off Burr's hands for $146 million, but the deal foundered over a dispute with the pilots' union. So it was that organized labor, which People had avoided for most of its brief life, helped to hasten its demise.

On September 15, 1986, with Frontier in bankruptcy, People Express was taken over by a competitor. The acquirer, Texas Air, was the parent company of Continental Airlines, from which Burr and his spunky band of entrepreneurs had sprung five years earlier.

It had been a bumpy ride for the founders and for the employees, but no less so for the investors. For each share of People Express—a stock that had sold as high as $25\frac{7}{8}$ in 1983—they received Texas Air common and preferred stock worth a little more than $4. Furthermore, if the hapless investors failed to dispose of their new securities in fairly short order, they encountered additional turbulence. Weighed down by massive debt taken on in a series of acquisitions, Texas Air landed in bankruptcy in 1990.

Can we derive a broader lesson from the ignominious end of a concept that initially seemed to have merit? Consider what it is that makes a concept stock so special.

The run-of-the-mill company listed on a national exchange has a lengthy, audited history of revenues and earnings. Its stock has limited potential for rapid appreciation precisely because its prospects are well defined. Chances are slender that the stock will ever be grossly misunderstood or undervalued, at least relative to other, similar stocks. Notwithstanding such characteristics, the most humdrum stock in the market may at any moment be struck by an unforeseeable calamity. You can be socked with a whopping loss just when you were about to die of boredom.

Concept stocks, by contrast, are hardly dull or predictable. They do not have clearly measurable records or prospects, nor have they been tested in a wide variety of economic climates. About the only way they resemble the conventional, uninspiring stocks is in their potential to produce nasty surprises.

Some people cannot bear to invest in anything unless they perceive a realistic possibility of losing 100% of their money. If you fit this description, then the bulk of your portfolio ought to consist of concept stocks. Otherwise, these high-risk, high-reward securities deserve a minor role in your investment strategy. You'll have fewer opportunities to get in on the ground floor, but you'll also lessen your risk of being buried in the cellar.

4

It's Lonely at the Top

Dislodgement and Death in the Executive Suite Produce Large but Uncertain Profits

*D*oes it trouble you that so much of this book is devoted to demolishing sacred cows? It's an understandable reaction. I know how disturbing it can be to discover that cherished beliefs about the market are utter fantasies.

Such an unsettling message has to be balanced by less distressing material. I therefore thought it would be a good idea to include one completely upbeat chapter. So get ready to hear some heartening news about a well-documented capital gains opportunity: This is your chance to join the savvy investors who cash in when eminent chief executives get canned.

The more illustrious the CEO, it seems, the greater the potential returns. Take Kenneth H. Olsen, who founded and then headed Digital Equipment Corp. for 35 years. "By some measures the most successful U.S. entrepreneur since Henry Ford" is how *The Wall Street Journal* described him.

On July 16, 1992, Olsen announced his decision to retire as president of DEC. That, at least, was the phrasing he used for official purposes. In a subsequent meeting with employees Olsen reportedly claimed that he was fired. Either way, the stock market loved the news. Digital common rose $2\frac{3}{8}$ to $40\frac{3}{4}$ on word that the computer industry pioneer was on his way out. The stock climbed another $2\frac{1}{4}$ points the following day, as investors continued to exult in Olsen's downfall.

In fact, the market seemingly couldn't wait for him to leave after three-and-a-half decades of devoted service. Earlier, DEC's stock had rallied to 38, from as low as $33\frac{1}{4}$ in June 1992, on rumors that the CEO would get the boot. (Oddly, one analyst nevertheless termed Olsen's resignation "completely unexpected.")

Why the buoyancy in DEC's stock? The company's "legendary founder" evidently had a few shortcomings. So said some long-time colleagues, who spoke on condition of anonymity. According to these and other observers, Olsen was "a strong-willed executive not used to being second-guessed." Other descriptions included "autocratic," "cantankerous," and "maddeningly stubborn."

The deposed chief had reportedly resisted cost-cutting efforts. It was further alleged that he had dragged his feet in introducing open systems. Finally, charged the press, Olsen had pushed aside any executive who potentially challenged his near-total control.

Well, nobody's perfect. At least Digital Equipment was solvent at the time that Kenneth Olsen stepped down. The same could not be said for R.H. Macy, as of the April 1992 retirement of Chairman Edward Finkelstein. Under the 43-year-veteran's tutelage, the department store chain had followed the familiar path from leveraged buyout (LBO) to Chapter 11. (One wag suggested that LBO was an acronym for "Let's bankrupt ourselves.")

Macy's was privately owned at the time of Finkelstein's not-quite-voluntary retirement. As a consequence, he was spared the ignominy of seeing his company's stock trade up on the news. There was a modest rally in the retailer's publicly traded bonds, however.

Perhaps by now you've decided that betting on the downfall of chief executives is distasteful. In that case, you'll be even more offended by a popular strategy with still greater capital gains potential. It consists of seeking profits from the chief executive's death. The opportunities available in this cold-blooded speculation were dramatized on March 2, 1992. That was the first trading day following Earl Scheib's death at the age of 85. In response to the passing of Earl Scheib Inc.'s beloved chairman/president, the stock leaped from $8\frac{1}{2}$ to $12\frac{1}{2}$. Volume soared to 108,400 shares, nearly 17 times the daily high of the previous month.

Sentiment took a back seat to past criticisms of Scheib's leadership. He had been slow in raising prices to offset the trend toward longer lasting (and therefore less frequently repeated) paint jobs.

Partly as a result, the company had been forced to cut its dividend by half.

Suddenly, the CEO's demise opened up new possibilities. Irwin Buchalter, Scheib's executor and his successor as chairman, ventured, "Stock buyers think there will be a change in the operations, and that it will be better."

Renowned money manager Mario Gabelli pointed to the opportunities implicit in the company's cash balance and low debt. He also drew attention to the real estate value represented by the land underlying its paint shops. A sale of Earl Scheib Inc. was "very likely," announced Gabelli, whose asset management firm happened to hold a 17.8% stake. But Donald R. Scheib, upon succeeding his father as president and CEO, denied that the company was for sale. The shares ended that day at $11\frac{1}{2}$, down one point from the peak. Before the month was over, the stock had closed as low as 10. Clearly, the passing of a chief executive may raise hopes that go unfulfilled.

Scheib's new president, by the way, expressed surprise that the company's stock had rallied following his father's death. "I thought it would go down," he said. The reaction might not have struck the younger Scheib as paradoxical, however, if he'd been tracking the record of ghoul-oriented investing. For instance, about two years before Earl Scheib died, Curtiss-Wright's stock jumped 14% on the death of its CEO. A spokesman characterized the response to the passing of 80-year-old Roland Berner as "a very morbid reaction."

Perhaps so, but it was no more unseemly than the 15% rise in Campbell Soup after the 1989 death of retired chairman John Dorrance. A son of the company's founder, Dorrance was revered as "a gentlemanly, compassionate man with a lot of moral commitment." More to the point, in the view of investors, Dorrance had controlled enough shares to block any takeover attempt. Speculators were betting that the remaining heirs would quarrel and bring about a sale of Campbell Soup.

Plainly, there's a lot of money to be made in the death of CEOs. Be aware, though, that like many other investment strategies, this one can require a lot of patience. After all, octogenarians figured prominently in two of the case studies we've discussed so far.

Occidental Petroleum's late chairman, Armand Hammer, kept the grave-dancers waiting even longer. He was 92 when he died in the saddle, following a series of speculative episodes revolving around his health.

While still a stripling of 77, Hammer had pleaded guilty to making illegal contributions to President Richard Nixon's reelection campaign. He appeared in court for his sentencing in a wheelchair, attached to a heart monitoring device. This evidence of Hammer's tenuous hold on life helped to win him leniency. He was sentenced to just a year's probation and a $3,000 fine. Apparently, the judge's mercy revived the Oxy chairman. Only a few weeks later, he was observed strolling briskly on a Moscow street.

Hammer's recovery was undoubtedly a disappointment to some speculators. They perceived Occidental as a crazy quilt of Hammer-conceived acquisitions. The pieces, they believed, would be worth more if the company were broken up. Divestments seemed unlikely as long as Hammer was in charge, however. It was also widely thought that the chairman was responsible for maintaining Oxy's dividend payout at an excessive level.

Investors who hoped to see Hammer out of the picture, one way or another, received some encouragement when financier David Murdock acquired a large stake in Oxy. For a while, it appeared that Murdock might try to shake up the company. In 1984, though, Occidental bought back his stock at a premium and Hammer remained at the helm.

Hopes were raised again in June 1987, when the chairman cracked three ribs in a slip in his bathtub. The stock rose after Hammer fell, finishing $4\frac{1}{2}$ points higher. Just a month later, however, Hammer was back on the job. Seeking to quell speculation, he invited a reporter to his office. "It's obvious I'm not dying," he declared, despite his equally obvious pain. "I'm in perfect health."

The scene was repeated in 1989 when the seemingly indestructible executive had a cardiac pacemaker inserted. Initially, Occidental was a bit vague about the reasons for Hammer's failure to show up for a scheduled meeting with financial analysts. As word of his operation leaked out, however, Oxy's stock climbed 11% on double its normal volume. Four days later, Hammer came in to work and denounced the "ridiculous" rumors of a takeover of

Occidental. He urged stockholders to be patient. The company was well positioned for a recovery in energy prices, said the chairman.

A few years earlier, Hammer had offered similar counsel to the New York Society of Security Analysts. At the same meeting, his then heir-apparent (one of about a dozen cast aside over the years) also had some advice. Oxy shareholders, said Robert Abboud, first had to discard the notion of Armand Hammer's mortality.

For a time, the remark seemed not entirely facetious. True, the chairman reportedly took to snoozing at management meetings in his later years. But by then, he had seemingly repealed the rule about death and taxes. The inevitable finally occurred in 1990, however. Hammer succumbed just as he was about to celebrate his Bar Mitzvah. The coming-of-age rite had been delayed some 79 years beyond the customary date. Here, plainly, was a man who felt he had all the time in the world.

Oxy's stock responded to Hammer's death much as speculators had long predicted. An order imbalance resulted in a late opening. Volume swelled to approximately 12 times the usual level, while Occidental's price climbed by about 9%. Once again, the dying-CEO strategy was vindicated. It was debatable, though, whether the rewards were commensurate with the length of the death watch. The experience demonstrates that although death is inevitable, it's no sure thing in terms of payoffs to investors.

One problem is that analysts don't always see a CEO's death as an unalloyed benefit. In some instances, they may even think the company will be better off if the boss survives. Consider the case of Wang Laboratories. It had a different twist, even though the company resembled the others in certain respects.

For one thing, Wang Laboratories's founder/chairman was as illustrious as any of those already mentioned. An Wang was the inventor of the magnetic computer memory, as well as a renowned philanthropist.

Also like some of the other companies examined here, Wang Laboratories faltered during the 1980s. The problem was its slow response to changing market conditions. Specifically, the company was late in switching its production from dedicated word processors to personal computers. The resulting financial strains forced Wang Laboratories to eliminate its dividend in 1989. In that same year, the elder Wang was apparently instrumental in the ouster of his son, Frederick Wang, as president and chief operating officer. Then, in 1990, An Wang died, never having surrendered the post of CEO.

Consistent with the pattern of the other case histories, Wang's stock rallied by 20% when Frederick Wang got the boot. (No comparable surge followed An Wang's death.) But Frederick Wang's departure represented only a temporary fix. Instead of turning around, the company continued to deteriorate. Wang Laboratories entered Chapter 11 in 1992.

Chairman Richard Miller attributed the bankruptcy partly to An Wang's decision to kick his son out of the president's spot. That act "irreparably" damaged Wang Laboratories's credibility, said Miller. "More damage was done than we thought at the time," he added. "It's been hard to get new customers." In other words, firing the boss can backfire.

But is that taking too long a view? If the market's immediate response to a firing is sure to be positive, perhaps it makes sense to grab a quick profit. Sometimes, though, you have to be awfully nimble, as shown by one final case study.

Shareholders of DWG Corp. could supply a number of reasons for wishing that chairman Victor Posner would exit. Chief among these was his rejection of a $22-a-share bid for the company in 1989. In August 1992, the stock was trading slightly below 10.

Another reason for wanting Posner out was that he seemed to be a jinx. Companies he became associated with had a tendency to go bankrupt. Evans Industries (1985) and Sharon Steel (1987) were prominent casualties. In the latter case, Posner agreed to return 13 Norman Rockwell paintings after the bankruptcy trustee accused him of plundering the company.

Such allegations were another reason for DWG's shareholders to feel some discomfort with Posner. In 1977, the Securities and Exchange Commission accused him of causing several publicly held companies to pick up the tab for $1.7 million of personal expenses for himself and two of his children. The family subsequently reimbursed the companies, without admitting or denying wrongdoing.

Finally, DWG stockholders may have felt that Posner simply didn't project the right public image. For example, in 1987 he pleaded no contest to charges of income tax evasion. The government claimed that he had dodged more than $1.2 million of taxes by inflating the value of land he donated to a Miami Bible college.

At any rate, DWG's stock responded favorably at first to the September 3, 1992, news that Posner would step down as chairman. He agreed to sell half of his shares in the soft drink/ restaurant/textile/propane/plastics company to Trian Group L.P., an investment partnership. The deal was presumed to end long-standing litigation in which Posner was accused of self-dealing and contempt of court.

In the initial burst of enthusiasm, investors bid DWG up to $12\frac{1}{8}$ from the previous day's close of $11\frac{1}{2}$. One analyst characterized Posner's impending departure as "good news for securities holders," citing sizable fees that the chairman had extracted. Others licked their chops at the prospects of carving up Posner's mélange of businesses in order to enhance shareholder value. DWG's legal bills also appeared to be headed for a sharp decline.

Fairly soon, though, it became clear that matters might not be so simple. Trian's vice chairman disavowed any plans to divest businesses. It also developed that Posner's agreement to sell half his stock was contingent on approval by shareholders, regulators, and a U.S. district court judge. Some stockholders immediately indicated they'd oppose the deal. An attorney for the plaintiffs in one suit against Posner vowed to continue litigating until the outgoing chairman agreed to return some of the money he'd allegedly bled from DWG.

By the end of the day on which the proposed stock sale was announced, DWG was *down* by an eighth from the preceding close, to $11\frac{3}{8}$. Investors who got in at the top could have lost 6% of their money in a matter of hours.

Betting on the death or dislodgment of a chief executive is a treacherous undertaking, after all. Not only do some of the CEOs keep you waiting for inordinately long periods, but the stocks don't always behave properly. As with many other formulas for certain profits, this one is less certain than it's cracked up to be.

5

Technical Difficulties

The Chartists' Case Rests on the Unproven Premise That Past Prices Hold Clues to the Future

Technical analysis has enriched the vocabulary of the financial markets. "Blowoff," "falling wedge," and "rigor mortis rally" are a few of the more vivid coinages. It is also true that technical analysis has enriched a number of famous prognosticators. The usual method is to publish a newsletter that purports to forecast the market's future by charting its past. What about investors seeking similar enrichment? As the Wall Street adage goes, "Two out of three ain't bad."

The professional technician (or "chartist") benefits greatly from the customary terms of debate. Almost invariably, the small investor's query is, "Which guru has discovered the True Method?" Rarely do market addicts question the underlying premise that prices follow predictable patterns.

Devotees of the various technical forecasters are outspoken in defending their favorites. On occasion, the letters-to-the-editor section of *Barron's* gets a bit overheated as a consequence. The master technicians encourage such partisanship. In fact, they contribute to it by lacing their self-aggrandizement with digs at competitors. ("Last May, when every other analyst in the universe was predicting a decline, I sent my subscribers an unequivocal 'Buy' signal.")

Since everybody makes a bad call once in a while, all technicians take their lumps from time to time. Even so, the chartists are better off keeping the fracas focused on which of them is number one. They have nothing to gain by raising a more basic question: Is any of their advice useful?

However, serious students of finance have addressed the question in excruciating detail. They have conducted interminable tests of the proposition that past prices hold clues to future fluctuations. In the process, the researchers have dared to consider the other possibility. Might it be the case, they ask, that trends do not display any particular tendency to continue?

This alternative view has been labeled the "random walk hypothesis." It suggests that the securities markets are "efficient" in taking into account all relevant information, including historical prices. By implication, chartists can gain no additional edge by identifying "sawtooths," "whipsaws," or other ostensibly significant patterns.

The research findings on this point represent considerably less than a ringing endorsement of the value of charting. In their textbook *Investment Analysis and Portfolio Management*, Jerome B. Cohen, Edward D. Zinbarg, and Arthur Zeikel write: "Most of the statistical investigations of the random walk hypothesis confirm the belief that successive price changes are generally statistically independent."

In plain language, it's questionable whether past trends have any bearing whatsoever on future prices. Cohen, Zinbarg, and Zeikel argue, however, that "this fact does not necessarily warrant a conclusion that technical analyses . . . are useless." Lesser men and women might be discouraged by such tepid support, but chartists carry on with undiminished zeal.

To be fair about it, the evidence is not entirely on the side of market efficiency. For one thing, statistical principles state that if prices were perfectly random, a graph of historical returns would produce a bell-shaped curve. Financial scholars generally concede that the reality is otherwise. Chance alone would not generate as many periods of very high and very low returns as the marketplace does. (Theoreticians colorfully refer to this phenomenon as the "fat tails" problem.)

The random walk hypothesis has also proven to be assailable through some highly sophisticated mathematical techniques. (More sophisticated, at least, than the typical technical analyst employs.) Notable among these is chaos theory. A powerful analytical tool, chaos theory has materially advanced the study of such scientific preoccupations as the molecular motion within a pot of boiling water. To date, however, chaos specialists have not cracked the market's code. According to Edgar F. Peters, author of *Chaos and Order in the Financial Markets: A New View of Cycles, Prices, and Market Volatility*, "Chaos theory says that markets are not efficient, but they are not forecastable."

For the most part, however, technical analysts have left the "quant jocks" and academicians to squabble among themselves. They have preferred to take their case to the People, who are not as well equipped to evaluate it.

Even more to the advantage of the chartists, many prospective newsletter subscribers are desperate to believe. As Mahatma Gandhi said, "To the hungry, God appears in the form of bread." Likewise, to investors who hope to turn a bit of capital into a bundle, a self-proclaimed financial messiah may look like the genuine article. Helping to bring the willing converts into the fold are the persuasive methods of technical analysis.

The chartist begins by sketching a hypothetical head-and-shoulders formation, skipping over, for the moment, the fact that actual price histories do not always display such a clearly recognizable pattern. (After extensive statistical smoothing, they do sometimes come close.) Next, the technical analyst explains that points and figures on the graph reflect psychological swings among masses of faceless investors. Suppose, for example, that a stock has traded down from the level at which a large volume of buying occurred in the past. As a result of the subsequent decline, vast numbers of discouraged shareholders are hoping just to get out even. Soon after the stock begins to rally, it will bump up against an impenetrable mass of sellers. Chartists claim that this phenomenon, known as "resistance," is discernible amidst their squiggles.

Most technicians apparently believe that the mere outlining of such scenarios validates their theories. As a rule, books about technical analysis do not unduly burden the reader with statistical verification. The most meticulous authors merely reproduce selective (and possibly unrepresentative) charts that superficially appear to confirm their propositions.

Observe as well that this explanation of resistance presumes that investors behave irrationally. After all, if shareholders think the stock is headed lower, they should sell immediately, rather than nurture hopes of breaking even. On the other hand, holders may believe the stock is likely to go higher than the price at which they happened to get in. In that case, they should not liquidate at precisely the moment that they will begin to realize a profit.

The implication that investors are irrational isn't something that technical analysts seek to downplay. On the contrary, they revel in it. Technicians gleefully ridicule the naiveté of the random walkers, who assume that market participants intelligently evaluate each new piece of information. In reality, say the chartists, the mob is forever lurching from euphoria to despair.

Conveniently, the portrayal of investors as impulsive losers is immensely flattering to the individuals whom the technical analysts hope to recruit. It is not this elect group, evidently, but rather some other crowd that behaves irrationally. Those who follow the master technicians will profit from the fickleness of the masses. Or, at the very least, they will enjoy the ego gratification of feeling superior to the multitudes.

Proselytizing technical analysts buttress their more tenuous arguments with testimonials. The chief qualification of individuals who offer these endorsements is unswerving faith in the debatable proposition that trends continue. To demolish any residual skepticism, the technicians brandish complimentary press clippings. Never mind that the gushing financial organs have a vested interest in investors' continued confidence in forecasting techniques. If people ceased to believe in technical analysis, they would have one less reason to subscribe to periodicals composed largely of interviews with prominent technicians. It's essentially the same reason that daily newspapers do not dwell on the question of the validity of horoscopes.

Astrological analogies are not altogether out of place in a discussion of technical analysis. Consider these comments from Michael D. Sheimo's *Dow Theory Redux: The Classic Investment Theory Revised & Updated for the 1990's:*

> Just as the ancients would consult with oracles, seers and prophets to know what might happen next, modern investors will consult the stock market indicators.

There are hundreds of indicators to choose from; some are economic, others are technical and some are literally 'out of this world.' There are some analysts who are reported to base investment advice on the alignment of the planets.

Notwithstanding some fringe elements, it might well be that technicians are on to something after all. Certainly, academic researchers cannot claim to have tested the merits of every single proposition of technical analysis. Nor will they ever reach that point, since new indicators and systems are being developed all the time.

Academic questions aside, a more practical problem confronts you as an investor: Assuming the chartists really have discovered some exploitable patterns in securities prices, can you learn to share in the riches by reading their books or attending their seminars? Your chances would be better if the technical prognosticators distilled their knowledge into explicit trading rules. Generally speaking, they don't. In the words of one technician, who charges thousands of dollars for his sessions, "If there were a mechanical system that worked successfully and consistently, it wouldn't be worth $30,000, it'd be worth $30 million."

In lieu of mechanical systems, the authors of technical treatises offer their sympathy in your efforts to master the market's complexities. For good measure, they toss in scores of charts, some homespun philosophy, and weighty phrases such as "double three corrective waves" and "fulcrum reversal patterns." Your difficulties begin only when you try to answer the question, "At this juncture, should I buy or sell?" But don't worry. You can always get an expert reading of the market's signals by subscribing to some technician's newsletter.

One way or another, books about technical analysis invariably concede that there are no hard-and-fast rules to follow. Here are a few typical disclaimers:

- "The creation of a scenario to explain movements in the stock market is almost always a guess—there are many possibilities." (Michael D. Sheimo)

- "It's not precise; no one knows whether this is all the subsurface strengthening there will be, or but the first of several messages developing." (Justin Mamis)
- "Certainly the Dow Theory is not infallible. No theory, no system, no approach is. . . . Ultimately the decision to buy or sell is yours." (The New York Institute of Finance)

Credit the chartists with honesty, at least. But don't assume they have any better idea than you do about which way the market is headed. The only thing we know for certain about technical analysis is that it's possible to make a living by publishing a newsletter on the subject.

Some of the master technicians put their own money at risk on their recommendations. This demonstrates sincerity, perhaps, but doesn't necessarily mean they'll be right. Your best bet concerning technical trading systems is to maintain a healthy skepticism. It's a good rule to follow when someone claims you can get rich by exploiting the other fellow's irrationality.

6

Take Me Out of
the Ballgame

The Skills That Win a
Stock Market Contest
May Be Poor Lessons
for Real Life

One valuable lesson I learned at
Harvard Business School involved the underlying seriousness of
investment games. For example, participating in a commodities
trading contest demonstrated to my satisfaction that a futures market was no place for dabbling. I also found that certain students did
not moderate their cutthroat tendencies merely because we were
dealing in play money. Still another sort of lesson emerged from a
school-wide stock market competition, which was sponsored by
the institutional brokerage firm of Mitchell, Hutchins Inc.

The stock market game gave Mitchell, Hutchins such a high
profile on campus that I perceived it to be among Wall Street's
premier houses. In at least one respect—the quality of its research—my impression was totally accurate. Mitchell, Hutchins
consistently took high honors in *Institutional Investor*'s annual
rankings of Wall Street analysts. The firm's size was another matter, however. Aptly described by the then-current phrase "research
boutique," Mitchell, Hutchins had the intimate feel of a small
business. As an underwriter of securities, it ranked far below the
industry leaders in volume.

Reflecting the firm's modest scale and its primarily institutional focus, Mitchell, Hutchins's name recognition was not as high
off campus as I had supposed. In fact, many of my friends never

quite mastered the pronunciation. A few perennially confused the company with Miller Huggins, manager of the immortal 1927 New York Yankees.

In any event, the Harvard Business School's stock market game was immensely successful, at least from the sponsor's standpoint. It greatly expanded awareness of Mitchell, Hutchins among potential recruits. Most of the contestants did not profit as directly as the firm did, although many had a lot of fun. Stock market novices who got involved did pick up some practical knowledge of the mechanics of speculating. On the whole, the division of benefits was typical of such exercises.

Based on this assessment, you might be inclined to dismiss investment competitions as harmless diversions. That conclusion may be too optimistic, however. Participants who take the games seriously are likely to emerge with distorted images of the financial markets. In particular, emulating the winner's strategy could prove costly in real life. The reason is that securities market games generally differ from actual investing in two essential respects.

First, the mock investors put no genuine capital at risk. They can, however, gain a reward in the form of a prize or simply through the glory of winning. The players do not need to weigh risk against reward, as in the real world. Instead, they have every incentive to go for the big score, regardless of the downside—for there is none.

This encouragement of "elephant hunting" is reinforced by the second artificial condition imposed in most investment contests. In order to be able to declare a winner before the audience's interest wanes, the sponsor ordinarily limits the length of the game, perhaps to a few months. Such a short horizon effectively foils the strategy of buying stocks with fundamental but unrecognized value. (Advocates of "basic value" investing generally caution that it may take the market a considerable time to correct an error of neglect.) The rules of the game, then, drive the players toward highly volatile, faddish securities. Patient ownership of solid but out-of-favor companies is almost guaranteed to be a losing strategy. In real life, by contrast, the latter approach is perhaps the answer most frequently given by successful investors when they are asked, "How did you do it?"

Admittedly, investment contests are not always won by reckless speculators. Sometimes the competition takes place during a horrendous bear market. If nobody is fortunate enough to pick one of the few stocks that soars in spite of the downdraft, the prize may go to a timid soul who remains 100% in Treasury bills throughout the period. A result of this sort underscores the silliness of awarding laurels to a 90-day wonder. It's the financial-market equivalent of ending a poker game after the first hand, in which a mediocre card player happened to be dealt a royal flush.

In truth, there's no significance whatsoever in a victory gained by owning cash equivalents during a single, short decline in the market. Certainly, the strategy would not succeed in a competition extending over many years, since common stocks easily outperform risk-free Treasury bills in the long run.

The victor might, on the other hand, characterize the winning T-bill strategy as a feat of astute market timing. To substantiate that claim, the self-proclaimed master of trends would have to repeat the success over subsequent periods. Otherwise, it would be impossible to prove that the "market call" was truly more than a lucky guess. Sponsors and fans of investment games don't care about such quibbles. They are unfazed when players triumph with strategies that would be ruinous under actual market conditions.

If verisimilitude is what's desired, the solution is simple: Restrict the competition to prominent professionals instead of letting a bunch of amateurs succeed in spite of themselves. *The Wall Street Journal* conducts an exhibition based on this principle. In the "Investment Dartboard," contestants aren't merely pitted against one another. They also compete against a portfolio selected by tossing darts at a list of stocks. On the positive side, this particular contest is ongoing, rather than short lived. It is therefore a somewhat more meaningful test of investment acumen than a two- or three-month investment game.

The *Journal* offsets that concession to the real world, however, by allowing the pros to pick just a single stock in each round. In managing actual portfolios, the *Journal's* contestants divide their risk among a number of different securities at any given time. They recognize that the stock with the greatest upside is usually one that also has a lot of downside. Accordingly, they don't want to bet all of their chips on it.

By way of analogy, baseball batters know that when they swing for home runs, their risk of striking out is high. They bunt or try for singles if the situation demands caution. The *Journal's* contest, in contrast, is akin to an old television series, *Home Run Derby*. On that program, batters scored points only when they knocked the ball out of the park. Gratifyingly, *Home Run Derby* never approached the popularity of baseball itself, a far more complex and subtle game.

Jonathan Steinberg, a participant in the *Journal's* one-stock contest, personifies the swing-for-the-fences mentality that stock market simulations foster. On March 5, 1992, the "Investment Dartboard" update included this comment:

> In 10 tries, Mr. Steinberg has finished first six times and last four times. Both his home runs and strikeouts have been memorable. He has picked the contest's biggest winners. In addition to Michaels Stores, they are Clearly Canadian Beverage Corp., up 193.3%, and Dell Computer Corp., up 117.2%. But he has also picked the contest's two biggest losers: Management Co. Entertainment Group, down 96.9%, and Financial News Network Inc., down 69.9%. (p. C5)

In the *Journal* reporter's judgment, Steinberg's picks had performed "admirably" in aggregate through that point. On average, they had posted 22.9% gains over six months, versus 14.8% for the other professionals in the contest and 4.4% for the Dow Jones Industrial Average. Most real-world clients would *expect* to earn a substantial premium on Steinberg's picks. Otherwise, they could live without the excitement of his "alternating between big gains and monster losses," as the *Journal* phrased it on September 6, 1991.

Of those two categories, by the way, guess which one Steinberg emphasizes in promoting his *Special Situations Report*? Here's an excerpt from an advertisement in the March 23, 1992, *Barron's*, offering access to his "unqualified *#1 stock recommendations*":

> Clearly Canadian Up 1,063% in 22 months
> Score Board Up 413% in 19 months
> Software Toolworks Up 165% in 8 months.

By capitalizing the word "Up," alone among the words that are not proper nouns, the copywriter leaves a clear impression about the direction in which Steinberg's selected stocks go. Devotees of investment competitions would form a more mixed impression, however.

Spotting such disparities is just one of the opportunities available to you in observing a stock market derby. By watching as the contestants jockey for immediate and imaginary profits, you can learn how *not* to manage a real portfolio for the long term. As a lark, you might even enter an investment competition. Just hope you don't win. If you suffer that misfortune, you may begin to believe you're on to something. Whatever you think you've discovered, it's probably nothing that will work consistently when you start playing for keeps.

7

It's an Ill Wind

*There's Often Money to Be Made in
Natural Disasters; The Trick Is
Figuring Out Whether to Buy
or Sell*

News of a natural disaster immediately prompts many people to ask, "How can I help?" With equal swiftness, astute investors begin to wonder, "How can I profit?" Seeking gains in devastation represents the ultimate form of looking at the bright side. This indomitable impulse spans a wide spectrum of human misery.

For example, when the Persian Gulf war broke out in 1991, stock purchasers went on the prowl for manufacturers of gas masks and poison antidotes. The destruction wreaked by the conflict suggested earnings increases for companies that were positioned to participate in the rebuilding of Kuwait. Even the AIDS epidemic has had a silver lining for speculators. Condom manufacturers were an obvious "play" in the early stages. Pharmaceutical and biotechnology companies have also emerged as vehicles for participating in the economic response to the crisis. All of this activity is fully in the spirit of the free enterprise system. As the saying goes, when you come to the edge of a cliff, you'll find an entrepreneur selling parachutes.

Financial markets necessarily adjust to all events that create, destroy, or redistribute wealth, including earthquakes, floods, and civil disturbances. Securities prices will be recalibrated to reflect such developments, even if some participants feel queasy about the process. But squeamishness is by no means a universal response to the prospect of profiting from the suffering of others.

Many investors begin to champ at the bit from the instant they hear of another impending catastrophe.

When Hurricane Andrew struck South Florida in the summer of 1992, for example, stockbrokers wasted no time in helping the financial markets adjust to the news. The research director of a Florida-based securities dealer reported that as soon as he got into his office, he received 100 calls from brokers, asking how they could profit from the disaster.

There was no shortage of creative ideas. The New York Mercantile Exchange's natural gas futures contract set a volume record, reflecting potential disruptions in Gulf Coast gas production. One brokerage firm recommended the stock of a Florida railroad that transported crushed stone and cement. Those materials were expected to be essential to the rebuilding effort. Other analysts saw opportunities in bank stocks, since many hurricane victims would have to borrow in order to put their lives back together. "It's not the kind of loan demand we'd like to have," conceded a spokesperson for one institution, but capital-gains-seeking investors were undeterred.

Unfortunately, noted the besieged Florida research director, people were carried away by their enthusiasm. Consequently, investors who had bought at the top ran the risk of being hung out to dry. "They better be praying for another hurricane next week," he said, "or they're going to be in a world of trouble."

Such excessive rejoicing over death and destruction is just one of several pitfalls of investing in disasters. Another danger is betting on plausible-sounding stories that don't necessarily have merit. In the case of the banks, for instance, Hurricane Andrew was not an unquestionable windfall. One economist noted that a lot of existing borrowers would lose their jobs and fall behind on their loan payments. There was also a downside to the obliteration of houses, which investors regarded as an unalloyed blessing for homebuilders. Many of the newly homeless would receive checks for the fully insured value of their houses and would pay off their mortgages, resulting in lost interest income for the banks.

Another dubious recommendation emanating from Hurricane Andrew was one that has frequently been proposed in connection with natural disasters. The concept is to sell U.S. Treasury bonds short. Underlying this idea is the premise that property and casualty (P&C) insurers must liquidate fixed-income holdings in order to pay off unusually large claims. In reality, say the P&C companies, claims are invariably paid out of cash on hand, interest income, and funds received from bond redemptions.

One professional interviewed in the aftermath of the Florida disaster noted that he'd been in the investment department of a major insurer for over 25 years. "Never in that time," he said, "have we been forced to liquidate investments to take care of claims." A spokesperson for another company dismissed as nonsense the talk of bond selling by insurance companies, pointing out that claims arising from natural disasters always got paid out over an extended period. Consequently, there was no need to raise cash quickly by dumping bonds. "I think there are some people trying to create a little uneasiness in the bond market," concluded the spokesperson.

Hurricane Andrew likewise stirred up little immediate reaction in the municipal bond sector. Tax-exempt specialists noted that a lot of the obligations of southern Florida municipalities were in the hands of small, buy-and-hold investors. (At any rate, some of the brokerage firms to which they might have tried to sell their bonds were shut down by the storm.) Traders did not rush to dump, either. "Hurricanes come and hurricanes go," said one.

Another disputable investment recommendation churned up by Hurricane Andrew was to buy the stocks of the P&C insurers. Like the idea of shorting Treasuries, this was a chestnut bandied about in previous natural disasters. It was also counter intuitive, since the most obvious effect of the storm for insurance companies was an increase in underwriting losses. The rationale for buying P&C stocks, instead of selling them in response to expected earnings reductions, was a hope that the underwriting cycle would be broken. That is, analysts argued that the insurers' shares had previously been held down by overly aggressive competition on rates. They suggested that the massive claims payouts arising from Andrew would finally force companies to charge higher premiums in order to maintain their earnings.

At least one Wall Street analyst deemed this scenario "likely," as opposed to merely "possible." A New York University finance professor predicted that insurance companies would use Andrew, as well as the subsequent Hurricane Iniki, to justify requests for premium increases on the order of 10% to 15%.

Many experts thought the prospect of a general hike in rates was unlikely, however. Fitch Investors Service noted that companies had excess capacity for underwriting insurance, thanks to recent gains on their stock and bond portfolios. Standard & Poor's concluded that Andrew probably would not push premiums up to high enough levels to improve the industry's profitability. In fact, a storm almost as fierce as Andrew was unleashed when one property and casualty insurer suggested the possibility of raising rates. An American International Group (AIG) internal memorandum, written on the day the hurricane hit the Florida coast, spoke of "an opportunity to get price increases now." Consumer advocate Ralph Nader got hold of the memo and cited it as evidence of a need to tighten federal regulation of the insurance industry. J. Robert Hunter, president of the National Insurance Consumer Organization, urged state insurance commissions to head off the "outrageous attempt by AIG to increase its already bloated profits."

The company denied that it was seeking to take advantage of the hurricane. AIG's chairman said that the Florida Department of Insurance's response to the affair painted "a grossly distorted picture." In any event, the momentum was clearly not with the notion of raising premiums.

On the other side of the coin, the insurers had to begin paying claims. In certain cases the exposures were huge. Continental Corp. was forced to cut its dividend for the first time in 139 years. Prudential Insurance Co. of America quadrupled its initial loss estimate to over $1 billion, prompting reviews of its bond ratings by Moody's Investors Service and Standard & Poor's. Moody's downgraded not only Allstate Insurance Group, but also Allstate's parent, Sears, Roebuck & Co. The estimated loss from Andrew just about wiped out the $722.5 million of profits contributed to Sears by Allstate in 1991.

According to some sources, the industry's potential underwriting losses were worse than they might have been in an earlier year. The threat to insurers' earnings had reportedly been heightened by previous cutbacks in the use of reinsurance. By way of explanation, primary insurance companies normally lay off a portion of the risk that they underwrite. They accomplish this by paying reinsurers to take over the exposure above a specified dollar level. The amount of exposure retained by the primary insurer determines the volume of *net premiums written* that it can record on its income statement. Apparently, some companies had tried to maintain growth in this revenue measure during the tough years preceding Andrew by keeping more than the customary amount of the risk for themselves. Investors could not have known the extent of this earnings hazard from reading the companies' financial statements. Disclosure on the matter was not sufficiently detailed.

Whatever the precise causes, the impact of Andrew-related earnings surprises was dramatic. About three weeks after the hurricane first struck Florida, Motor Club of America dropped a bombshell. Reinsurance would cover only about $20 million of the $50 million in claims that its MCA Insurance unit expected to receive. The resulting loss would wipe out Motor Club's entire investment in its P&C insurance company.

One industry analyst called Motor Club's exposure "shocking," relative to the company's size. Management estimated that shareholders' equity would fall from roughly $29 million to about $8 million. In response to the news, Motor Club's stock plummeted 64% in a single day. So much for speculators' dreams of vast profits on the wings of premium increases!

From the experience of the insurance stocks, we learn two important lessons. First, a proposed method for capitalizing on disasters may have a logical rationale but still not work. Second, a reasonable-sounding strategy can be undermined by hidden risks. The latter factor affected another group viewed as an Andrew play, the housing-related stocks.

In the initial euphoria generated by the catastrophe, cash flooded into the shares of Florida-oriented homebuilders. The speculation extended to some companies with extremely modest involvement in the area hit by the hurricane. Also catching the wave were manufactured housing companies, as well as producers of all sorts of construction materials. Elcor was up 26% in one week on an expected surge in demand for roofing shingles. Trading volume expanded nearly a hundredfold in the stock of Dycom

Industries. The electrical construction company was quickly on the scene in Florida, deactivating fallen utility lines. Taking into account the potential earnings to be derived from putting up new lines, investors pushed Dycom's stock to more than double its previous level. The most prominent gainer, however, was Lennar. The company's stock quickly broke its 52-week high. As the largest homebuilder in hurricane-devastated Dade County, Lennar was a logical issuer for investors to focus on. The company enjoyed a good reputation, having been named Company of the Year in 1991 by two Florida publications. Chairman Leonard Miller had taken Man of the Year honors.

These accolades intensified the shock felt when the homeowners in a Lennar development sued the company for negligence. They alleged that their houses were defective and consequently had suffered worse damage in the hurricane than they should have. Lennar promptly denounced the suit as "totally without merit" and resolved to contest it vigorously. The company even vowed to seek compensation for any costs incurred in the litigation.

Nevertheless, Lennar's stock plunged on news of the lawsuit. On September 3, the shares closed at $23\frac{1}{2}$, down 22% from the post-hurricane peak close of $30\frac{1}{8}$ on August 27. As a matter of fact, the final September 3 price was down 16% from the close on the Friday preceding Hurricane Andrew. A disaster that was first perceived as a boon had proven to be a net detriment to the stock. Certainly, the reversal was not entirely foreseeable, but there were a few straws in the wind prior to the lawsuit by residents of the Hampshire Homes development. For one thing, some securities analysts had characterized the initial surge in Lennar shares as early or overdone. They'd pointed out that Lennar's traditional business was constructing blocks of 100 new homes at a time. The main task that would be called for by Andrew was the rebuilding of individual homes.

If anything, these analysts had said, Lennar's costs would rise in its new-construction activities, since rebuilding would increase the demand for labor and supplies. Furthermore, at a price of $30\frac{1}{8}$, Lennar was trading at twice the multiple of estimated earnings of many other homebuilders.

Even more to the point than these warning signs was the fact that the share-wrecking litigation wasn't entirely new. The Hampshire Homes residents had initially sued Lennar more than a year before the hurricane hit. At that point, they'd alleged that the builder's use of untreated wood and ungalvanized steel bolts had caused their houses to rot before their time. The original suit was still pending when Hurricane Andrew ended the rotting problem for many South Florida homeowners.

Along with Dade County homeowners, many investors also incurred losses in the wake of the hurricane. In some cases, the culprit was faulty logic. Other attempts to capitalize on the disaster backfired because of previously unrecognized risks.

It all goes to show that the victims of a fire, famine, or flood aren't to be found exclusively in the disaster zone. Thousands of miles away, a natural calamity can be quite an uncomfortable affair for people who merely wanted to make a quick buck off it. Plainly, there are many far less harrowing ways of investing your money.

8

Gambler's Blues

When Investment Turns to Speculation, Betting Isn't Far Behind

The scene is a psychiatrist's office. He is meeting for the first time with a compulsive gambler. Never before has the doctor accepted a patient with this particular problem. He has found that as a rule, gambling addicts run out of money before seeking treatment. In this case, however, the gambler's wife threatened to divorce him unless he agreed to go into therapy. Knowing that the spouse is handling the financial end, the psychiatrist feels confident of getting paid.

Almost immediately upon entering the office, the new patient demands to know how much the treatment will cost.

"One hundred fifty dollars a session," answers the psychiatrist.

"Tell my wife two hundred, instead," replies the gambler. "I'll split the extra fifty dollars with you."

* * *

The patient in this story (which happens to be true) continued to focus on finagling money to feed his habit, rather than on trying to shake it. His brief fling with psychiatric counseling proved unfruitful on both scores. Sadly, the tale could be repeated, with heart-rending variations, literally millions of times. As many as 3% of adult Americans have serious gambling habits.

If you're wondering whether a discussion of betting addictions belongs in a book on investments, consider a pertinent statistic. It comes from Dr. Robert Custer, who founded the first treatment program for compulsive gambling. He reports that 20% of his patients who have the problem got started in the financial markets. Speculating in stocks and bonds doesn't always lead to getting hooked on harder stuff, but causation is a moot point for many investors. They buy and sell securities in a manner that's essentially indistinguishable from gambling.

It might pay to take a hard look at your own investment habits. You could find uncomfortable parallels with the classic winning, losing, and desperation phases that characterize the problem gambler. To a compulsive bettor, the best thing in the world is to gamble and win. Second best is to gamble and lose. "Gambling is much better than sex. No comparison," says one reformed horseracing addict. (Let's hope you don't feel as strongly as that about the stock market. But are emotional "kicks" part of the appeal for you?)

The most severe psychological deterioration sets in when a gambler begins to "chase his losses." This consists of betting more and more in a desperate attempt to get back to even. (Do you habitually average down after making a bad investment?)

Sociologist Henry R. Lesieur, a long-time researcher into problem gambling, is quoted by Dennis Breo, in the November 10, 1989, issue of the *Journal of the American Medical Association*, as saying that what usually pushes an addictive bettor over the edge is a loss that he considers "illogical." Suppose, for example, that a gambler meticulously handicaps a football game. As his team goes for the winning field goal, the ball hits the crossbar and misses by an inch. "Well, this type of loss represents a severe injury to the gambler's self-esteem," Lesieur explains, "and now he begins to furiously try to win his money back *without* handicapping the games. Of course, he loses more and more."

If you haven't yet seen your own behavior reflected, your speculative impulses are probably under control. But are you perhaps prey to the gambler's legendary superstitiousness? Rationally, we know that each number in a lottery has an equivalent chance of being the winner. Yet the introduction of lotteries by the majority of states has stimulated sales of "dream books." These publications purport to recommend lucky numbers based on objects that appear in the slumbers of the credulous. (You've never bought a security on a hunch, have you?)

Don't be ashamed if you've occasionally fallen into one or more of the traps listed in parentheses. Even Wall Street professionals can succumb to the fatal attraction of irrational risks. Early in my career I received a vivid, firsthand confirmation of that fact.

Along with some co-workers, I visited a festival in Manhattan's Little Italy section. The attractions included the usual midway amusements. Anyone with a gift for squirting water into the mouths of toy clowns could go home with an armload of adorable stuffed animals. One game, however, had a more peculiar fascination. A contestant wagered on the roll of a set of six-sided sticks. Each facet of these elongated dice contained a series of numbers. The player won if the numbers on all face-up sides exceeded a specified sum.

My analysis of the game was simple. The prize was not a stuffed animal, but rather a color television set. I reasoned that if players had any realistic chance of winning, the proprietor would long since have gone broke.

The TV set also figured prominently in the thinking of my friends, who quickly elbowed their way to the front of the line. By the time they had dropped 30 or 40 dollars, I assumed they would be ready to move on. I was mistaken, however. It was at this point that the surpassing brilliance of the game's inventor became apparent. According to the rules, a player could retain all points accumulated on previous rolls by buying one more chance. The threshold for victory, naturally, rose to a higher level with each roll. Thanks to the cunning arrangement of the numbers on the sticks, the sucker's accumulated score appeared always to be within one roll of the jackpot. The illusion was strong enough to keep players plunking down their cash until it ran out, as my colleagues proved.

Their excesses might be excused by the festival's prevailing carnival atmosphere. Unfortunately, though, people do not automatically lose the gambling impulse the moment they turn from sideshows to the securities market. Huge payoffs are no less enticing in financial speculation than they are in roulette.

Around the same time as the incident in Little Italy, I ran into a college classmate. He could scarcely wait to tell me about his spectacular success in the market. "Last year, I made $20,000 trading in options," he proudly related. "Of course, I lost $30,000 on my *unprofitable* trades. But now I've figured out what I was doing wrong. This year, I'm going to clean up."

The bug had bitten him worse than I would have believed. "I've also arranged to manage money for a few of my friends," he went on. "I'm just waiting to accumulate a little more cash. Then, I'll quit my practice and start trading options full time."

Here once again, albeit in a different form, was the illusion of perpetually verging on profitability. From a psychological standpoint, speculating in options was even more alluring than the numbered-sticks game. Not only were the stakes higher, but the contest contained a larger element of skill.

It's almost redundant to add that the odds eventually caught up with my college pal. The next time I saw him, he had little to say about options. No longer was he prepared to chuck his promising legal career. His system had been no match for high volatility and the relentless drain of commissions.

This is not to suggest that options are inherently too risky to mess with. In fact, they can be used specifically for reducing risk—that is, to hedge a position in the underlying securities. The catch is that if someone is shedding risk, somebody else is acquiring risk in the transaction. Are you the right person for that role?

A poker player's adage may help you to answer that question. It says that the evening's eventual winner will be the player who sits down at the outset with the biggest bankroll. As the pots grow and the distribution of chips fluctuates wildly, the individual with the most staying power will have a distinct advantage.

By extension, it's hazardous to speculate when your competitors are far better capitalized than you. Institutional investors generally fit that description. You may be further handicapped by the need to concentrate on other things (such as your job) during trading hours. Being a few hours late in receiving pertinent information isn't a catastrophe when you're investing in fundamental value for the long term. It may be a completely different story when you're seeking quick profits in a volatile instrument.

Still, there's an undeniable appeal in betting against impossible odds—at least for some people there is. As for myself, I get as much of a thrill out of reading an actuarial table as I do from playing roulette. The house's edge guarantees that over time the bettors will lose money at a predictable rate. There's not much excitement for me in seeing the action confirm well-established laws of probability.

Viewed in these terms, the house's side is far more appealing than the gambler's. Unfortunately, obtaining a casino operator's license requires immense capital, as well as an unimpeachable character. Hitting this combination is a longshot, to say the least.

In the investment area, by contrast, anybody can be the house. It doesn't require starting a brokerage firm, although collecting commissions on other people's risk taking is one good strategy. Another and more generally available alternative is to capture the built-in positive return on capital. Like the casino's margin or the bookmaker's vigorish, this is a modest but reliable earnings stream.

Why does a diversified portfolio of sound investments inevitably grow in value over the long run? One explanation is that people have the alternative of spending their money to obtain instant gratification. Choosing instead to invest capital means deferring pleasures while somebody else uses it. The only obvious reason to delay gratification is in order to be even more gratified later on. As a result, the folks who want to borrow money for a while must promise to pay back a larger amount in the future. Economic theorizing aside, the positive payback on patient, conservative investing is one of the few things you can count on in the securities markets. If you're truly aiming to build your net worth, you have to devote a portion of your assets to slow appreciation and low turnover. When that foundation is in place, it makes sense to commit some of your funds to higher-risk, higher-return investments. But if you cross over the line into irrational speculation, don't delude yourself that you're genuinely trying to increase your wealth. It may even be time to seek professional help.

Part Two

NUMBERS
RACKETS

9

Out of the Blue

Short-Run Changes in Earnings
Forecasts May Not Be the Best
Basis for Your Investment Decisions

At the opposite extreme from
companies that claim to be undervalued due to lack of attention
lies the institutional stock par excellence, International Business
Machines. By no stretch of the imagination could the world's largest computer manufacturer be considered overlooked. The 1991
Standard Periodical Directory lists nine journals and newsletters devoted solely to the affairs of "Big Blue." IBM attracts extensive
coverage by securities analysts as well. As of March 14, 1991, 34
analysts contributed quarterly earnings-per-share forecasts on the
company to the *Institutional Brokers Estimate System* (IBES), published by Lynch, Jones & Ryan of New York.

Many other prominent corporations had significantly less coverage by this measure (e.g., Eastman Kodak with 25 published
estimates, Lockheed with 22, and Xerox with just 16). On the
whole, then, investors ought to have felt confident that IBM's stock
was not mispriced as a result of analytical neglect.

The 34 IBES estimates for IBM's 1991 first quarter, dated two
weeks prior to the end of the period, had a mean average of $1.84,
about flat with the $1.81 recorded one year earlier. Having studied
the available information concerning the company's prospects, no
analyst saw a need to deviate by more than 10% (rounded) from
the consensus. The full range of estimates was from a high of $2.01
to the most bearish forecast of $1.65 a share.

On March 19, 1991, IBM stunned the analysts with the revelation that the most pessimistic of their group was in fact too opti-

mistic by about 80%. Instead of matching its first-quarter 1990 results, the company now expected that its earnings would fall by half, to around $0.90. That day, one of the most closely watched stocks in the market plunged by almost 10% in response to news that caught every analyst by surprise.

Under different circumstances, a 10% decline wouldn't have been terribly distressing. (Except, naturally, to investors who happened to own the stock in question.) Suppose, for instance, that a price discontinuity of 10% or so had resulted from some unforeseeable shock. Examples might include an oil tanker collision or an unexpected legal decision. A consequent lurch in the stock price would not have contradicted any economic theories about how the financial markets respond to new information. Alternatively, an instant 10% devaluation wouldn't have caused much of a stir if it had occurred in an obscure and illiquid stock. That sort of event would have merely reinforced the popular belief that thin research coverage creates exploitable mispricings.

However, some basic assumptions are challenged by the IBM incident. Six billion dollars of market value suddenly went up in smoke, without any shock that the company failed to foresee. The triggering event was an announcement by the company about its earnings prospects. For a company as widely monitored as IBM, it seems surprising that securities analysts were caught so severely off guard.

Certainly, things don't happen that way in the economics textbooks. According to theorists of the capital markets, securities prices are constantly incorporating new information. Barring unpredictable shocks, changes in earnings expectations should be incremental and evolutionary. In that sort of world, it makes sense that portfolio managers vie to be first to learn of minor forecast revisions by the leading analysts. The climactic change in the IBM earnings estimates casts some doubt on the benefits of early notification about shifts in nuance.

At least one analyst quoted in the press blamed IBM for surprising him and his peers. Significantly, he also faulted Big Blue for having done the same thing on previous occasions. This statement has a disturbing implication for the whole process of earnings forecasting. It suggests that analysts often find it difficult, working from the outside, to anticipate even the major swings. Companies less scrupulous than IBM might take unfair advantage of their opaqueness. They could manipulate their securities prices by controlling the outside estimates of their earnings.

The scenario is hardly far-fetched, given the inherent difficulties of short-term forecasting. IBM, for example, is hard to fathom because of its vast size and complexity. Additionally, Big Blue's net income is highly sensitive to modest (and hard-to-predict) fluctuations in operating margins. As a matter of fact, even after the scales fell from analysts' eyes on March 19, IBM's outlook was not entirely clarified. When actual earnings per share of $0.93 were announced on April 14, some analysts cut their 1991 full-year estimates again. In response, the stock dropped by $2\frac{1}{8}$ to $108\frac{1}{2}$.

IBM's second slump occurred even though earnings came in a bit above the $0.90 that management had spoken of earlier. Underlying the change was the fact that along with the official earnings, the company provided a breakdown of sales. It revealed a larger-than-expected 17% fall in the hardware sector. As a consequence, analysts once more revised their forecasts.

Perhaps the real lesson of the IBM incident has to do with the value of earnings estimates and reports. Variations in 90-day chunks of corporate performance shed only limited light on intrinsic securities values. Like most statistical series, quarterly earnings figures contain a certain amount of "noise." (This term refers to minor fluctuations that convey nothing meaningful regarding longer-term trends.)

Theoretically, the price of a company's common stock reflects its earnings in all future periods. It appears, therefore, that investors lavish too much attention on quarterly numbers. This premise is supported by the latitude inherent in financial reporting standards. Management's discretionary decisions can move reported earnings across a wide range, with no particular mooring to economic reality.

Reflecting these and other problems, there is an active debate surrounding the value of quarterly earnings figures. (The matter was even raised as a campaign issue by presidential aspirant Paul Tsongas, in May 1991.) One aspect of the question is not a matter of debate, however. It's pretty clear that you can lose money by overreacting to minor shifts in quarterly earnings estimates. Many times, revised forecasts produce a spurious impression that a company's intrinsic value has changed. By responding to that illusion, you'll wind up paying commissions to execute unproductive trades.

For your own protection, you should use analysts' opinions with discretion. Resist the temptation to react to every minor ripple in the earnings stream. While you're worrying about statistical noise, the truly significant changes in value may be about to hit you out of the Blue.

10

Fundamental Assumptions

*Poring Over Financial Statements
Can Be Rewarding, Provided the
Statements Are on the Level*

"*F*undamental analysis" consists of evaluating companies' securities by studying their financial statements. If you believe that getting ahead is mostly a matter of hard work, you'll probably find fundamental analysis the most appealing style of investing. At the very least, you'll like the clichés associated with it.

When you engage in fundamental analysis, you'll *roll up your sleeves* and *get your hands dirty*. You'll *take the company apart* and go over its numbers *with a fine-toothed comb*. You'll search for *basic value*, emphasizing *hard assets* and a *solid earnings record*.

Unfortunately, you won't always derive as much satisfaction from your results as you do from your display of sturdy virtues. The problem is that not all of the companies issuing the financial statements share your ideals. Some of them use *liberal accounting practices*. Others *paint glowing pictures* of grim situations. A few just flat out *cook the books*.

How can corporations get away with misleading financial reporting right under the noses of their auditors, the Financial Accounting Standards Board, and the Securities and Exchange Commission? In the case of outright fraud, the answer is that surveillance can never be totally effective against individuals who are willing to risk prison terms if caught. The more common hazards for investors are the nasty surprises lurking in statements that appear to satisfy the rules.

Consider, for example, the September 27, 1991, announcement by Community Psychiatric Centers that it had earned a mighty one-cent-per-share profit in its latest quarter. Investors were evidently disturbed by the fact that this figure represented a 98% decline from the company's previous-year results. Community Psychiatric's stock price promptly fell by $6\frac{1}{2}$ points to $17\frac{1}{4}$.

The profit plunge did not reflect a sudden drop in the number of people requiring psychiatric attention. Like most providers of mental health care, Community Psychiatric was feeling some pressure on patient admissions and prices in 1991, but its year-over-year revenue decline was only 5%. The much sharper slide in reported earnings resulted largely from an addition to reserves for accounts receivable. In less technical language, this means that Community Psychiatric reported profits in one period based on the assumption that it would eventually get paid for services it had already rendered. Later, the company modified its assumption and decided that a portion of those profits had not been profits after all.

Note that this sort of shock can occur without any violation of the standards for financial reporting. On the contrary, an essential feature of the accrual method of accounting is the estimation of certain items. Examples include future losses on bad debts and the rate of wear and tear on plants and equipment. The theory is that accruing revenues and expenses provides a truer picture of profitability than simply recording the cash going out or coming in.

Unfortunately, estimates are by definition prone to error. Community Psychiatric's stockholders learned just how costly an error can be when the aggregate value of their shares fell by $430 million in two days. (The total includes a $2\frac{3}{4}$-point drop in the stock price on the day before the earnings release. Investors got nervous because the report came later than expected—a classic signal that trouble might be brewing.)

If you're trying to beat the market through fundamental analysis, you need to be aware that the Community Psychiatric affair was far from unique. All corporations' annual reports reflect assumptions that are subject to change. And change they do.

Around the same time Community Psychiatric was concluding that it had been too optimistic about prospects for collecting from its customers, Citicorp was having similar misgivings about its foreign borrowers. The banking giant accordingly wrote off $745 million of its $2 billion of medium- and long-term loans to Brazil. Citicorp's abrupt change of heart about the value of its loan portfolio coincided with mammoth charges for restructuring of operations. In addition, a decision to eliminate dividends on the company's common stock left shareholders feeling dejected. As if to assuage their pain, Citicorp simultaneously produced a $122 million accounting gain by revising its method of valuing the investments of its venture capital subsidiaries. Management did nothing to enhance the actual economic value of the investments. It merely adopted a less conservative approach for recording them on its balance sheet, switching to *fair value* from *the lower of cost or fair value.*

The accounting rules fully sanction such instantaneous creation and destruction of purported wealth. Potential misuse of this discretion is constrained by the obligation to obtain an auditor's seal of approval for financial statements.

Latitude regarding assumptions can be a benefit to investors when used by upright corporate managers. Actual and potential shareholders are helped by a company's prompt recognition of unforeseen changes in economic value. But the timing of a decision to write off assets or to adopt an alternative accounting method is inherently subjective. Abuses can easily arise. A company can, for example, exploit its discretionary power to mask gradual erosion in value. Inevitably, in such cases, the gap between reality and the balance sheet expands to a dimension that ceases to be credible. At that point, the stock price collapses in a convulsive revision of past statements.

Your interest as a fundamentals-oriented investor is to be standing somewhere else when the debris comes crashing down. Fortunately, there are two fairly useful rules to follow if you want to avoid being the fall guy. First, consider a company's record when you assess the reliability of its financial reporting. If you get bagged by a management team that has a long history of producing nasty surprises, you share the blame. By way of illustration, *The Wall Street Journal* on October 16, 1991, ran a front-page article under the headline, "Hollywood Mystery: Woes at Orion Stayed

Invisible for Years." A subhead read, "Studio Apparently Resorted to Aggressive Accounting as Its Business Faltered." According to the *Journal*, Orion Pictures "postponed big losses by inflating the value of its TV and film inventory." When the losses could no longer be put off, the company announced that it would report a "substantial" loss in its latest quarter.

Just by chance, I had used Orion Pictures as an example of postponement of inevitable losses in my book *Financial Statement Analysis: A Practitioner's Guide*, published about six months before the *Journal*'s exposé. The events I described took place in the studio's 1981–1985 fiscal years. During that period, Orion consistently reported profits of about $7 million annually, then tumbled to a $31.9 million loss in fiscal 1986.

At least one Wall Street analyst correctly foretold the company's reversal of fortune. John Tinker, who was then working at Balis & Zorn, Inc., detected in Orion's financial statements some strong evidence that the studio was slow in writing off its box office flops.

Even if your research had uncovered neither my book nor Tinker's 1985 report, you still could have known that Orion's financial statements needed to be approached warily. As the *Journal*'s October 16, 1991, article reported, "In April, 1987, the Securities and Exchange Commission became curious enough about Orion's accounting to investigate its policy on writedowns." Ultimately, the SEC found nothing illegal, but you were free to regard the company's numbers with intense skepticism from that day forward. Paying attention to Orion's history would have been a wise policy, as it turned out.

A second common thread among accounting surprises is their tendency to coincide with other signs of deterioration. It seems that as a company's operating problems mount, so does its boldness in interpreting the rules for financial reporting. Therefore, you should be doubly cautious about relying on fundamental analysis when a company may be fundamentally unsound. In all of the cases discussed in this chapter, there were good reasons to be on red alert before the bomb dropped.

Community Psychiatric's 98% earnings decline broke a 22-year streak of quarterly increases, yet the calamity was not entirely unforeseeable. Financial reports of other hospital chains had already shown the ravages of public and private efforts to contain health care costs.

Citicorp, too, had suffered from well-publicized industry problems. In fact, its Brazilian loan problems were old hat by 1991, as real estate and leveraged buyout loans had garnered a greater share of investors' angst. Standard & Poor's gave a clear signal of deterioration in April 1990, when it downgraded the institution's debt. The rating agency cited Citicorp's low levels of capital and loan loss reserves relative to those of its competitors. Later the same year, S&P took Citicorp down another notch, based on an expectation of further deterioration in asset quality. For a time, that seemed like the bottom. A couple of months before Citicorp's October 15, 1991, bombshell, however, S&P switched its rating outlook from stable to negative.

As for Orion Pictures, investors had only to watch the 1991 Academy Awards broadcast to realize that all was not well. Comedian Billy Crystal joked that the nominated films included "Awakenings," the story of someone coming out of a coma; "Reversal of Fortune," which dealt with someone going into a coma; and Orion's "Dances with Wolves," a movie made by a studio in a coma. (Another clue was the drop in the company's share price from over 15 to less than 2 in the year preceding the October 15, 1991, announcement.)

In summary, the fundamental approach is laudable as an embodiment of self-reliance and the nose-to-the-grindstone philosophy. If the stock market were perfectly just, high returns would accrue to investors who painstakingly studied companies' financial statements. Unfortunately, the statements are not always on the square. Even when they conform to all of the applicable accounting standards, as attested to by leading accounting firms, they may rest on estimates and assumptions that will later change. You may avoid being victimized if you study not only the company's annual report but also the company's credibility as an issuer of financial statements.

11

Droll Models

Forecasting Methods Often Oversimplify Reality

How would you like to be in a showdown with the fastest gun this side of the Pecos? Just to make it interesting, give yourself a slight handicap: Let your opponent begin with his six-shooter loaded, while allowing yourself to load up only after the other fellow shouts, "Draw!"

If this kind of sport appeals to you, consider entering the exciting field of financial-market forecasting. Your task will be to predict economic events that are likely to influence securities prices. The challenge is that the prices themselves represent a consensus forecast of the very events you're attempting to predict.

When fast-breaking news alters the outlook, investors can revise their collective forecast almost immediately. They simply bid prices up or drive them down. Their transactions occur in far less time than it takes you to consult your computer and publish your updated forecast. In other words, while you're putting your ammunition into the chamber, the market is plugging you full of hot lead.

Conceivably, though, you can succeed as an oracle without being exceptionally quick on the draw. By its nature, the crowd's instantaneous response can't reflect a carefully thought-out analysis. Over time, a well-designed forecasting model should easily beat traders who shoot from the hip.

This reasoning is the basis for many forecasting systems, yet it contains a fundamental flaw. In reality, success does not depend merely on conducting a more complex analysis than traders can perform in the split second following a news bulletin. What you really need, if you hope to beat the pack consistently, is a forecasting model that can deal adequately with the complex world economy. That implies a model nearly as complex as the economy itself.

Professional forecasters may protest that I'm setting an impossibly high standard. Global economic activity, after all, consists of millions of daily interactions. Furthermore, new factors are constantly entering the picture. Examples include newly constructed factories, technological advances, changes in government regulations, and many more. It's simply not feasible to incorporate every variable that might someday be relevant. Accordingly, keeping things on a manageable scale is essential to making any headway whatsoever. As long as a model addresses the major cause-and-effect relationships, it should capture the main trends. Leaving out the minutiae will presumably produce only trivial errors.

Let's grant for the moment the argument that it's okay to neglect minor factors in order to concentrate on the big picture. There are at least two things that can go wrong. History shows that these vulnerabilities are not hypothetical.

The first problem is that cause-and-effect relationships aren't necessarily consistent over time. Frequently, the reason is that human behavior changes in unforeseen ways. In the late 1970s, for example, Americans failed to save at the rate that the models assumed they would. Maybe people figured it made no sense to hold on to cash that was quickly losing its value through inflation. Whatever its cause, the drop in the U.S. savings rate wasn't anticipated by the forecasters. Consumer spending consequently persisted at a higher level than the models had predicted. The second reason that models sometimes get even the big things wrong is that they necessarily leave out a lot of details. By simplifying reality, forecasting systems omit subtleties that occasionally prove critical. Such flaws are not necessarily limited to individual models. Some are common to virtually every practitioner. Consider the underestimation of mortgage prepayment rates in early 1992 by all major investment banks.

By way of background, the value of mortgage-backed debt securities depends heavily on the speed with which homeowners repay the principal on their loans. Contractually speaking, the borrowers can typically take 30 years to pay off their balances in full. On average, though, they liquidate the obligations much more rapidly. Some causes of the prepayments are reasonably predictable. First-time home buyers commonly move up to bigger houses as their incomes rise. In the process, they extinguish their existing mortgages. A similar process occurs when workers take new jobs that require them to relocate. Retirees, too, may move out of their homes well before their mortgages are fully amortized.

These sources of turnover in the housing stock are fairly steady. Demographic changes (fewer first-time buyers, more retirees, etc.) alter prepayment rates only gradually. Certain other factors create considerable volatility, however. In particular, when interest rates decline, many homeowners pay off their balances by obtaining new, cheaper mortgages. This refinancing can cause prepayments to rise far above normal levels.

By 1991, mortgage-backed securities specialists had extensively studied the historical connection between interest rates and prepayments. Their models contained well-supported assumptions about the amount by which prepayments would rise, given a stated decline in yields on 10-year Treasury obligations.

Despite all the work that went into them, the models substantially underestimated the surge in prepayments that occurred in early 1992. For example, consider the class consisting of mortgages originated in 1986 and carrying 10% interest rates. What if the Wall Street pundits had known beforehand that 10-year Treasury yields were going to fall by 1.11 percentage points in the 12 months ending June 1992? On average, the 12-month forecasts they made in mid-1991 still would have been more than 50% too low. The source of the forecasting error was the simplifying assumption that all interest rates would move up or down by equivalent amounts. In fact, while 10-year Treasury yields declined by 1.11 points (from 8.24% to 7.13%), 5-year yields fell by 1.62 points (from 7.91% to 6.29%). Holders of shorter-term mortgages, which had become increasingly common during the 1980s, responded more to the drop in 5-year yields than to the smaller drop in 10-year yields.

Existing models foresaw none of this. Far more than the predicted number of homeowners prepaid their mortgages in early 1992.

Clearly, it's possible to correct a model's oversights. Likewise, forecasters can adjust their methods to reflect changes in behavior. It's not feasible, however, to construct a model that completely accounts for the complexity of the global economy.

This is not to say that forecasting has no value. On the contrary, looking forward is essential for manufacturing companies. A key to their success is planning production in advance of demand. Note, however, that a manufacturer doesn't ordinarily lock itself into a "single-point" forecast. Suppose that the company budgets sales of 10 million units. It will also prepare for the possibility of actual demand coming in at 11 million. The extra production can be achieved by scheduling overtime or through subcontracting. If, on the other hand, demand slips to 9 million units, management may use layoffs to close the gap.

In the manufacturing context, much of a forecast's value lies in telling management how much flexibility is required. More dramatic measures would be called for, in our example, if near-term demand were to surge to 15 million units or dwindle to 5 million. The company might then need to construct new capacity or close one of its facilities. Merely by assigning low probabilities to the extreme scenarios, a forecaster can aid management's contingency planning immensely.

Forecasts of the financial markets would probably be more helpful if they, too, presented ranges of possibilities. Practically speaking, you probably won't overhaul your portfolio if your favorite pundit's forecast switches from a 20% gain in the stock market to a 25% rise. That sort of difference is of interest mainly to the prognosticators themselves, who will later quibble about which of them was closest to the mark. But it may matter a great deal to you whether the probability of a massive sell-off is 5% or 30%. If you'd be devastated by a big loss, the latter assessment would probably send you scurrying into cash.

Regrettably, it's not easy to obtain forecasts that place odds on a range of possible outcomes. When economists are surveyed, the boxes they're asked to fill in generally involve only "rates and dates." The question is simply, "Where will the Dow be on December 31?" This is a case of a question that's too simple.

Simplification, as we've already seen, can lead to serious fore-casting errors. Predictive models must cut reality down to a size they can deal with. To the extent that you rely on models, make sure to hedge your bets. Doing otherwise is equivalent to playing with a loaded gun.

12

Improbable Though It Seems

Basic Laws of Probability Give Lie to Most Claims of Superior Investment Performance

*H*ere's a great-sounding invest- ment: A mutual fund that unfailingly achieves better returns than the median fund in its category. The method underlying this re- markable record is simple. Through many years of trial-and-error, the fund's manager has perfected a conservative, value-oriented system of picking stocks. Because a cornerstone of her strategy is to limit risk, she avoids the high-flyers that sometimes triple or quadruple in value. Consequently, her fund is never at the very top of the quarterly or annual performance sweepstakes. On the other hand, she rarely picks a security that loses 70% or 80% of its value.

The manager's slow-but-sure approach has created an intrigu- ing investment opportunity. By owning her fund, you can expect to outperform 50% or more of all mutual fund shareholders year in and year out. Over time, you should far outdistance the specu- lators, who occasionally finish in the top 10% only to fall to the bottom 10% the following year.

Naturally, there are no guarantees when it comes to future results. But this manager has an authenticated track record to back up her claims. Since perfecting her formula three years ago, she has outperformed the median stock mutual fund in every annual survey.

* * *

As salespitches go, "Shoot for the top half" is fairly under-stated. It appeals less overtly than many marketing campaigns do to the fatal something-for-nothing instinct. Even so, the case for the self-proclaimed median-beating fund suffers from at least one se-rious defect in logic. Every year, by definition, half of the mutual funds in a peer group finish above the median. The "winners" invariably include many funds that were "losers" (below-median performers) in the preceding year. A single period's results simply can't tell you whether a manager made it to the top half by virtue of a genuinely superior investment strategy. Some of this year's winners are certain to fall to the bottom half next year. They will probably do so while continuing to employ the same techniques that placed them above the median in the current year. This will give rise to a strong suspicion that their moment of glory was a function of luck, rather than skill.

The slow-but-sure manager, however, is not basing her claims on finishing in the top half for a single year. She has accomplished the feat three years in a row. Doesn't that lend some credence to the story that she has found a formula that really works?

Not necessarily. To understand why, let's analyze the rank-ings of a hypothetical group of competing mutual funds over three years. Applying a few basic laws of probability will aid the analysis.

Suppose for a moment that no manager in the peer group enjoys a real edge in picking stocks or timing the market's ups and downs. Under these conditions, each manager has a 50% chance of placing in the top half during the first year.

At the end of the first year, the race starts all over again. Good performance in Year 1 does not imply any sort of "head start" in Year 2. If we stick to our premise that no manager in the group possesses a genuinely superior formula, then everyone continues to have a 50% chance of finishing in the top half during the coming year. This applies as fully to Year 1's top-halfers as to its bottom-halfers. Accordingly, 50% of Year 1's above-median performers should achieve above-median results in Year 2, as well. By this reasoning, each manager in the peer group has a one-in-four chance of reaching the top half in both Year 1 and Year 2. Continu-ing the logic to the third and final year, 50% of the managers who beat the median in both Year 1 and Year 2 should do so again in Year 3. That is, one-half of one-quarter of all funds—one-eighth of the total—should have top-half performance for three years in a row. The slow-but-sure manager will probably have some company in the three-time winners' circle.

Depending on your point of view, a one-in-eight chance of above-median performance may look like either mediocre or excellent odds. On the one hand, you probably wouldn't go into business as a mutual fund manager on the mere hope of ending up among the lucky one-eighth in your peer group. Imagine, however, that you are a financial reporter who wishes to write a profile of a "hot" manager. There is a high probability that at any given time, some fund will have outperformed half of its competitors for three years running.

The slow-but-sure manager may sincerely believe that she has at long last discovered the secret of consistent top-half performance. Three years is simply not enough time to prove or disprove the proposition, however. It may be that although the manager is working very hard, her theories are unfounded. Perhaps the validation she thinks she is hearing as prices rise is really the sound of the market mocking her.

* * *

As I promised a few paragraphs back, I have brought the discussion this far by applying only the most basic laws of probability. Notwithstanding its simplicity, the analysis you've just read exposes a fallacy that is repeated every day in the financial markets. Investment advisers regularly win new clients on the strength of performance records that are not demonstrably better than chance results. Market forecasters routinely persuade investors of their excellence by stringing together just a few correct predictions.

If these representations of superior skill can be discredited so easily, why do people persist in relying on them? Some investors simply do not understand the basic principles of probability. Others, I suspect, know a fair amount about probability but do not perceive its connection with investments.

This conceptual gap is understandable. Thinking about probability is easy enough when the discussion is limited to coin flipping and dice rolling (the two primary obsessions of the authors of elementary statistics textbooks). Rational individuals will readily concede that the likelihood of rolling a seven is in no way affected by the efforts of the roller. It's quite another matter, however, to conceive of investment managers' results as being controlled in large measure by chance. Surely, you would think, they derive some benefit from their intensive study of economic trends and historical price movements.

Perhaps so, but the conclusion is not self-evident. Investing contains a larger chance element than you might imagine. In this regard, playing the market resembles many other highly skilled games. Consider the "hot hands" phenomenon in basketball. Everyone who has played or watched the game knows that the ability to sink baskets runs in streaks. From time to time, a player hits several straight shots and becomes so self-confident that missing seems to become almost impossible.

The only problem with this nearly universal perception is that serious research has refuted it. Stanford University psychologist Amos Tversky and his associates studied every field goal attempt by the Philadelphia 76ers over a season and a half. Making one basket, they found, did not improve a player's chances of sinking the next one. Neither did making two. Nor three.

What about those longer streaks of eight, nine, or ten in a row? A player who on average sinks 55% of his attempts has a 30.25% chance (.55 x .55) of making two baskets in a row. The same player has a 16.64% chance (.55 x .55 x .55) of making three in a row, assuming that his accuracy is not improving with each one he sinks. Clearly, the probabilities get pretty small when we extend the calculation to long streaks. A National Basketball Association team takes thousands of shots in a season. The odds are that a few exceptionally long streaks will occur over the course of a season, even if the likelihood of success does not mount with each successful attempt. Tversky found that the 76ers' streaks were neither more numerous nor lengthier than chance alone would have predicted.

This suggests that players reel off strings of 10 or 12 consecutive baskets because the laws of probability say they must. Inevitably, a player in the midst of a streak feels an elevated sense of self-assurance. He feels "hot" and credits that feeling for his continuing success. Statistical analysis, however, suggests that he has the cause and effect reversed.

Similarly counter-intuitive conclusions emerge from a careful look at baseball statistics. Jean Lemaire, a professor of actuarial science at the Wharton School of the University of Pennsylvania, gives the example of a .265 hitter who is benched after going 0 for 11. This slump is not really an indication that he is batting less competently than usual. If he comes to the plate 600 times during the season, the probability is over 99% that he will go 0 for 11 at least once. Approximately half of the league's .265 hitters will go 0 for 17 at some point in the season. Their droughts will not reflect temporarily reduced skill, but rather the predictable consequences of hitting safely 265 times out of 1,000, on average.

Hitless streaks, like long sequences of successful jump shots, will cease to amaze you if you decide to pursue the subject of probability. You will likewise be less in awe of a three-year record of top-half investment performance. In reality, it is no more remarkable an achievement than tossing "heads" three times in a row. Armed with this understanding, you will resist the manager's claims of being able to beat the median unfailingly. And resist you should. There is considerable doubt that a hot hand in the investment game promises future success.

Edgar W. Barksdale and William L. Green, managing directors of RCB International in Stamford, Connecticut, conducted a detailed study of the relationship between past and future performance. Their sample included more than 144 equity portfolios managed by 135 firms. All of the portfolios were in existence over the full 15-year period of the study.

Barksdale and Green measured the portfolios' returns over each 10-year period beginning in 1975 through 1990: They then asked whether managers who performed well in the first half of a decade also tended to do well in the second half. Their results were far from a ringing endorsement of the hot hands hypothesis.

Of the managers who finished in the top 20% for the half decade 1976–1980, only 52% finished in the top *half* during 1981–1986. Furthermore, that was the best second-half performance for the top quintile in any decade-long period of Barksdale and Green's study. Just 31% of the top-fifth finishers of 1975–1979 made the top half in 1980–1984.

How about the *bottom* quintile of managers? In the 1975 through 1984 decade, 57% produced above-median returns during the second half of the period. Just as good performance did not confer a better-than-even chance of subsequent good performance, poor performance did not assure continued mediocrity.

* * *

A little sophistication regarding probability can go a long way in assessing the claims of investment managers and market pundits. Consumer protection exists up to a point, but after that, you have to protect yourself.

It's easy to fall prey to the "hot hands" illusion. A Dow forecaster can garner a lot of publicity by correctly calling two or three swings in succession. When you see the newly anointed prophet profiled in *Barron's*, you may forget that a lot more evidence is needed to establish that this genius's predictions have any validity whatsoever. The chances are extremely good, however, that a few more forecasts will restore your faith in the power of probability.

13

Beware the Bond Rating Bashers

Criticism of the Rating Agencies Rarely Springs from a Disinterested Quest for Truth

Bond ratings carry immense power in the financial markets. Corporations and municipalities quake at the prospect of being downgraded, fearing that their borrowing costs will rise in consequence. In certain instances, a reduction in ratings can cut off credit altogether. Even sovereign nations are mindful of how their monetary and fiscal policies may affect the rating agencies' opinions.

The high stakes involved make bond ratings a controversial topic. As in many comparable situations, the people engaged in the controversy are sometimes a bit casual with the facts. When you read criticisms of the agencies and their methods, remember that objectivity is usually not foremost in the minds of the critics. A few case studies should help to drive home the point.

On November 25, 1991, Moody's Investors Service upgraded the subordinated debt of Calmar Inc. from B3 to B2. Around the same time, the rating agency's leading competitor was also having a change of heart regarding the manufacturer of plastic pump sprays. Standard & Poor's was not thinking of mimicking Moody's upward revision, however. On the contrary, S&P reported on November 27 that it had switched from a positive to a negative outlook on Calmar. What's more, Standard & Poor's already carried a lower rating on Calmar (CCC+) than Moody's had prior to the upgrade. By contemplating a downgrade, S&P was edging toward a still wider disparity vis-à-vis its rival.

The two agencies were basing their opinions on the same financial statements, yet they regarded Calmar's credit quality quite differently. Moody's perceived "potential for further growth." S&P, in contrast, saw earnings growth that had virtually halted in 1990's poor economic climate.

This example establishes an important fact: Bond ratings are not derived by applying rigid numerical formulas to financial data. Instead, the Moody's and S&P methodologies rest heavily on subjective judgments. As a result, the agencies frequently reach contrasting conclusions. With several other players in the credit rating game as well (A.M. Best, Duff & Phelps, and Fitch Investors Service, among others), the potential for differences of opinion is vast.

On the face of it, disparities in ratings might seem avoidable and unnecessary. Wouldn't it be easier for the agencies to load companies' financial ratios into a computer and pull out purely objective credit ratings? That sounds like a fairer approach from the bond issuers' standpoint.

The flaw in this reasoning is that the only objective numbers available are those that deal with the past. Bondholders already know whether a company faithfully met its obligations last year and the year before. What they really care about is whether the company will continue to pay on schedule in the future. In some cases, the prospects for timely payment have little to do with historical ratios such as earnings to interest.

Imagine, for instance, that a company is facing potentially huge legal liabilities. (Let's define "huge" to mean "greater than shareholders' equity.") Litigation can be a lengthy affair. Years may pass before the company either writes a check for the damages or decides to establish a reserve. Until that point, the lawsuit will not affect the company's income statement, aside from lawyers' fees. There is a clear danger, however, that the plaintiffs will ultimately prevail. If that happens, a bankruptcy filing may be the only way to preserve some value for shareholders. In the meantime, the rating agencies cannot ignore the threat of default merely because the ratio of earnings to interest charges hasn't fallen yet.

This scenario is by no means hypothetical. Texaco's 1987 bankruptcy filing sprang directly from a lawsuit related to its 1984 acquisition of Getty Oil. The plaintiff, Pennzoil, was awarded a whopping $8.5 billion, plus interest and costs. Prior to the Pennzoil judgment, Moody's and S&P had rated Texaco A1 and A+, respectively. Those ratings connoted "upper medium grade" and "a strong capacity to pay interest and repay principal." Once the threat to Texaco's solvency became apparent, the agencies lowered the company to the speculative-quality ratings of Ba1 and B. They wisely looked past the historical numbers to consider a far more important credit factor.

The Texaco case shows that Moody's and S&P might reach grossly wrong conclusions if they did everything by the numbers. Furthermore, they would set themselves up for abuse if, in the name of objectivity, they relied solely on financial ratios. A purely quantitative system, after all, would have to include precise numerical cutoffs for each rating category. Otherwise, it would not be perceived as fair. Once Moody's and S&P pinned themselves down, companies would play accounting games in order to hit the targets. Among other ploys, they would liberalize their assumptions regarding the value of inventories and receivables. By putting a qualitative component into their ratings, the agencies reduce corporations' incentives to engage in such high jinks. Companies know they will gain nothing by manufacturing good numbers through shoddy accounting practices.

On the whole, then, a bit of subjectivity adds a lot of accuracy to bond ratings. However, by relying on human judgment, the rating agencies expose themselves to sniping by disgruntled issuers. For example, a company may complain that it has a lower rating than a competitor with weaker historical numbers. Realistically, a disparity of this sort is not likely to have escaped the attention of the Moody's and S&P credit analysts. The agencies constantly monitor numerical comparisons between companies. In all probability, the alleged discrepancy has arisen because the rating agencies believe certain qualitative factors outweigh the quantitative comparisons.

Nevertheless, a vast audience is prepared to believe that the protesting company's low rating represents an oversight. There are millions of investors who understandably have not devoted long hours to studying the agencies' methods. To them, it seems plausible that the ratings are simply out of line with the company's financial ratios.

The public's unfamiliarity with the subtleties of the rating process is a boon to senior executives of companies that get downgraded. Corporate managers rightly fear that if shareholders regarded the agencies' rating reductions as fair, they might blame management for the financial deterioration. Shareholders will rarely reach such conclusions, however, if they read the company press releases that "explain" the agencies' misguided actions.

From the rating agency's viewpoint, it's no fun to be castigated for downplaying financial ratios that lead to an absurd conclusion. What's really galling, though, is catching flak for exactly the opposite reason at the same time. This occurs when a company is rated lower than a competitor and also has worse financial ratios. Management's standard strategy in such cases is to blame the agencies for being too mechanical. "Moody's and S&P are backward-looking," goes the refrain of a company that compares unfavorably on the numbers. "The agencies give too little credit for the most important asset of all, the resourcefulness of management."

A company that bases its argument on something as intangible as management resourcefulness is making a statement about the rating process. It is endorsing the proposition that the agencies should consider subjective factors. Don't be surprised if the company subsequently changes its tune. A year or two down the road, it may demand to be upgraded on the basis of purely objective financial ratios. Management will then scream if the agencies dwell on unfavorable qualitative considerations. Inconsistency is a hallmark of the rating-agency bashers.

Another example of self-contradiction by the agencies' critics involves evidence from the marketplace. Every so often, a bond analyst employed by a brokerage firm claims that a certain issue is overrated by Moody's and S&P. Typically, the evidence offered is that the bond is trading at a higher yield (implying higher risk) than other bonds of the same rating. The market, concludes the analyst, is saying that the agencies are wrong.

Note, however, that the same analyst earns his livelihood by recommending bonds that he believes are trading below their intrinsic value. In that role, he is claiming that the *market* is wrong, at least some of the time. If the bond market is not infallible, can it truly be used as a test of the rating agencies' accuracy?

There's a second reason for doubting that the market is a good stick to use for beating the agencies. Moody's and S&P make no attempt to align their ratings with fluctuating quotations. The agencies don't purport to offer investment advice. Doesn't it seem unfair to criticize them for failing to deliver on a promise they've never made?

As Moody's and S&P readily acknowledge, their ratings reflect only a few of the factors that determine a bond's price in the secondary market. First and foremost, the agencies focus on default risk. They also consider an issue's seniority in the capital structure and, to an extent, the potential for recovery of principal in the event of default.

Bond traders, on the other hand, take into account several additional variables. One particularly important consideration is a bond's par amount outstanding. A $500 million issue will ordinarily be more liquid—that is, easier to buy or sell—than a $50 million issue. Investors are willing to accept less return in exchange for superior liquidity. So, all other things (including ratings) being equal, the larger issue should trade at a lower yield than the smaller issue.

Does this situation, in which two identically rated bonds trade at different yields, mean that one of them is misrated? Hardly. The agencies are simply saying that the two issuers have comparable default risk. They recognize that several other nonrating factors will also influence prices.

These ideas may be hard to accept if you're used to reading corporations' self-interested denunciations of the rating agencies. Perhaps you are still inclined to take it as proof that Moody's and S&P have blundered if their ratings fail to correspond to market prices. If so, consider the following case.

XYZ Corporation announces it will issue 10-year bonds to replace some of its short-term bank debt. By lengthening its liabilities, the company will reduce the risk of encountering a cash squeeze. The danger of a default on XYZ's bonds should therefore decline. Moody's and S&P hail the news as a favorable development for the company's credit quality, yet the company's outstanding bonds decline in price.

How can the bonds slump while their quality is rising? It's simply a case of the market anticipating increased supply. Many of the likely buyers of the new XYZ bonds want to swap out of old XYZ issues that they already own. To set themselves up to accommodate those trades, brokerage firms are selling the outstanding XYZ paper short.

Regrettably, the relationship between ratings and prices is just one of many sources of misunderstandings about the agencies. Perhaps the most serious of these is the tendency to view ratings as predictions. To understand why they're nothing of the kind, think about this analogy from the life insurance business.

Actuaries view 25 year olds in nonhazardous occupations as relatively good underwriting risks. Nevertheless, a predictable portion of the individuals in that category will die within the next few years. Some will unexpectedly contract incurable diseases, while others will be involved in fatal automobile accidents. An unforeseeable death within a low-mortality-risk group does not demonstrate that the actuaries erred. They never suggested that a particular individual had a 0% probability of dying within the next year or decade. All that the actuaries said was that, on average, the 25 year olds would outlive the obese, 80-year-old professional drag racers. As long as forecasts of that sort prove accurate in aggregate terms, the actuaries can justly claim to have done their job well. If one of the 25 year olds is struck by lightning, nobody claims that the actuaries made a false prediction.

Like actuarial assessments, ratings place individuals (in this case, bonds) within defined risk categories. The ratings merely indicate that issues in higher-risk categories are more prone to default than those in lower-risk categories. Moody's and S&P do not attempt to divine which bonds within a particular rating group will survive and which will not.

For an issue in the lowest-risk category (triple-A), the probability of a failure is exceedingly small, but it is not zero. The 1987 default of Texaco, which was rated Aaa by Moody's as late as 1983, demonstrates that a top credit rating does not imply immunity to default. Keep these facts in mind when you hear one of the most common forms of rating-agency bashing: "QRS Corporation has just filed for bankruptcy. Yet only a year ago, Moody's rated the company Ba, just one step below investment grade. The agency gave investors no warning."

In reality, Moody's Ba rating implied about a 1-in-50 chance of default at QRS within one year. That was the same probability (based on long-range statistics) that applied to every other Ba issuer. Moody's did not try to predict which of its Ba issuers would go belly up. In that respect, the agency was like the actuaries who refrained from marking for death specific individuals within their category of 50-year-old heavy smokers.

As with the actuaries, the true test of a rating agency is the relationship between its rating categories. That is, do Ba issuers demonstrate a greater propensity to default than Baa issuers and a lower propensity than B issuers? The answer is yes. A Baa company has approximately a 1-in-550 chance of failing to meet its obligations within the coming year, making it about one-eleventh as risky as a Ba company. For a B issuer, the probability of default within 12 months is about 1 in 11.

Incidentally, both Moody's and Standard & Poor's have good records for downgrading bonds in advance of defaults. Whatever their ratings one year or five years prior to bankruptcy, companies usually fall to the single-B category or lower before going bust. As a bondholder, you may find that the most valuable information you receive is the signal that credit quality is deteriorating. The absolute level of the rating can be less important than the trend. If S&P drops an issue from B+ to B, consider yourself warned that a highly speculative issue has just become even more speculative. Don't quibble about whether a B– would be more appropriate.

Above all, don't ignore advice that may save you money merely because others delight in bashing the rating agencies. Much of their criticism reflects misunderstanding of Moody's and Standard & Poor's methods. Of the remainder, at least a portion represents conscious misrepresentation. The rating-agency bashers have mastered the trick of using bizarre anomalies to discredit the entire process. Don't let yourself become a pawn in their self-serving machinations. Along with its acknowledged imperfections, the rating process contains time-tested wisdom. You can profit if you invest a little time in understanding it.

14

The Missing Link

*Predicting the Economy's
Direction Won't Enable You to
Beat the Market*

*H*ow much would you pay for a
crystal ball that could foretell the direction of the U.S. economy?
Probably a pretty sizable sum, judging by investors' preoccupation
with the outlook for interest rates and the gross domestic product
(GDP).

Electronic news services compete to be swiftest in reporting the
latest economic indicators (industrial production, money supply
growth, etc.), with margins of victory measured in seconds. It is
typical, at an investment seminar, to see the coveted luncheon
speaker's spot awarded to a prominent economic prognosticator.
Banks, brokerage firms, and money management firms make these
seers' pronouncements the centerpieces of their market strategies.

Surely, you would think, the information that is sought through
all of this peering into the future must be extremely valuable. In
truth, you might have a hard time exploiting a crystal ball of the
economy in the financial markets. Suppose, for example, that during 1950–1990 you had always known, as of January 1, whether
real gross national product (GNP) would rise or fall during the
coming year. ("Real," in economists' parlance, means an actual
increase or decrease in output, with the effects of inflation stripped
away. GNP was the series widely followed before government
statisticians switched their focus to GDP.) Suppose further that in
each year you had bet on the Standard & Poor's 500 to move in the
same direction as real GNP.

The benefits of perfect foreknowledge? You would have made money in 25 years but lost money in 16. Clearly, knowing the direction of the economy cannot by itself make you rich.

Still, you may point out, 25 out of 41 is a 61% success rate. If you can be assured of being right even 51% of the time, the cliché goes, you're bound to prosper.

Following that reasoning, you'll do better simply by betting that the S&P will rise every single year. During the same 1950–1990 period, that mindless strategy was a winner 83% of the time. Knowing which way the economy is headed, in other words, merely enables you to do worse than an investor who hasn't the faintest idea.

But what if you knew not only whether the GNP was moving up or down but also whether it was moving a little or a lot? Then you could clean up by being long only during the biggest rallies and short only during the most dramatic declines. Or could you? Consider this: The average rise in GNP during the 34 up years between 1950 and 1990 was 4.2%. Therefore, 1989's 2.5% rise was below average. Nevertheless, the S&P 500 jumped 32% in that year—its third largest gain in the four-decade period. On the other hand, in 1984 real GNP grew by a well-above-average 6.8% while the S&P 500 posted its third smallest increase (1.1%).

In short, you would not have gotten wealthy by coordinating your biggest bets with the biggest swings in GNP. As a matter of fact, that strategy would have caused you to plunk down extra cash at some highly inopportune times. During the 1950–1990 period, for instance, there were four years in which an above-average rise in real GNP was accompanied by an absolute decline in stock prices.

This is not to say that there is no connection at all between the stock market and the economy. The 61% rate of correspondence mentioned above results from comparing each year's GNP with its stock market trend in the same year. A more accurate relationship involves anticipation. Comparing the direction of GNP with the S&P 500's performance in the *preceding* year produces a match in 36 out of 41 years, or an 88% rate.

Unfortunately, clarifying the sequence makes it harder, rather than easier, to make money with your crystal ball. If it were the economy that led the stock market, then your ability to forecast one year ahead would be invaluable. Instead, the stock market is the leader and the economy the follower. Therefore, your ability to forecast the direction of GNP in the coming year gives you information about what the stock market did *last* year. To make matters worse, the information gives the wrong signal about 12% of the time. On this basis, the value of your crystal ball is less than the price of *The Wall Street Journal* published on the first day of the new year. That edition provides a record (and an accurate one, at that) of the previous year's stock market results.

If economic forecasts are both fallible and potentially irrelevant, you may wish to consider whether you are devoting too much time to worrying about them. Consider, too, that impeccably constructed forecasts can be obliterated by unanticipated shocks such as Iraq's hostile takeover of Kuwait in 1990.

After you've reflected upon these hazards, think a bit about the problems of revisions. GDP figures are highly susceptible to revision subsequent to their initial reporting dates. This raises some sticky problems about what it is, exactly, that you're trying to beat to the punch.

Market timing based on short-run economic forecasts appears, on the whole, to be a chancy approach to investing. Nothing compels you to try, even though the business media and many investment research publications make the economic outlook seem paramount. Nor are you obliged to alter your mix of stocks, bonds, and cash simply because the experts have changed their near-term estimates of business growth. Your time and energy, not to mention your commission dollars, may be far better spent on other aspects of your financial affairs.

Part Three

SMOKE AND MIRRORS

15

How to Run a
Boiler Room

*Studying the Methods of Successful
Con Artists Can Help You to Avoid
Becoming a Victim*

Boiler rooms represent one of the longest running and most successful forms of enterprise in the financial services industry. They arose early in the 20th century, when the growing popularity of telephones spawned armies of high-pressure callers pushing securities of dubious value.

A similarly shady type of operation, the bucket shop, has been prevalent in the commodities markets since the 1870s. Bucketeers originally specialized in taking customer orders, then not executing them. They pocketed the cash that their victims "invested" in losing trades, sometimes manipulating prices to guarantee that the losers would outnumber the winners.

The vigor of these illicit businesses is attested to by the more or less constant investigations into their activities. *Barron's* has even commented that tips on bucket shop scams are "a dime a dozen." The implication is that such leads are scarcely worth following up on unless the alleged perpetrators have devised something truly novel and despicable.

How can you break into this lucrative field? The annals of regulatory efforts to stamp out dishonest brokers provide many valuable pointers. Not all of the allegations recounted below were proven in court, but they constitute a superb training manual for bucketeers, all the same. (By the way, you can also profit from studying these true-life techniques if you happen to be an investor who would like to avoid falling prey to swindlers.)

Getting Started

To get started in the bucket shop business, you first take over the offices and personnel of another bucket shop that has recently been shut down by the authorities. Not only will you economize on organizational expenses, but you can recruit some highly seasoned hands in the process. After all, it is often the case, when ill-reputed brokerage houses are exposed, that the principals are no strangers to disciplinary actions. "The trouble with these bucket shops," said a spokesperson for the Commodity Futures Trading Commission in 1985, "is that when you shut one down, the owners scatter and start up new firms in other states. It's like hitting mercury with a hammer."

Basic Marketing Techniques

You build your customer base through a massive cold-calling effort. Encourage brokers to make 100 to 400 calls a day. (Experts differ regarding the optimal level.) Reinforce the brokers' dedication to their task by having a manager patrol the sales floor, checking on tallies of completed calls. Punish those who are not either dialing or talking to prospects by suspending their telephone privileges for one day. Establish the guideline that callers are not to hang up until the prospect either buys or dies.

Employ either of two proven strategies for maximizing the business generated by your phone assault:

1. Win your customers' confidence by initially recommending trades in well-known stocks listed on the New York Stock Exchange. Later on, push speculative over-the-counter issues in which you control the market. Strongly discourage selling of these stocks. Make unauthorized trades in customers' accounts if you cannot otherwise keep prices within the desired range.

2. Establish credibility with prospects by instructing the broker to solicit no orders on the first call. Instruct him to make a follow-up call, to alert the prospect that a recommendation will be coming in a week to 10 days. When the fateful

day arrives, provide the name of a thinly traded "house stock," as in Strategy 1.

Supplement your telephone solicitation with a bait-and-switch campaign in the print media. Advertise a genuinely good value in a low-risk security. When prospects respond, tell them the advertised special sold out early in the day. Recommend that they instead invest in an unadvertised item that you have in inventory (which you can mark up unconscionably).

On newly floated penny stocks (those typically selling for less than $3 a share), 200% markups are not unprecedented. To maximize your profit margin, have brokers at one branch stampede customers into dumping the same stocks that brokers at another branch are talking up. Your trading profit is the product of gross margin and turnover, so remember to keep churning those accounts.

If you follow this prescription closely, you might begin to encounter resistance to your penny stocks. Investors might start to associate low-priced shares with hyperaggressive sales techniques. In that case, be flexible. Engineer reverse stock splits (one for three, one for ten, etc.) in order to raise share prices to more respectable-sounding levels.

Incidentally, a good way to create a manipulable house stock is to acquire the nearly worthless shares of a public company. Change its name and switch its business to some currently hot industry. This approach enables you to escape the bothersome Securities and Exchange Commission scrutiny that accompanies an initial public offering.

Advanced Marketing Techniques

Now you're ready for some advanced marketing techniques. For example, push the stock of a company that claims to have a secret process for turning sand into gold. If a geologist denounces the claim as "a scam and a fraud," pay no heed. Instead, tell customers that the process is producing substantial amounts of gold and that they should hang on to their stock. Meanwhile, unload your own shares at a handsome profit.

Sell the sizzle. Tell customers that the company you're touting has discovered a cure for cancer. Say that along with their stock investors will receive foreign licensing rights for the cure. If your prospects wonder whether the venture might be risky, overstate the amount of cash on the company's balance sheet by 30 to 40 times.

Associate any stock you are promoting with some hot new product. Suppose, for example, that a company distributes tapes and records. If compact discs represent a higher-growth business, tell customers that the company also sells those, whether or not it's true.

Tell customers that your investment ideas originate with a brilliant in-house research analyst. Describe him as being fat, bald, and slovenly, but possessing one of the keenest minds on Wall Street. Ignore the fact that you have no analysts on your staff.

If prospects refuse to buy from you, arrange to have their utilities turned off. (Remember, these are not made-up examples, but are drawn from actual accounts of questionable brokerage firm practices.)

Public Relations

If you've followed all these marketing tips, you should now be ready to pursue an aggressive public relations strategy. When the Securities and Exchange Commission charges you with running a boiler room operation, denounce the allegations as tired, unsupported, and completely unfair. Issue your denunciation through your attorney, preferably a former high official of the SEC. Congratulate yourself on having had the foresight to raise vast campaign funds for influential politicians. If the regulators persist in snooping around, condemn their efforts as a witch hunt. Threaten to sue them for hounding you. Suggest that you are performing a public service by holding them accountable.

What should you do if a few hundred thousand pages of legal documents relating to your case disappear from the SEC's office? Why, you should express your suspicion that someone at the SEC maliciously destroyed the files in order to make it impossible for you to defend your firm. Announce that you will take sworn depositions from SEC employees and vow that you will not let them "get away with it."

If another batch of documents disappears a few years later, brush off the incident on the grounds that the latest investigation merely rehashes old charges. This need not actually be true.

Landing on Your Feet

Finally, when the rug inevitably gets pulled from under you, be prepared to land on your feet. No matter how tenaciously you attempt to undermine the regulators' efforts, they may in the end succeed in closing down your operation. It's one of the hazards of being in the boiler room business. So when the boom gets lowered, immediately reopen under a new name with the same facilities and personnel. (See "Getting Started.")

A Parting Thought

Boiler rooms and bucket shops use the same techniques year after year, name change after name change, for two basic reasons. First, the tried-and-true methods get results. If a particular strategy succeeds in permanently separating customers from their money, don't ask questions. Just use it. The second reason that the best ruses never go out of style is that there are always new sheep to be shorn. For every victim who has wised up, there are many prospects who have not yet been burned in a boiler shop.

Don't spoil the market by letting this bucketeers' manual fall into the wrong hands. Keep your potential customers in the dark for as long as possible. As long as they remain ignorant, the same old scams will continue to work with new generations of investors. With any luck, the opportunity could last forever.

16

Two-Timers and Second Chances

Why It's a Good Thing That Market Timing Isn't Mandatory

You receive a letter from an expert on the stock market. The low-key missive doesn't suggest that you invest your funds through his firm. Nor does it even indicate how you might do so. Instead, the letter simply informs you that the expert's forecasting model calls for the Dow Jones Industrial Average to rise in the coming month.

When a similar letter arrives one month later, you are curious to read it, given that the Dow has in fact rallied since the previous forecast. This time the model is bearish. Once again, no solicitation accompanies the free investment advice.

As the market proceeds to sell off, you begin to watch the mail with keen anticipation each day, wondering when it will contain another letter from the astute prognosticator. At long last, an announcement that the model has again turned bullish arrives. Along with it comes the news that you will be receiving no more complimentary recommendations. Reading further, you find instructions for sending money. It will be invested in accordance with the buy-and-sell signals generated by the remarkable forecasting system you have now seen in action.

The minimum required investment mentioned in the letter is a significantly larger amount than you would ordinarily commit. You therefore decide it would be prudent to wait until the month's end, just to make certain the model is accurate. As the Dow finishes the month sharply higher, however, you decide you'd better not procrastinate. Undeterred by the expert's comparatively high commission rates (they will be dwarfed by the profits you can expect to earn!), you mail off the biggest investment-related check you have ever written.

Several months later, you manage to retrieve what remains of your capital. To your dismay, it has been severely depleted by commissions incurred through rapid turnover in your account. Instead of generating profits far above your transaction costs, the expert's formerly flawless forecasting system has suddenly and mysteriously broken down. In the most recent period, it has called the Dow's moves correctly only about half the time.

You curse your luck for having turned your money over to the genius just before he lost his golden touch. The discredited expert is wasting no time bemoaning his false predictions, however. Instead, he's mailing out free "Buy" recommendations to 1,000 new names on his purchased mailing list. Simultaneously, he's dispatching free "Sell" recommendations to a different 1,000 names.

The truth is that the direct mail guru has economized. He's forgone the research and development costs required to create an elaborate forecasting model. He neither knows nor cares whether the Dow will finish the month higher or lower. If higher it is, then 500 of the previous month's "Buy" signal recipients will receive another letter saying that the fictitious model predicts a continued rally. The other 500 will be sent a "Sell" signal. As a further cost-saving measure, the expert will decline to follow up with the 1,000 individuals who received the incorrect prediction in the first month.

In the final iteration, 250 lucky recipients will receive a third consecutive correct recommendation. A predictable number of them will, as you did, pony up the minimum investment.

* * *

Other writers have described this classic scam, including John Allen Paulos in *Innumeracy: Mathematical Illiteracy and Its Consequences*. (That's a book that all serious investors should read, by the way.) Fortunately, the letter-writing trick is illegal, so you probably won't be victimized so blatantly.

However, key elements of the deception are present in many perfectly legal marketing techniques. In effect, the strategy of writing back only to the winners is of interest to the law enforcement agencies mainly because it is so crude. More refined shell games avoid any criminal taint, even though they can still be costly to you.

Worst of all, disseminators of some of the most treacherous recommendations are themselves taken in by the illusion. This makes it doubly difficult for investors to protect themselves. When the press adds its authority to the process, even a cautious, conservative investor can easily be caught in the trap.

Such pitfalls are especially worth keeping in mind when you evaluate the advice of bona fide stock market forecasters. These include legions of legitimate strategists, newsletter writers, and investment advisers. Unlike the con artists, whose aim is to create an illusion of foreknowledge, the legitimate practitioners are genuinely trying to make money for their clients. Most people who do this sort of thing for a living sincerely believe that their recommendations produce better returns than raw guesswork. Evidence to the contrary, such as a succession of horrendously wrong calls, doesn't necessarily undermine the self-assurance of typical market timers. There is, after all, the eternal hope that by analyzing their errors they'll achieve the last bit of fine-tuning needed to perfect their models.

But what if a burned and now-skeptical public doesn't share a market timer's confidence that the few remaining bugs are about to be eliminated? That's the time for the failed prognosticator to dust off a classic *mea culpa*: "The reason I miscalled the market was that my model's output was so far from the consensus that I didn't have the courage to go with it. Believe you me, I'll never make that mistake again." Put another way, "I was wrong because I was right."

It isn't feasible, within the confines of this chapter, to settle once and for all the classic question about market timing: Do investors who try to catch the tops and bottoms merely spend more on commissions than other types of investors, or do they really have a chance of outperforming steady, low-turnover strategies?

It's hardly a radical innovation to be skeptical about the market-timing prowess of self-proclaimed experts. Before World War II, for example, Henry W. Dunn, of the investment management firm of Scudder, Stevens & Clark, wrote in an investment letter from that company:

> [W]ith all the effort which has been expended on attempts to discover or devise new and better methods of forecasting or to develop greater skill in the use of the old methods, guessing the next move of the stock market, with due reference to the two vital factors of direction and timing, remains little more than a gamble.

Perhaps you'll reject out of hand the suggestion that it's futile to bet on the direction of the market. It defies reason, you may say, to imagine that millions of investors are so deluded as to value advice that's utterly without value. If you're of this mind, you'll probably find it equally improbable that the press incessantly interviews forecasters who have no better idea where the market is going than Aunt Sally has.

Stop and consider. Have you ever seen an independently verified, complete forecasting record of any of the celebrated masters of market timing? If so, you're part of a privileged minority. Did the track record include a reliable calculation of the profits (net of trading costs) that you could have earned by following the expert's advice?

Certainly, the typically brief and laudatory introduction to a published or televised interview with an "acknowledged expert" contains no such documentation, much less an attempt to adjust the results for risk. The omission is understandable. Mark Hulbert, whose *Hulbert Financial Digest* tracks the recommendations of investment newsletters, had this to say about the market timers (*Forbes*, July 20, 1992): "Not a single one beat a buy-and-hold over the past ten years. Followers of these letters may have gotten fun and excitement from all their trading, but they didn't get paid for all that time and effort."

* * *

There's a purpose behind discussing a phony forecasting scam and good-faith market-timing efforts in a single chapter. I certainly don't mean to equate the two in moral terms. Rather, I want to underscore the fact that their economic impact may be similar, even though only one intends harm.

No one would seriously deny the prudence of checking out an investment firm's reputation before entrusting money to it. My point is that you should be every bit as careful in investigating the track record before staking your capital on a market-timer's advice. There's a good chance that if you do take such precautions, you'll decide not to adopt a strategy of trying to profit from swings in the Dow.

17

When Audits Win No Plaudits

Just How Independent Are the Independent Validations of Companies' Financial Statements?

*I*t is axiomatic that stories about undervalued securities vastly outnumber undervalued securities. Many a company can correctly point out that its stock trades at a lower price/earnings multiple than the shares of its industry peers. Only rarely, however, can management argue convincingly that the disparity represents a genuine mispricing. In many instances, the market is simply refusing to take the company's financial statements at face value. It's entirely possible for investors to be assigning a multiple of 15× to a corporation with reported earnings of $3.00 a share, even though its stock is trading at 30 instead of 45. The solution to this riddle is not that people have suddenly forgotten their multiplication tables. Rather, they believe the company has overstated its profits by 50%. A 15× multiple, applied to the legitimate earnings of $2.00 a share, produces the observed—and appropriate—stock price of 30.

But wait just a minute, you might say. We're not talking about a forecast of *next* year's earnings. Honest people could certainly disagree about that. The evaluation we're discussing is based on last year's profit. This is a figure that has already been certified by a nationally recognized accounting firm. If the auditors have confirmed that net income per share was $3.00, is there any reason to doubt it?

As a matter of fact, there are several good reasons to be skeptical about financial statements, even when they are audited. Indeed, many veteran readers of annual reports consider the phrase "independent auditors" a contradiction in terms.

Practically speaking, it is the company's management that chooses its accounting firm, even though shareholders officially get to approve or reject the selection. Under the circumstances, it should come as no surprise if the auditors feel beholden to management, despite their mandate to serve the company's stockholders.

Ethical standards and the threat of litigation control this potential conflict of interest, but only up to a point. Certifying a financial statement requires exercising a great deal of judgment in grey areas of the accounting code. You needn't be a hardened cynic to infer that auditors give most of the close calls to management.

Bear in mind, too, that quarterly financial statements are not generally audited. Nevertheless, between one annual report and the next, investors rely on interim figures for fine-tuning their future earnings estimates. The fourth quarter, which is the time of the year when the auditors arrive on the scene, also happens to be the high season for revisions to earlier statements.

Whatever the underlying causes, skepticism about financial statements is vindicated on a fairly frequent basis. Countless incidents have demonstrated that a dollar of reported profits can easily prove to be worth less than 100 cents once the dust has settled.

Late in 1991, for example, First Financial Management revised its earnings per share for the first nine months of the year from $2.11 to $1.89. The information services company explained that it had lost track of a few items in the process of consolidating 19 acquired companies. In combining the units into a single subsidiary, management had altered its accounting systems and eliminated some of its accounting staff.

Looking for the silver lining in an episode he termed "embarrassing," First Financial Management's chairman pointed out that no funds had been misappropriated. Investors nevertheless took a dim view of the matter. The company's stock fell 10% on news of the earnings revision.

If 10% doesn't strike you as a particularly calamitous drop, how would you feel about a one-day decline of 62%? That was the fate of Chambers Development's Class B shares on March 18, 1992, after the company announced revisions in certain accounting practices. The changes slashed 1991 earnings per share from 83 cents to a mere 3 cents.

Prior to the change, the waste management company had "capitalized" certain indirect expenditures associated with the development of new landfill sites. This meant that in calculating profits, Chambers didn't immediately deduct 100% of its executives' salaries, travel expenditures, legal bills, and public relations outlays. Management deemed it appropriate to match these costs against the revenues that the projects would produce in future periods. Otherwise, the company reasoned, expenses would be overstated (and profits understated) during the landfills' development periods.

Chambers's practice of postponing certain expenses was not inconsistent with accounting theory. The company's auditing firm, Grant Thornton, signed off on the practice. In fact, Chambers "led the world to believe they were using conservative accounting standards," according to James Patton, an accounting professor at the University of Pittsburgh.

The issue nevertheless generated an internal debate when Chambers hired a managing partner of Grant Thornton to be its chief financial officer. Shortly thereafter, according to another partner of the accounting firm, discussions took place on the subject of capitalizing indirect development costs. In the partner's recounting, Grant Thornton merely concurred that changing the accounting treatment was one of the options available to Chambers. Unnamed sources quoted by *The Wall Street Journal*, however, said that the auditors refused to certify the 1991 results, thereby forcing the company into its 96% reduction in reported earnings per share.

Whether Grant Thornton merely offered its opinion or actually precipitated the writedown, its reward for upholding the accounting standards was not pleasant. On April 13, Chambers dismissed the firm as its auditor.

Management offered no public explanation for the firing. We might speculate, however, that a contributing factor was the $493 million paper loss sustained by the company's chairman and his two sons in the wake of the accounting change. Chambers's chief financial officer likewise took a hit on his stock, while getting sacked in the bargain.

By the time all of this firing took place, Chambers's stock was down even further. The company was contemplating additional accounting changes that threatened to wipe out even its measly 3-cents-a-share profit. Analysts were focusing on another category of capitalized expenses—interest on debt—and wondering whether Chambers could really turn a profit on landfills after recognizing all of the associated costs. (Doubts on this point increased when a subsequent filing with the Securities and Exchange Commission raised the possibility that Chambers had capitalized some of the indirect development costs *twice*.) For good measure, the SEC was looking into unusual activity in the company's stock and options during the days preceding its shift in accounting procedures.

Shareholders had little to cheer about in the interaction between Chambers Development and its auditor. They could take solace, however, in the fact that the management/accountant relationship worked out even more poorly in another prominent incident of roughly the same period. The company involved was a high-flying retailer, Cascade International.

Cascade's relationship with its auditor was quite amicable. This was made easier by the fact that the accounting operation in question was a one-man practice. "We know of no other firm of this size that is not audited by a Big Six accounting firm," was the comment of the *Overpriced Stock Service* newsletter (as quoted by David Poppe, "Is Apparel Retailer Paying Price for Deception?"). Sole practitioner Bernard H. Levy had the inside track on Cascade's accounting business, however, having handled the personal taxes of the company's founder and chairman, Victor Incendy.

So intimate was the client/auditor relationship, in fact, that Levy stood at Incendy's right hand in a photograph of Cascade's management team published in the *Miami Review*. Also beyond the call of duty for an independent auditor was Levy's accompanying of Cascade executives on "road show" presentations to investors. (He later disputed published suggestions that he had helped to promote the company's stock, however.)

From all appearances, Levy had good reason to be proud of his close association with Cascade International. In a June 3, 1991, *Business Week* article, an enthusiast characterized Cascade shares as "one of the hottest bargains around," despite having zoomed from $2\frac{3}{4}$ to $8\frac{1}{8}$ within the space of a few months. The "still undervalued stock," the expert said, had a shot at doubling within 6 to 12 months. In short order, Cascade shares climbed to $11\frac{3}{4}$ on the strength of a deal to create a chain of specialty shops featuring Oleg Cassini's designs.

Soon afterward, however, the stock fell all the way back to $2\frac{3}{4}$. Victor Incendy disappeared amidst allegations of inflated sales figures and unlawful issuance of stock. Furthermore, the chairman was not all that was missing. Many of the 126 stores and 245 cosmetics counters reported by Cascade appeared to be figments of Incendy's imagination. For example, California sales tax records listed just 18 of the 29 outlets that Cascade claimed to be operating in that state.

Questions about the true number of Cascade shops had arisen long before the chairman's disappearance. As far back as 1987, brokers at Thomson McKinnon Securities had been unable to verify the company's store count. One broker reported that he had contacted employees of the Fashion Bug retailing chain, which supposedly housed 220 of Cascade's cosmetics counters. According to the broker, the workers said they had never heard of Cascade or its Jean Cosmetics unit. Cascade's attorney replied to stock analysts' subsequent criticisms by saying that releasing the addresses of the company's stores would amount to giving its competitors a road map. The retailer's executives, he added, were "unwilling to have their operations torn apart for the benefit of the analyst community."

Other discrepancies heightened suspicions about the accuracy of Cascade's disclosures. In its fiscal 1990 annual report, for instance, the company had described its Jean Cosmetics unit as "vertically integrated." But the fiscal 1991 report, in a seeming contradiction, said Jean engaged "independent contractors to manufacture and package its proprietary cosmetics." Also, according to press reports, Cascade told analysts in 1991 that its top-performing cosmetics counters were selling approximately $55,000 of merchandise per year. The fiscal 1991 annual report, however, indicated *average* volume of approximately $66,000.

Confronted with such evidence of inaccurate reporting, Incendy adopted a tactic that is common among managers who find themselves under attack. He counterattacked. Short sellers had conspired with a certain analyst, Incendy alleged, "to plant negative, unsupported commentary" about his company. "This may be one area in which the regulatory authorities ought to devote additional attention in their cleanup of the Wall Street community and the abuses which can take place," he offered helpfully.

While waiting for the authorities to heed his suggestion, Incendy threatened to sue the *Overpriced Stock Service* for defamation. The company launched an investigation into the backgrounds and motives of its accusers and promised to lodge serious allegations against them. Fumed the chairman, "I resent that my word is questioned and I have to prove what I am saying against the word of crooks."

Notwithstanding Incendy's injured tone, Cascade's public relations firm suggested that the company offer some hard data to quell investors' concerns about its financial reports. When the requested information did not emerge, the firm resigned the account, helping to precipitate a sharp sell-off in Cascade's stock.

There is little to indicate that auditor Levy shared the skepticism voiced by analysts, investors, journalists, and Cascade's own public relations firm. By his own account, he believed that certain financial figures supplied to him by Incendy, which he later perceived to be inaccurate, had come directly from accountants in various states. In conducting his audit, Levy said, he visited 10 of the company's purported 245 cosmetics counters and a few of its stores. "Obviously, I didn't do everything I should have done," he concluded. (This was something of a pattern with Levy, as it turned out. In 1989, New York regulators had fined him $1,000 and put him on one year's probation for failing to file a client's tax return).

Following a bankruptcy filing by Cascade, interim chairman Aaron Karp reported that the previous two years' revenues and earnings had been reported incorrectly. In fact, he said, it would be impossible to prepare accurate audits for either year. Here, indeed, was a cautionary tale against relying absolutely on certified financial statements.

In conclusion, the next time you hear a company complain about its unjustifiably low P/E multiple, find out whether analysts are complaining about the quality of the company's financial reporting. If management appears to respond defensively to such questions, it's best to err on the side of skepticism.

Undoubtedly, the Cascade episode is an extreme example of the problems that can arise in auditing. It does not, however, represent the worst conceivable example, and it certainly will not be the last time investors lose money on a cheap stock that gets cheaper when the market finds out what the auditors missed.

18

Pass the Trash

Don't Become a
Victim of Involuntary
Risk Transfer

The savings and loan (S&L) crisis that erupted in the 1980s was a godsend to the crime-and-corruption branch of the press corps. Politicians joined in the fun by thundering against the greedy executives who had looted the thrifts. Television audiences relished the spectacle of former Lincoln Savings chief Charles Keating, clad in a prisoner's uniform, indignantly proclaiming his innocence. The whole affair seemed to validate Bertolt Brecht's remark that robbing a bank cannot compare with the opportunity of owning a bank.

You'll miss some valuable investment insights, however, if you suppose that simple theft was responsible for the entire S&L debacle. The missing hundreds of billions of dollars, which taxpayers were compelled to replace, did not vanish exclusively through midnight raids on the vaults. On the contrary, much of the institutions' capital vaporized in lawful transactions. It just so happened that many of these transactions worked out more favorably for the thrifts' managers than for the thrifts themselves.

Understanding the financial stratagems that helped to bankrupt the S&Ls may help you to dodge a great many investment landmines. The common feature in all of them is transfer of risk from somebody else to you. Financial theory says that you receive a bigger share of an investment's potential rewards whenever you assume a larger portion of the risk. In practice, however, that won't always happen unless you figure out on your own that risk is being transferred.

For S&L operators, there were historically two huge risks in the business of taking in deposits and lending the proceeds to home-buyers. First, the borrowers might not repay their loans. Second, interest rates on savings accounts might rise above the rates on existing mortgages, which were locked in for a number of years. If that occurred, the institution would be collecting less interest than it was paying out. The resulting losses would erode the sharehold-ers' capital, perhaps even causing the thrift to fail. In 1979, when interest rates began to gyrate wildly, widespread insolvency be-came a plausible forecast of the future of the savings and loan industry.

Notwithstanding these genuine risks, S&Ls attracted many as-tute entrepreneurs. They understood that the thrifts possessed vast profit potential, provided the opportunities were properly ex-ploited. Over the years, Congress had authorized savings and loan associations to engage in a widening range of businesses. Some of the newly available activities, including commercial real estate lending and mortgage-backed bond trading, could be extremely lucrative. The higher-margin businesses were also riskier than tra-ditional home mortgage lending, but that fact did not deter the new breed of S&L operators. They had several means of transfer-ring the risk to others while keeping the potential rewards for themselves.

To begin with, S&L owners were obliged to risk only a com-paratively small amount of their own capital. With equity of just 5% of a savings and loan association's assets, they could capture all of the associated profits. If adverse conditions—or bad credit judgment—wiped out their thin sliver of equity, any additional losses would be borne by the Federal Savings and Loan Insurance Corporation.

Aggressive S&L owners endeavored to pull out even the modest amount of capital they had at risk. One popular method was to extract huge salaries and bonuses. Naturally, the thrift regulators might squawk if top management's compensation seemed excessive in light of the institution's financial performance. Under the free enterprise system, however, owner-managers who vastly increased their firms' profitability were indisputably enti-tled to share in the benefits. Making loans that competitors rejected as too risky was one quick way of boosting profits—at least for a while.

Let's imagine that a shopping mall developer acquires land purely on speculation. He has no retailers committed in advance to becoming tenants and no equity to invest in the project. The developer does, however, have a friend at the local S&L.

Based on a liberal appraisal, the S&L lends the developer 100% of the property's purchase price. For good measure, the institution also lends the developer enough to make the interest payments. The developer promptly returns the latter funds to the thrift, which now has a loan in good standing on its books.

You may not perceive that this shuttling of money back and forth has created any economic value. Nevertheless, the accountants label it revenue. A portion of it flows down to the bottom line to create an immediate profit. The profit, in turn, justifies additional incentive-based compensation for the thrift's management. It also increases the institution's capital, which enables the managers to practice their prestidigitation on a larger scale. If the S&L operators generate enough compensation for themselves before the loans default, they may recoup all of the capital that they invested in the S&L.

Best of all, there is always a chance that these "time-bomb" loans will not default. If the economy should unexpectedly boom, the developers may find their malls fully leased. They will remain current on their interest and even pay back the principal. The S&L will then record bona fide profits, enriching the owner-managers, who may then sell the successful institution for a massive gain.

The venture will go down in the annals of laissez-faire capitalism as a case of boldness rewarded. In reality, though, the entrepreneurs risked little capital. They immediately set to work eliminating even the small potential for loss by generating dubious profits. Had the thrift failed, the owners would have walked away unscathed, bequeathing the capital shortfall to the deposit insurers. The S&L owners were truly betting with other people's money.

Their co-schemers, the developers, played much the same game. With none of their own capital at risk, the real estate operatives could afford to build malls and office buildings that were likely to remain empty for years. During construction, they could pay themselves reasonable salaries out of borrowed funds. If tenants stepped forward upon the project's completion, the developers would reap legitimate profits to boot. If not, they could flip the keys to the S&L and proceed to the next deal.

As an investor, you have many opportunities to serve as the patsy in deals that employ similar risk-transfer techniques. Sometimes the vehicle is a small growth company making an initial public offering. On other occasions, it may be a limited partnership involving natural resources or works of art.

In all cases, you should avoid transactions that allow the organizers to hog the profits while ducking any possible losses. Typically, they do so through large salaries and consulting fees that effectively return to them all of the capital that they have ostensibly put at risk. When a deal's structure permits the controlling parties to eliminate all of their personal exposure, it invites them to take excessive operating risks. After all, if they're playing with your money, rather than their own, why not go for the biggest possible payoff?

Be careful to distinguish between risk sharing that is inequitable and that which is merely unequal. Many legitimate investment partnerships have "promote" features for managers who contribute their expertise. The partnership agreement in such a venture entitles the organizers to a share of the profits that's more than proportionate to their equity investment. You can benefit from the promote if it genuinely creates an incentive for the managers to make the venture successful.

To differentiate between reasonable splits and abusive risk transfers, you have to do some comparison shopping. Are the fees and proposed division of profits in line with norms for similar deals? If so, you have some assurance of being compensated for your risk at a rate established in a competitive market.

Be aware that markets occasionally get overheated. If a particular type of investment performs exceptionally well for a few years, demand for it tends to escalate. Once investors become convinced that the value of gold or antiques or baseball cards will continue to skyrocket, they may become inattentive to the fees and profit splits. Additionally, a booming asset category may attract buyers who lack previous experience in the field. These conditions create a vast pool of investors who are unfamiliar with—or unconcerned about— traditional risk-sharing arrangements. The predictable result is a shift of terms in favor of deal organizers and to the detriment of deal participants.

A classic example of this phenomenon occurred in the late 1980s in leveraged buyouts (LBOs). On the strength of impressive results in the preceding years, LBO organizers were able to increase their upfront fees. A parallel shift in risk sharing occurred in the high-yield bond financings that accompanied many of the large LBOs. Some equity holders were actually able to take money out at the same time that they were inviting bond buyers to put money in.

Promoters cannot be blamed for doing deals on terms that the market will bear. Remember, you have no obligation to participate. There is, after all, only one reason to agree to terms less favorable than were offered in the past. You might conceivably be able to justify some concessions on fees and splits if the potential profit has risen above its normal range. Usually the facts are quite the opposite. Deal terms generally change to the disadvantage of investors when a class of assets has performed exceptionally well for several years in succession. Following a big runup, the investment category will ordinarily have below-average appreciation prospects.

To summarize, be on the lookout for operators who are trying to transfer risk to you without your knowledge or consent. Don't be so dazzled by the upside in an investment that you bargain it all away. And remember that in the savings and loan debacle, not all of the losses were created by crooks. As is usually the case in such affairs, the real scandal was the part that was legal.

19

Buzzwords and BOMFOG

Slippery Language Can Conceal Major Investment Hazards

Have you ever noticed how many terms of obfuscation begin with the letter B? Examples include "babble," "bunkum," "bombast," "blather," "bluster," "blarney," "blabber," "balderdash," and "baloney." In the more blunt category, there's the term that used to be bowdlerized (when folks still bothered to) into "bullfeathers."

The late Nelson Rockefeller added to this already lengthy list in 1964, when he spoke repeatedly of a "Brotherhood of Man under the Fatherhood of God." Reporters, who had hoped to hear a more concrete proposal regarding civil rights, lampooned Rockefeller's lofty rhetoric as "BOMFOG."

Keep in mind this rich linguistic tradition the next time you're annoyed by the buzzwords with which companies habitually bombard investors. Be tolerant of euphemisms that glamorize the mundane or trivialize the calamitous. Just consider how dull the discourse between corporations and shareholders would be if the language were purged of such delightful dodges.

Buzzwords proliferate whenever an investment concept gets hot—and for good reason. Catchphrases are much cheaper than capital investments as a way to become identified with a high-multiple industry.

In the early 1980s, for example, energy prices were skyrocketing. Countless corporations sought to jump onto the bandwagon. A few went so far as to acquire oil companies. Many others took the more economical route of disclosing for the first time that their revenues were largely energy-*related*. "Energy-related" was a marvelously imprecise term, encompassing everything from home insulation to molybdenum (the hard-to-pronounce metal used in the specialty steels required for the drilling of extra-deep wells).

To a large extent, the place where energy-related companies were helping to explore for oil and gas was the *Sunbelt*. With energy prices seemingly in a permanently upward spiral, that favored region could count on spectacular population growth and prosperity. Retailers were soon vying to demonstrate the extent of their concentration in Sunbelt states. Fortunately for the corporate communications profession, there was no official definition of which states comprised the Sunbelt. If a retailer wanted to include its Kentucky stores in the count, it was free to do so.

When oil prices collapsed, however, companies lost their zeal to be identified with either energy or the Sunbelt. Banks that were saddled with Sunbelt real estate loans began emphasizing how little exposure they had in Texas. Or, if they had unwisely bet the ranch on the Lone Star State, they noted that their loan portfolios were less concentrated in energy-dependent Houston than in the more economically diverse Dallas-Fort Worth area. Their stocks got hammered all the same.

Business downturns give special impetus to the use of buzzwords. Building materials companies recast themselves as counter-recessionary suppliers to the *remodel-and-repair* market. Automotive parts producers burble that they will thrive by selling *aftermarket* goods. Demand will boom, they gush, as consumers wear out original equipment by waiting longer to trade in their cars. Paper manufacturers proclaim (historical precedent to the contrary notwithstanding) that this time around they will avoid ruinous price cutting through *industry statesmanship*.

The hostile takeover boom of the 1980s produced another creative burst of buzzword coinage. Many corporations amended their bylaws to create barriers to hostile raiders. But few, if any, called the measures "antitakeover provisions." That would have smacked of entrenching management. Instead, companies instituted *shareholder rights* and *fair price* amendments.

Ultimately, buzzwords endure because they provide genuine value to companies. They dissuade investors from simple-minded, commonsense (and correct) interpretations of bad news. Furthermore, successful spin control through the use of buzzwords is a great confidence builder. It encourages corporations to escalate to the next level, heavy BOMFOG.

The variety of doubletalk most favored for setting shareholders straight is shallow boosterism. Its hallmark is the proposition that there are no problems, only challenges. With language borrowed from the corporate pep rally, investor relations officers can reassure nervous portfolio managers, even when their fears are well justified. Developments that objectively reduce a company's future earnings prospects can be repositioned as exciting new growth opportunities.

Suppose, for the sake of illustration, that an apparel manufacturer's most important chain store outlet goes bust and shuts down. The good news, investors will learn, is that the clothing maker will henceforth be less dependent on a single large customer. Similarly, it may be a blessing in disguise when industrial companies shut down in droves in a natural gas pipeline's territory. The company's future revenues will be skewed to the stable home and commercial sectors, where demand is less sensitive to economic conditions.

I had a memorable experience with a company turning a negative into a positive in 1982. On a visit to Union Carbide, I raised the question of environmental hazards. This issue was actually a strength for the company, I was told. The truly dangerous chemicals were in the halogen family, which Carbide was not involved with.

In December 1984, Union Carbide's affiliated plant in Bhopal, India, suffered an industrial accident that was labeled the worst in history. According to Indian authorities, more than 3,000 people died. Claims against the company ran into the billions for a time, while the near-term impact on shareholders was a $400 million loss of market value. The only consolation was that no halogen-based chemicals were involved. Sevin, a fertilizer, proved to be highly lethal, however.

Around the same time, the hospital management industry was putting the silver-lining technique to excellent use. The companies actually made it sound plausible that they would benefit from a Draconian, federally imposed austerity program.

In response to mounting public concern about rising health care costs, Congress tied Medicare reimbursements to a prospective payments system. No longer could a hospital simply tote up the cost of a patient's care, tack on a profit, and present its bill. The payment level was now based on a standard cost. To make money on the deal, the hospital would have to devise some means of providing the service for an amount less than the predetermined reimbursement.

Ordinarily, going off a cost-plus system is viewed as a detriment to a company's earnings prospects. Investors, in their simpleminded way, prefer guaranteed profits to uncertainty. The logic didn't hold in the hospital industry, however. At least, such was the view propagated by the hospital management companies. The industry experts explained that the true losers under the prospective payments system would be the nonprofit hospitals. Hampered by the inefficient stewardship of charitable organizations, they would be unable to develop competitive cost structures. The for-profit operators would gobble them up, generating dramatic revenue and earnings growth in the process.

But wasn't there a danger in the pressure to keep treatment costs within the guidelines? Presumably, the for-profit hospitals would be compelled to discharge patients more quickly than in the past. That would mean a decline in occupancy rates. In most industries, underutilized capacity means substandard profits. Once again, the hospital management companies successfully bomfogged investors out of a logical conclusion. Capacity utilization, said their spokespeople, simply didn't apply to health care.

Judging by *The Wall Street Journal*'s March 11, 1983, "Heard on the Street" column, many investment professionals embraced the industry's view. One expert predicted 20% annual earnings gains by the companies. This would be achieved in part, he reasoned, by acquisitions of "Little Sisters of the Poor" hospitals that would go by the boards. Another health care specialist predicted that the highly efficient for-profit hospitals would increase their margins under the new reimbursement system.

As if to confirm this rosy picture, hospital stocks were moving up. In fact, there was only one sour note in the *Journal* story. An investment adviser noted the heavy insider selling at two of the leading companies during the preceding six months. On that basis, he was not recommending their shares, even though his fundamental analysis indicated that earnings would "grow, grow, grow."

The adviser's conclusion was borne out over the next few years. On October 2, 1985, Hospital Corp. of America (HCA) conceded that its earnings would not grow and grow, but would instead be flat in 1986. At the root of the problem, said management, was a continuing decline in occupancy rates.

HCA's announcement was "definitely a shock," according to one analyst, notwithstanding the fears voiced years earlier about the end of the cost-plus system. And if HCA's news was a shock, American Medical International's earnings release on the same day was a massive trauma. AMI's quarterly profits had fallen by 38% on a year-over-year basis, even though revenue was up 18%. So much for the thesis that margins would widen.

The insider sellers had been on the right track after all. On the day of the HCA and AMI bombshells, the major hospital management stocks plummeted by 10% to 20%. The group accounted for three of the session's four most active New York Stock Exchange issues. All told, four hospital chains dropped an aggregate market value of $1.5 billion in a single day.

Clearly, the hospital management companies' reduction in value had been a long time in the making. The deterioration had begun at least as far back as 1983. Skillful management of perceptions, however, had considerably delayed the market's recognition of the altered circumstances. Corporate communications officers performed extraordinarily well in staving off the debacle for as long as they did.

For investors, the bright spot in all of these incidents is the opportunity they provide to profit from experience. Financial markets repeatedly demonstrate the power of buzzwords and BOMFOG in lending authority to mistaken premises. If you keep your ears open for delusive language, you may sidestep a few can't-miss situations just before they crater.

20

Incentive-Debased Pay

There's No Perfect Solution to the Puzzle of Compensation Systems for Financial Advisers

*P*eople who sell stocks and bonds for a living vary widely in their backgrounds, personalities, and investment knowledge. They work for firms that differ from one another in scale and operating strategies. One trait is nearly universal among securities salespeople, however: Whatever the compensation system is, they understand it extremely well. They quickly adapt their behavior in response to any modification in the incentives. Economists need look no further if they seek a real-life demonstration of rational self-interest.

Suppose, for instance, that a firm switches its corporate bond salespeople from salary plus subjective bonus to commissions based on volume. Trading revenues will almost certainly show the hoped-for increase. Trading profits may go the other way, however. This paradox ultimately derives from the fact that corporate bonds have limited liquidity. As a consequence, brokerage firms that deal in the corporate bond sector carry sizable securities inventories. Otherwise, they'd find it difficult to fill salespeople's orders, since ready sellers aren't always available.

Generally speaking, when institutions want to buy round lots of bonds they go directly to brokerage firms. This is in contrast to the equity market, where the exchanges play a dominant role. In short, there's no central auction market for corporate bonds. Traders must instead rely on sporadic reports of over-the-counter transactions to determine appropriate bid and offer levels.

In this environment, the salesforce's incentives may conflict with the trading desk's. Observe what happens if the salespeople induce their traders to sell bonds, out of inventory, at excessively low prices. (This can occur if the salepeople hear material news and respond before the traders get wind of it.) If the desk repeatedly lets bonds go at less than full value, the salespeople's volume will rise. After all, profit-maximizing institutional investors are glad to direct business to firms that let them buy too cheap. Fugitive commodity trader Marc Rich captured the essence of this volume-maximizing strategy when he remarked that anyone could sell a dollar for 99 cents.

As portrayed here, a commission system works favorably for both the salespeople and their customers. Clearly, however, the bond desk cannot make money by habitually engaging in transactions that are too good for the investors. Before long, the traders will be demanding that the salespeople's compensation be linked to the desk's trading profits. They will argue that the salesforce ought to be compensated only for generating *profitable* volume.

Based on this scenario, a commission system might appear to represent a portfolio manager's dream come true. Yet many portfolio managers would characterize the arrangement as a nightmare. As it turns out, commission salespeople's perverse incentives aren't limited to trying to take advantage of their own traders. In the single-minded pursuit of volume, salespeople may also try to talk customers into uneconomic trades. "Churning," as the practice is known, is a complaint frequently lodged against shady stockbrokers by individual investors.

Is the salary plus subjective bonus system then the preferable setup, from the customer's standpoint? Not necessarily. Some portfolio managers value the independence that a commission system affords to salespeople. If a commission salesperson doesn't believe that a particular investment is appropriate for her customer, she can decline to push it. That may mean forgoing a juicy commission. As an offsetting benefit, however, she will preserve a relationship based on trust.

A subjective bonus system, on the other hand, is likely to reflect the brokerage firm's priorities. These may include underwritings that, whatever their merits, do not suit the needs of all investors.

The well-intentioned salesperson may now face a heavier penalty for trying to put her customer first. If she doesn't make an all-out effort on a deal that's important to her firm, her bonus may suffer. This is not to say that the firm will ignore the contribution she makes by cultivating strong relationships. Striking the right balance at bonus time will not be an easy task, however.

In the end, there's probably no perfect solution to the puzzle of compensation systems. Investors, brokerage firms, and salespeople all have legitimate interests in the matter. It's impossible to reconcile them completely.

Similar shortcomings pop up in compensation arrangements between investors and money managers. Conflicts arise despite the clearly fiduciary nature of these relationships. Typically, the client pays a fee calculated as a percentage of his portfolio's market value. The manager's compensation is not based on the number of trades in the account. He therefore has no incentive to churn. Instead, the manager's means of realizing higher income is by making money for his client. That's because under a flat-percentage arrangement the fee rises if the value of the portfolio increases. A money manager's incentive, in short, is to do exactly what's in the client's interest.

As with so many aspects of investments, the reality sometimes falls short of the theory. Managers know that even with the best of intentions increasing clients' wealth is a chancy proposition. Accordingly, they may be tempted to pursue other, more dependable income-enhancing opportunities. Not all of these alternative approaches are ethical or even legal. At the sleazier end of the scale, bribery is one potential source of incremental income for money managers. An unscrupulous investment adviser might accept a kickback for selecting a particular firm's investment products. Undisclosed self-dealing with an affiliated brokerage firm is another practice that puts the client's interest in the back seat.

Most conflicts of interest in the money management business are not this crude, however. If you hire an investment adviser, you have to be extremely alert to detect behavior that works to your disadvantage. The more subtle types of conflicts typically result from the manager's desire to hold on to your business. On the face of it, client retention might seem like an extremely positive motivation. Presumably, the surest way to keep you in the fold is to make money for you. Where, then, is the conflict?

One snag is that the manager may have an incentive to be excessively risk averse, relative to your needs. Suppose, for example, that you have a high and secure income, with no major expenditures facing you. Under the circumstances, your need for liquidity is likely to be small. From a purely financial standpoint, you're in a good position to seek above-average returns by taking above-average risks.

Psychologically speaking, it may be a different story. An experienced money manager knows that you'll appreciate the "high-risk/high-reward" concept better in a bull market than in a bear market. Just wait until the averages fall and your "high-beta" holdings fall by an even greater percentage. You may forget that your portfolio is performing exactly as it's supposed to. You'll probably begin to wonder whether you need a new adviser.

In theory, the money manager's correct response is to explain one more time, in a calm voice, why it's rational for you to tolerate prudent risks. As a practical matter, it's hard to do this when you're screaming at him. Aside from enduring your unpleasant reaction, the investment adviser will probably lose your business. That's the downside of providing you with superior long-term returns at the expense of periodically underperforming the averages. Against this downside, the money manager must weigh the upside—a modest fee increase after a good year.

From the money manager's standpoint, the path of least resistance is to forget about achieving the highest possible returns over the long run. The more important objective, if he doesn't want to get fired, is to avoid doing worse than the market in any period. That means reducing risk below a level that you're perfectly capable of handling. Your returns will suffer as well.

Often, money managers carry risk avoidance a step further. They keep their clients' portfolios free not only of risk, but even of the appearance of risk. Better to have you lose money in IBM, they reason, than in a stock you've never heard of. The investment merits of the securities are a secondary consideration.

Unfortunately, a money manager cannot entirely avoid trouble by staying within the bounds of the market averages. A manager who succeeds in that goal may be denounced as a "closet indexer"—one who produces just about the same results as the Standard & Poor's 500. The problem is that overt indexers charge less for their services than managers who strive to beat the averages. Particularly in the fee-conscious institutional market, it's hard to command a premium for trying to outperform the S&P but failing.

One solution is for the manager to substitute the illusion of superior performance for the more-difficult-to-achieve reality. This strategy is known as "gaming the index." To understand how it works, you first have to know that the evaluation of investment returns is a controversial topic. It's no simple matter to determine whether a manager has legitimately beaten the market. Part of the problem is that there's no consensus about which index best represents the relevant universe of securities.

One of the few things the experts agree on is that the widely used S&P 500 is a problematic benchmark. The most obvious of its limitations is that it excludes smaller-capitalization stocks. A sizable body of research indicates that over long periods, small stocks produce higher returns than large stocks. The methodology of some of the studies has been challenged, but let's assume that their general conclusion is correct. Do the higher returns mean that small stocks are better investments than big stocks? Not really. The research also shows that small stocks are more volatile than big stocks. It's the old risk/reward tradeoff: You get a higher return, but you pay for it by incurring bigger swings in principal value.

Now let's consider a money manager whose performance is measured against the S&P 500. If he invests in a mixture of large stocks and small stocks, then over time his average return should be higher than the large-stock-only S&P. His portfolio may also be a lot riskier than the S&P, but he needn't dwell on that point. (Technically, the increase in risk will be mitigated to the extent that large-cap stocks and small-cap stocks do not move perfectly in tandem. The diversification effect will somewhat moderate the overall portfolio's fluctuations.)

In an up market, the hybrid of large- and small-cap stocks is likely to go up more than the S&P. The manager can do even better by buying call options. Like small stocks, options are outside of, and riskier than, the index. The manager who follows the hybrid strategy can justify his fee by pointing to his above-average returns during the bull market. In reality, though, there's nothing superior about his performance. He has merely traded off risk for return. But as long as the ruse works, he's not going to complain.

If you think the money manager has finally licked his problems, think again. For one thing, pension plan sponsors are getting more sophisticated all the time. As time goes on, he'll find it increasingly difficult to brag about superior returns while concealing the extra risk. But that's a long-term worry. A much more pressing problem is the inevitability of a market decline.

It was bad enough when you were screaming at him for underperforming the averages in a bear market. At least he had told you beforehand that he was pursuing a high-risk strategy. Imagine how the pension plan sponsor will react when his portfolio's asset value declines by more than the S&P. Without clearly disclosing the fact, the manager has deliberately created a portfolio that's riskier than the benchmark by which he's being evaluated.

One response is simply to let the day of reckoning come. The manager will get fired and replaced by a different adviser. But his successor will be in the same boat. The pension plan sponsor will continue to demand that its managers beat the averages on the upside, while doing no worse than the benchmark on the downside. Eventually, the new manager will get fired, too.

Since the universe of investment advisory firms is finite, the pension plan sponsors will keep rotating through the same group. A manager whose performance remains near the middle of the pack will always be in the running to get hired. And there will always be a lot of hiring going on, because there will always be a lot of firing.

For bolder managers, there's an alternative to fatalistically waiting to get canned. What does a quarterback do when his back is to the goal line, 30 seconds remain on the clock, and his team is down by six points? There's no choice but to throw the "bomb," a long pass that might miraculously produce a touchdown. It might result in an interception instead, but at such a late stage in the game the quarterback might as well go for broke.

The money manager faces a similar choice when he's been wrong on the market all year. With 90 days left to go, modestly outperforming the averages won't be good enough. He has to do spectacularly well in the final quarter to offset his poor performance in the first three. At this point, an outright gamble begins to look sensible. Suppose the manager expects interest rates to fall in the next three months. Ordinarily, he might make a small bet on that conviction by buying some intermediate-term Treasury bonds. Staying with maturities of 5 or 10 years would limit his downside. But now, in a desperate attempt to salvage the year, the manager loads up on 30-year bonds. These will produce the biggest payoff if he's right and rates decline.

If rates instead go up, it will cost the client a bundle. But what the heck? The manager will lose the client for certain if he doesn't score big in the final quarter. Long bonds are the portfolio manager's equivalent of the quarterback's long bomb.

An even more audacious end-game strategy is available to a manager who's on a hot, rather than a cold streak. The ideal candidate is a pure market timer who's currently working as a portfolio manager for a major investment advisory firm. Imagine that over the past few years this individual has made totally unhedged bets on the direction of the market. She has repeatedly swung back and forth between 100% cash and fully invested. Whether by skill or by luck, her timing has been close to perfect. She's miles ahead of the Dow, with nearly the best five-year returns among all managers. *Barron's* has profiled her, and she's even been approached by book publishers. This is the ideal time for her to strike out on her own.

At first blush, it sounds risky. She'll be building her business on the premise that her golden touch will continue. History shows astronomically long odds against maintaining a string of correct market calls indefinitely. Perhaps she's better off staying in place as an extremely well paid employee.

A closer look, however, suggests that the economics are pretty attractive, regardless of her prospects as a market timer. For one thing, she won't have to spend much money on marketing. She can count on bringing a few of her top clients along to her new shop. Since they're already impressed with her skills as a money manager, she won't have to rent fancy office space. Nor will she need much of a staff, since she doesn't attempt to pick stocks through fundamental research. At most, she'll require a recent college graduate to help run her computer models, plus a secretary.

Even when you throw in incidental expenses, there's plenty left over as profit if she starts out with $500 million or so to manage. At ½% annually, her fee will sound cheap, considering her record of outperforming the averages by 10 or 20 percentage points a year. Assuming that fortune continues to befriend the manager, she'll probably pull in some new clients. Her revenues will then rise from their initial $2.5-million-a-year level. But suppose she starts to miscall the market?

It's by no means a disaster for the manager to be wrong, at least not right away. Clients don't typically fire an investment adviser for a single year of bad performance. If the manager keeps her firm alive for just two years, she'll rake in $5 million. Even after expenses and taxes, she'll be able to retire in comparative comfort. Not bad for a worst-case scenario.

As I trust you've concluded by now, it's impossible to design a foolproof compensation arrangement. Certainly, you should prefer a setup that promises to benefit both parties. If the other party is only in it for the short term, however, that party is likely to benefit more than you will. While it's important to know the deal, it's at least equally important to know with whom you're dealing.

_____ *Part Four* _____

FOR YOUR
(MIS)INFORMATION

21

All the News That's Fit—And Then Some

Financial Journalists Have a Lot More to Worry About Than Simply Getting the Facts Straight

"**R**oy Rogers is back in the saddle again at Hardee's Food Systems Inc.," announced *The Wall Street Journal* on March 3, 1992. In response to popular demand, Hardee's was reinstating the singing cowboy's name and menu at a number of Washington/Baltimore-area restaurants. Earlier, the hamburger chain had tried to convert the units to its own brand.

A month-and-a-half later (April 20, 1992), the *New York Times* reported the "news" that Hardee's was restoring the Washington/Baltimore restaurants to their original trademark. The lead paragraph of the article was catchy: "Roy Rogers is back in the saddle again."

Perhaps it's churlish to add that the badlands ballad, "Back in the Saddle Again," was recorded by Roy's cinematic rival, Gene Autry. But maybe not. Compared with some of the sins attributed to the press, lack of originality and questionable motifs are minor offenses.

More serious allegations against financial journalists include misrepresentation, slanting, and quoting out of context. One nice thing about big, blatant falsehoods is that they're comparatively easy to spot. (If you don't detect the flaw on your own, there's always a chance that some aggrieved party will write a letter to the editor.) The truly treacherous traps of journalism are more subtle and, surprisingly often, inadvertent.

As an example, reporters are sometimes accused of twisting the words of people they interview. In certain cases, though, it can be equally misleading to accept a statement at face value and reproduce it.

A common variety of deceptive literalism involves earnings releases. When corporations report their quarterly financial results, they are obliged to be truthful. But there are no laws specifying the order in which they must tell the truth. If net income was down but pretax profits were up, guess which item will be highlighted in the opening paragraph? Next quarter, earnings may be down by every measure. In that case, the press release will probably highlight the rise in sales. Over time, a reporter who passively transcribes the company's press releases creates the impression that the company never has a down quarter.

If routine earnings reports can trip up journalists, imagine what happens when the stories begin to get complex. A major problem is that it's simply not feasible for reporters to become experts on every subject they write about. Consequently, they have no choice but to rely on recognized authorities. That's one reason why the articles in business publications are chock-full of quotations. Unfortunately, there's no guarantee that the individuals most willing to talk to reporters are also the best informed on their subjects. The most frequently quoted so-called "experts" may merely be the ones with the strongest desire to see their names in print.

True publicity hounds know that the surest way to get quoted is to be quotable. This can mean having a knack for inventing (or borrowing) colorful metaphors. ("Trying to determine XYZ Company's true growth rate is like trying to nail Jell-O to a wall.") Quotability can also consist of a willingness to stake out extreme positions on issues. Reporters, after all, don't want to write bland stories any more than readers want to read them.

Clearly, relying on the most obliging authorities has its drawbacks. Certain professional constraints make it difficult for journalists to avoid the practice, however. For one thing, editors generally instruct reporters not to inject their own opinions into factual news stories. Quoting an expert can be an effective way of working in necessary interpretation. (As we have already seen, a listing of the facts entirely without comment can be just as misleading as a deliberately slanted account.)

Using quotations to put the facts into context is fine, as long as the journalist is attempting to write a balanced story. Some reporters, however, are skilled in eliciting statements that support their personal views on the news. Suppose an interviewee fails to provide the hoped-for slant. To an enterprising journalist, this presents nothing more than a minor inconvenience. The reporter simply switches to questions that begin, "Can you completely rule out the possibility that . . . ?" This tactic produces quotes that appear to validate extreme interpretations without necessarily violating journalistic ethics. That is, the practice falls slightly short of putting words into people's mouths.

There's another possible reason that business scribes rely so heavily on quotations. Overworked (or lazy) reporters seemingly feel that the technique gets them off the hook on accuracy. Surely, no accredited journalism school teaches any such principle. But it's only human for reporters under deadline pressure to skip the step of seeking a corroborating comment.

Can it really be true that newspapers sometimes print stories without checking the facts? You would hate to think it happened very often, especially if you base investment decisions on information you glean from the press. From the publication's viewpoint, however, there's a tradeoff. At times, it's possible either to be 100% certain about the facts or to scoop the competition, but not to do both. Waiting another day to check niggling details may mean missing a chance to break a big story. Editors look bad if they fill their pages with follow-up articles on bombshells that appeared first in other periodicals.

The press baron Joseph Pulitzer (1847–1911) had an unequivocal solution to dilemmas of this sort. Accuracy, he declared, was to a newspaper what chastity was to a woman. (A wag noted, however, that a newspaper could always print a retraction.)

Fortunately, not every media *faux pas* results in monetary losses or bruised egos. Imagine, for example, how gratified Time-Warner's late chairman Steven Ross must have felt when his photograph appeared in a *Pensions & Investments* gallery of likely future winners of the Nobel Prize in economics. On the other hand,

Stephen A. Ross might have felt justifiably miffed. As the originator of the groundbreaking Arbitrage Pricing Theory, he was probably more entitled to consideration for the laurels than his near namesake. (*P&I* subsequently ran Stephen's photo in its "Corrections & Clarifications" column.)

Disputes about the facts are not always harmless sources of amusement. On April 27, 1992, Ryka Inc.'s president alleged that a misstatement in the *Boston Herald* was responsible for a 24% drop in the price of her company's stock. The *Herald* had claimed that the developer and marketer of women's athletic footwear was planning on calling its warrants. In reality, insisted Sheri Poe-Brieske, Ryka was not forcing holders to exercise the instruments.

Strictly speaking, it's impossible to tell whether Ryka's stock nosedived solely because of the *Herald's* comment about the warrants. Investors were probably not reassured by the story's suggestion of a cash crunch. Poe-Brieske acknowledged that as a "stopgap measure" she was injecting $1 million of her own money into the company. In August, 1992, moreover, Ryka did announce the redemption of its warrants. From the company's standpoint, the problem with the *Herald* article may have been farsightedness, rather than supposed inaccuracy.

By another standard, the Ryka article upheld the noblest traditions of financial journalism. That is, the piece was saturated with double meanings involving the company's line of business. The wordplay began with the headline: "Footwear Company Ready for Next Step." It continued with the observation that Ryka was "running through a lot of money," but "gaining a toehold" in major shoe stores. Furthermore, the company seemed to be "making strides" and was about to "jump into the cheerleading market" with shoes especially designed for standing on someone else's shoulders.

Business reporters delight in this brand of humor. Editors evidently believe the readers do, as well. Punning is particularly encouraged in articles about manufacturers of intimate apparel and other innately comical goods.

Ryka's shareholders may not entirely appreciate the lighter side of the *Herald* article. They should recognize, however, that it's a privilege for the company to be mentioned at all. Most corporate executives would love to get profiled in a major metropolitan daily. They lose untold hours of sleep wondering why the newspapers ignore them while lavishing attention on their rivals.

Their bewilderment is well founded. To the layman, newsworthiness seems to be a sufficient basis for deciding which stories to run. Editors have a broader set of criteria, however. For one thing, they value scoops far more than news that's being printed elsewhere. Astute press relations officers use this fact to draw special attention to their news. A publication that gets an exclusive is likely to give a story more space than it would otherwise receive. Perhaps even more than it deserves. Rival newspapers, having been scooped, may bury the item in an inside page or not run it at all. Therefore, unless you read every pertinent periodical, you'll probably miss a lot of useful information.

Don't infer from this, however, that journalists are indifferent to your interests. On the contrary, they tend to be champions of the small investor. They want you to make money in the market. Above all, they want you to *believe* you can make money in the market. They're especially pleased if you conclude that the way to do it is to comb the newspapers for insights by the leading experts.

Ever solicitous of your well-being, they fret about what would happen if you lost faith in the frequently quoted market prognosticators. You'd become despondent. You'd cease to be obsessed with market data. You might even cancel your subscription.

Happily, you'll almost never see the financial press expressing skepticism about your prospects for beating the averages. Your own investment record may be dismal, but the newspapers have a ready explanation. Depending on the current fashion, the culprits may be insiders or program traders. One way or another, however, your grief is caused by the big-money interests throwing their weight around.

Reassured, perhaps, by this populist view of the market, you may continue to seek your fortune in the financial pages. If you do, remember that the information you find there is not infallible. "The journalist's job," said Adlai Stevenson, "is to separate the wheat from the chaff and then print the chaff." Plainly, part of the task of interpreting the news remains with you.

22

Missing Records

Newsletter Writers Are Not Held to the Same Standard as Investment Advisers

*F*ederal securities regulations will provide you a valuable protection if you ever decide to hire an investment adviser. No one who solicits your business in this area is permitted to show you an incomplete or misleading investment track record. This safeguard reduces your risk of developing unwarranted confidence in a money manager's prowess.

Suppose, for example, that an investment adviser woos you with the historical returns on a highly successful fund she manages. She cannot lawfully conceal the fact that five other funds she has managed over the same period have performed atrociously. Withholding that information would misrepresent her record.

If your means are relatively modest, you may think this discussion is irrelevant to you. Many investment advisers would decline to take you on as a client unless you had a fairly sizable portfolio, say half a million dollars or so. But even if you lack the wherewithal to hire an adviser, you may feel a need for expert advice. Subscribing to an investment newsletter could be a highly cost effective means of obtaining that advice.

Whether you get your investment counseling in person or from a newsletter, there is one constant—the need to investigate the expert's record. You might therefore logically expect the rules that money managers must follow when presenting their past performance to apply to newsletter writers as well.

The U.S. Supreme Court doesn't see it that way. In 1985, the justices exempted investment newsletters that are not published by brokerage firms from the Investment Advisers Act of 1940. Congress is free to extend the Act's authority to pundits who dispense undifferentiated recommendations to subscribers. For now, however, as Stephen Wermail pointed out in *The Wall Street Journal*, the law of the land is that the Securities and Exchange Commission can regulate only "persons engaged in the investment-advisory profession—those who provide personalized advice attuned to a client's concerns."

The case that brought investment newsletters to the attention of the Supreme Court arose when the SEC revoked a certain investment adviser's registration. (This action followed the adviser's conviction for tampering with evidence, misappropriating a client's funds, and failing to register with state officials.) For good measure, the SEC then asked a federal appeals court to prohibit the miscreant from publishing newsletters that included advice about specific securities. The appeals court obliged, but its decision was reversed by the Supreme Court. Notwithstanding the ex-adviser's "unsavory history," said the high court justices, his right to peddle printed recommendations was protected by the First Amendment.

As things stand, authors of investment newsletters have no obligation to publish complete records of their past recommendations. One way to capitalize on this freedom is to print bullish and bearish comments in rapid succession, then to develop selective recall. In this way, it is theoretically possible for every newsletter to have predicted the 508-point drop in the Dow Jones Industrial Average on October 19, 1987. The number claiming to have foreseen the calamity has not yet reached 100%, but it has grown over time.

Consider the following phrasing by Mark Hulbert, monitor of newsletter recommendations, in his December 28, 1987, *Forbes* column. Referring to the renowned Elliott Wave theorist, Hulbert wrote, "[Robert] Prechter, of course, is currently famous for his stock market timing, *which by my count*, got him out of the market before the crash." (The italics are mine.) Evidently, the "Buy" and

"Sell" signals disseminated in newsletters are sometimes matters of interpretation.

Advisers who actually run portfolios, to their sorrow, cannot so readily exploit the benefits of fence straddling. Managers who chronically hedge can never score big by calling the market correctly—their gains are always offset by losses. As a result, their investment performance is invariably middling. Bound by the Investment Advisers Act, they must report it that way as well. Their vacillating counterparts in the newsletter business, on the other hand, have license to portray themselves as forecasting geniuses.

Perhaps it would be unwise to deny the newsletter gurus their creativity, even when it comes to representing their performance. Are most subscribers, after all, solely concerned with the substance of the newsletters' recommendations? More likely, entertainment value has something to do with the success of these publications.

Creativity and entertainment are even more important when a successful newsletter spawns investment seminars. Putting on a good show can make up for a string of bad calls. Nobody has exemplified this principle better than the celebrated purveyor of newsletters and seminars Joseph E. Granville. His antics have made him a unique and beloved character, even if his recommendations haven't always made his clients rich. (Perhaps he'd have done better by using astrology, which he has confessed to believing in but does not factor into his forecasts.)

Here is a partial list of the stage devices that Granville employed in his heyday:

- Blinking bow ties.
- Electrified sunglasses.
- Boxer shorts with imprinted stock market quotations.
- Balloons.
- A hand grenade.
- A chimpanzee.
- A six-year-old singer.
- Bikini-clad models.

- Juggling.
- Ventriloquism.
- Granville playing the piano.
- Granville saying to the audience, "Touch me and be wealthy."
- Granville dropping his tuxedo trousers to read stock quotations printed on his boxer shorts.
- Granville dressing up like Moses to deliver his Ten Commandments of investing.
- Granville dressing up as Ayatollah Khomeini.
- Granville dressing up as a chicken.
- Granville appearing to walk on water.
- Granville entering the stage in a coffin draped in ticker tape.
- Advice on investing in the stock market.

Regarding that last point, here are a few assessments of Granville's prophetic powers that have appeared over the years:

- "He emerged from the bear market of the early 1970s with a dubious record. During those years, he kept urging subscribers to buy stocks even though the market continued to sink." (*Time*, 1981)
- "After his January prediction that stocks would fall 'straight down,' stocks staged a rally that cost Granville 1,300 subscribers to his weekly market newsletter." (*Newsweek*, 1981)
- ". . . a flamboyant and not very reliable tout." (*Business Week*, 1985)
- "Joe Granville is now famous for missing the start of the great bull market in the summer of 1982 and resolutely staying bearish until early last year." (*Barron's*, 1987)
- "According to *Hulbert Financial Digest*, which rates 100 stock-market newsletters, any investors who followed the *Granville Market Letter*'s advice over the last $4\frac{1}{2}$ years would have lost 46.9 percent of their common-stock holdings. During the same

period, the Dow Jones industrial average climbed 256.3 percent." (*U.S. News & World Report*, 1987)

- ". . . over the past nine years, Joe's record was the worst of all newsletters." (*Ingram's*, 1990)

In fairness, Granville has made some correct forecasts over the years. Most notably, in early 1981 he predicted a sharp decline. The market promptly fell a then-staggering 23.80 points on the largest one-day trading volume ever recorded up until that time on the New York Stock Exchange. Calls to 3,000 Granville clients on the preceding night urging them to sell their stocks probably helped to fulfill the seer's prophecy.

When he branched out into earthquake predicting, Granville actually made a correct call (August 1979). His subsequent forecast of a California quake measuring 8.5 on the Richter Scale did not pan out, however. Neither did his bold prediction that, "I will never make another major mistake in the market again." Still to come was his dismissal of the great bull market that began in 1982 as a "sucker's rally."

There is abundant evidence by now of Joe Granville's fallibility. Even the master himself admits to having sometimes misinterpreted his own theory. But the theory, he contends, is "absolutely impeccable, perfect." Still, the suspicion lingers that under rigorous analysis his record would prove to be no better than the results of a coin-flipping strategy.

Luckily for Granville, his right to omit that record from his newsletter is protected by the Supreme Court's 1985 decision. As far back as 1981, *Time* accused Granville of conveniently forgetting his poor performance during the 1970s. (The magazine was referring to his market calls, not to his piano playing or his chicken impression.)

In 1985, Granville gave as his reason for not personally trading stocks a desire to maintain his objectivity. Fear of leaving tracks was not a stated motive. If nonparticipation gave Granville an advantage over investment advisers, who were obliged to stake real money on their convictions, it was not the only professional edge that he enjoyed. Brokerage firms complained that if they were to emulate Granville's technique of reinforcing his bearish forecasts with middle-of-the-night calls to clients, regulators would rebuke them for using "extravagant and inflammatory language."

Clearly, there is no level playing field for purveyors of investment advice. Granville, who became a market pundit after failing an entrance exam for a broker training program, can rebound endlessly from past embarrassments. A money manager registered under the Investment Advisers Act cannot escape the burden of history as easily. Remember this when you're wondering whether you're likely to recoup your subscription fee by following the advice offered in an investment newsletter.

23

Everyone's a Winner

*Seemingly Objective Rankings of
Mutual Fund Performance Can
Produce Widely Varying Results*

As sales of mutual funds have
boomed in recent years, business magazines have eagerly capitalized on the trend. Annual and quarterly mutual fund surveys are
now a mainstay of these publications.

From the publishers' viewpoint, special issues devoted to the
performance sweepstakes provide great opportunities to sell advertising. The advertisers, in turn, can promote their funds to a
vast and highly targeted audience. The only remaining question is
whether investors derive any benefit from the mutual fund rankings.

Certainly, the surveys contain voluminous information about
past performance. *Forbes,* for example, reports each fund's total
return over the most recent 12 months and over the past decade.
The self-described "Capitalist Tool" also evaluates funds on the
basis of their performance in up markets and in down markets,
while *Money* and *Business Week* add three-year and five-year histories. The magazine surveys are likewise excellent sources for such
data as the funds' size, turnover, largest holdings, maximum initial
sales charges, and toll-free "800" numbers.

If you're like most investors, though, what you really want to
know is which fund will make you the most money *in the future.*
Unfortunately, the surveys all omit this indispensable bit of information. In so doing, they quite properly heed the disclaimer invariably found in mutual fund prospectuses: "Past performance is no
guarantee of future results."

The underlying truth of that well-worn phrase emerges force-fully from Table 23.1, *Barron's* list of the 10 best-performing funds for selected periods. Evidently, there is little reason to expect that a fund ranked in the top 10 for the past decade will be a standout in the current year as well. *Not a single leader* of the 10-year period made the 10-best list in either the most recent year or most recent quarter shown.

To a large extent, the rapid turnover among the top performers reflects the shifting fortunes of various market subsectors. Six of the 1986–1990 top 10, for instance, are funds specializing in Pacific Basin stocks. In 1990, that concept was not as hot as health care- or deutschemark-denominated funds, which together accounted for four of the one-year leaders. Those same two categories produced only one leader during 1990's fourth quarter, when new conditions pushed growth and technology funds to the forefront.

As if the instability of the rankings were not enough of a problem, selecting a fund is further complicated by risk adjustment. The idea is to blow the whistle on funds that generate high returns but perform erratically. Risk adjustment is simple in concept, but because the various surveys use different methods, they frequently generate conflicting conclusions.

By way of illustration, Table 23.2 lists the 10 funds that per-formed best on a risk-adjusted basis during the five years pre-ceding *Money's* February 1991 survey. *Business Week's* survey, published the same month, classified just two of *Money's* cream-of-the-crop funds as "Superior" in terms of risk-adjusted perform-ance. Thirty-three other funds won *Business Week's* "Superior" designation, but none of them made it into *Money's* top 10. Two of *Money's* top 10 funds were "Below-Average" by *Business Week's* reckoning and one was actually ranked "Poor."

Is the implication, then, that you should take the risk-adjusted figures with a grain of salt and concentrate primarily on the raw returns? Perhaps, but even at this most basic level the surveys often disagree about which fund deserves the laurels.

Forbes, for instance, puts out its annual survey in September, rather than in February, as most of the other publications do. Fur-thermore, *Forbes's* long-term measurement period is not a neat 10-year span. Its 1991 survey measured returns between Novem-

TABLE 23.1
Barron's Top 10 Mutual Funds*

Ten Years	Five Years	One Year	Last Quarter
1. Fidelity Magellan	GT Global Japan	Fidelity Select: Bio Tech	Fidelity Select: Developing Communications
2. Merrill Pacific: A	Financial Portfolios: Health	Fidelity Bond Performance	Unified Growth
3. Phoenix: Growth	GT Global Pacific	Shearson Currency: Pound	Fidelity Select
			Fidelity Select: Technology
4. CGMA Capital Development	Nomura Pacific Basin	Financial Portfolios: Health	Fidelity Select: Computer
5. Sequoia Fund	Merrill Pacific: A	Fidelity Select: Health	Fidelity Select: Software
6. Fidelity Destiny I	First Investors Global	Kemper Global Income	Fidelity Select: Medical
7. Quest for Value	Fidelity Destiny II	Equity Strategies	Equity Portfolios and Growth
8. Japan Fund	Fidelity Select: Food	Shearson Currency: Deutschemark	Financial Portfolios: Health
9. Oppenheimer Target	Oppenheimer Gold & Specialty Mining	Fidelity Deutschemark Performance	Putnam New Opportunities
10. Lindner Dividend	Japan Fund	Scudder Global: International Bond	MFS Lifetime Emerging Growth

*Ranked by percentage change as of February 11, 1991.
Source: Data extracted from *Barron's* (February 11, 1991).

TABLE 23.2
Comparison of Risk-Adjusted Return Ratings

Money's Top 10 Five-Year, Risk-Adjusted Returns February 1991	*Business Week* Ratings Five-Year, Risk-Adjusted Total Returns versus Standard & Poor's 500 February 18, 1991
1. Fidelity Magellan	Above Average
2. Merrill Pacific: A	Superior
3. Phoenix: Growth	Very Good
4. CGMA Capital Development	Below Average
5. Sequoia Fund	Very Good
6. Fidelity Destiny	Average
7. Quest for Value	Below Average
8. Japan Fund	Superior
9. Oppenheimer Target	Poor
10. Lindner Dividend	Very Good

ber 1980 and June 1991, for example. (This may appear to be a somewhat arbitrarily selected span, but when you get down to it, so is the period January 1981 to December 1990.) Such seemingly minor timing differences between *Forbes* and its rivals can give rise to marked dissimilarities in reported returns.

Another reason why historical return calculations vary involves the choice between compounded and annual methods. Table 23.3 contrasts the two approaches by analyzing the performance of a pair of fictitious funds. Both funds produce returns solely in the form of capital gains, generating no dividend or interest income.

Had you invested $100 in Fund A at the beginning of the period and made no withdrawals, your shares would have risen in value to $114 by the end of the third year. The annual compounded growth rate simply tells you that you could have accumulated an identical amount by initially investing at a fixed rate of 4.5%.

TABLE 23.3
Alternative Measures of Return

		Fund A		Fund B	
		Initial Investment	(Year-Over-Year Change)	Initial Investment	(Year-Over-Year Change)
Beginning value:		$100		$100	
Value at end of year:	1	$ 85	(−15%)	$108	(+8%)
	2	$ 93	(+9%)	$114	(+6%)
	3	$114	(+23%)	$117	(+2%)
Compound annual growth rate: (Derived from compound interest table)		+4.5%		+5.4%	
Average annual return		$\dfrac{-15\% + 9\% + 23\%}{3}$ $= \textbf{+5.7\%}$		$\dfrac{8\% + 6\% + 2\%}{3}$ $= \textbf{+5.3\%}$	

On the face of it, Fund B had a better record over the period. It turned a $100 investment into $117 over three years, representing a 5.4% compounded annual growth rate.

Keeping score by the average annual return method produces the opposite conclusion, however: Fund A's 5.7% yearly average tops Fund B's 5.3%. (Note as well the sizable gap—4.5% versus 5.7%—between Fund A's returns, as calculated by the two alternative methods.)

Which method, the compounded or the average, is more correct? The truthful answer is that each has its advantages and disadvantages. Compounded annual growth possesses considerable intuitive appeal but is highly sensitive to the base date that you happen to choose. If the calculation begins in a year in which technology stocks were unusually depressed, technology funds may show far higher compounded rates of return than they are likely to produce in the future. Averaging the annual returns tends to mitigate problems involving unrepresentative base dates. Table 23.3 shows, however, that the average annual method may favor a fund that has huge year-to-year swings over a steadier performer.

Leaving aside the question of their relative merits, the essential point about the two methods of calculating returns is that they produce different rankings. To cite one dramatic example, Japan Fund takes eighth place in the February 1991 *Barron's* and *Money* surveys (Table 23.4). Both of these publications use compounded annual growth rate calculations. At *Business Week* and *Forbes*, which employ the average annual method, Japan Fund ranks third and second, respectively.

Consumers may view such inconsistencies either as a benefit (diversity of opinion) or as a problem (conflicting results). If the inconsistencies are a problem, the key players have little to gain from solving it. Business magazines must somehow differentiate their surveys from one another if they are to compete effectively for potential readers and advertisers. Mutual fund management companies are probably better off having multiple chances to capture the top ranking than they would be in a standardized, winner-take-all ranking system.

Since the magazine publishers are content to continue dispensing contradictory advice, your best course is probably to rely on

TABLE 23.4
How Do Competing Surveys Rank the *Barron's* Top 10?
(10-Year Total Returns)

	Barron's February 11, 1991	Business Week February 18, 1991	Forbes September 12, 1991	Money February, 1991
Fidelity Magellan	1	1	3	1
Merrill Pacific: A	2	2	1†	2
Phoenix: Growth	3	4	5*	3
CGMA Capital Development	4	5*	4	4
Sequoia Fund	5	5*	7	5
Fidelity Destiny II	6	8	5*	6
Quest for Value	7	5*	8	7
Japan Fund	8	3	2	8
Oppenheimer Target	9	Not ranked	Not ranked	9
Lindner Dividend	10	9	Not ranked	10

*Tied for position.
†September 1982 through June 1991 only.

them primarily for data. Even if the surveys agreed about which funds performed best in the past, their implied picks would not be guaranteed to excel in the future.

You can spend your time most profitably by determining which asset categories (growth stocks, bonds, international, etc.) best serve your financial objectives. Within these categories, you should pick specific funds with at least one eye on fees.

Note that the magazine surveys contain no representations of reliability in spotting next year's top funds. If the publishers really knew, they could sell the information for a lot more than the newsstand price of a mutual fund special issue.

— 24 —

Going By the Book
Can Be Hazardous

Lax Standards in the
Publication of Investment
Advice Puts the Onus of Quality
Checking on You

Nothing that is written about investments comes with a guarantee of reliability. Certain kinds of publications warrant greater confidence than others, however. A key factor is the degree of editorial scrutiny that the material receives before it appears in print. Regrettably, books aimed at nonprofessional investors often undergo surprisingly little quality control.

The most rigorously tested analysis of the securities markets is the research published in refereed journals. Much of the content of these academic periodicals (*The Journal of Finance, Journal of Financial and Quantitative Analysis,* etc.) is extremely technical. As a general investor, you would likely find the studies esoteric and of limited relevance. Still, you can benefit by knowing a bit about the standards applied by a scholarly journal's editors and referees (expert readers) in determining whether or not an article ought to be published. The contrast with the review process for many "how-to" investment books is stark.

Let's suppose a potential contributor conducts a test, based on historical data, of a so-called "trading rule." (Classic examples include buying stocks with low price/earnings ratios and shorting newly floated closed-end mutual funds.) The author may put a great deal of effort into demonstrating that a particular strategy has outperformed the Standard & Poor's 500. Hard work alone, however, will not persuade the journal's editors to acknowledge the findings as valid.

For one thing, they will consider the length of the test period. A trading rule may have worked well in the past solely because of unusual market conditions that prevailed for just a few years. If so, the strategy would have little chance of replicating its success in the future. Another problem with trading rules is that they may produce above-average returns simply by subjecting investors to above-average risks. Strategies that generate these sorts of results do not qualify as better mousetraps. You can achieve the identical effect (higher returns at the cost of higher risk) without recourse to clever trading techniques. For example, you can switch from high-grade bonds to medium-grade bonds or from large-capitalization stocks to more volatile small-capitalization stocks.

Given these and other pitfalls, it takes a lot of sophisticated statistical analysis to prove that a trading rule really works. Researchers often fail, on their first try, to support their conclusions to the complete satisfaction of the editors and referees. They must then revise their work and resubmit it, perhaps only to be sent back to the drawing board yet again. Months or even years may pass before their research finally appears in print.

Authors who steer clear of academe encounter far fewer obstacles. Commercial publishers quite understandably tend to be concerned about production schedules and costs. While publishers generally like to be known for editorial excellence, most do not pursue that objective to the extreme of dealing directly with niggling points of theory. After all, authors have incentives to preserve their own professional reputations. They might therefore be expected to exercise care in their research.

Relying on the authors to police themselves works reasonably well, provided the authors are both capable and honest. These two conditions are not always satisfied, however. Horrific consequences can proceed from the absence of other checks in the system.

Consider the case of Srully Blotnick. By the age of 46, pop psychologist Blotnick had written five books. One, *The Corporate*

Steeplechase: Predictable Crises in a Business Career, reportedly sold 50,000 copies. A *New York Times* reviewer deemed it the finest book he had ever read on the subject of career management. Blotnick also authored an investment-oriented column in *Forbes* and had received the ultimate professional accolade, a guest spot on the *Phil Donahue Show.*

In 1987, Blotnick, the author of *Otherwise Engaged: The Private Lives of Successful Career Women,* became the subject of some interesting revelations about his own life. For starters, it turned out that his doctorate in psychology had come from an unaccredited correspondence school. A New York state agency promptly launched a criminal investigation to determine whether Blotnick had described himself as a psychologist without having the proper licensing.

Besides impeaching Blotnick's credentials, an investigative reporter for the *New York Daily News* cast doubt on the authenticity of his research. Blotnick's books were supposedly based on interviews of more than 8,000 individuals over 29 years. But according to Eleanor Singer, president of the American Association for Public Opinion Research, Blotnick could not possibly have carried out the studies he described without far greater resources than he had at his disposal. Barbara Gutek, a Claremont College psychology professor, concluded that Blotnick's findings had no validity. She also remarked that certain passages of his books "almost read like soft-core porn."

Blotnick denounced the *Daily News* allegations as "malicious reporting," which he vowed to refute point by point. He protested that he was being held to an inappropriate standard, explaining, "I have never said my study is scientific." In further defense of his integrity, he noted that he spent all of his time and money on interviewing his subjects. "I don't play golf or tennis. I don't own a BMW. I don't take expensive vacations in Acapulco."

Pretty soon, he wasn't writing a column for *Forbes,* either. According to Blotnick, that relationship ended because he refused to let the magazine verify his data by calling his interviewees, who had agreed to participate in his research on condition of confidentiality. Even before the 1987 exposé, however, *Forbes* had evidently felt some qualms about him. A few years earlier, an editor had learned about Blotnick's mail-order degree and deleted the "Dr." from his byline.

For investors, the most significant revelation in the Blotnick affair was the reaction of the book publishers. *Mea culpas* were hardly the order of the day. An executive of Blotnick's first publisher, Facts on File, admitted that his company had never attempted to review the correspondence-school graduate's survey techniques. Blotnick's position as a *Forbes* columnist had given him credibility, added the official. Similarly, Blotnick's next publisher, Viking Penguin, said it had seen no need to check out the would-be psychologist's research methods, since it presumed that Facts on File had already done so.

The American Association for Public Opinion Research's Singer emphatically stated her conviction that, given the opportunity, an expert in survey techniques could have detected the problems in Blotnick's books prior to publication. Facts on File was not about to adopt the critical manner of the university presses, however. "Ninety-nine percent of what we do is based on faith," its executive explained.

While this casualness is not universal among publishers, neither is it unique. In my sideline of reviewing securities-related books for the *Financial Analysts Journal*, I find that quality control in the popular investment advice category leaves much to be desired. A case in point involves a book entitled *Beating the Dow: A High-Return, Low-Risk Method for Investing in the Dow Jones Industrial Stocks with as Little as $5,000*. The publisher was evidently less concerned than I was, when I reviewed the book, about the author's apparent aversion to checking his facts.

Referring to McDonald's, the self-proclaimed Dow-beater writes, "I don't know how many billion hamburgers they have sold to date [they know, though; look at their sign the next time you drive by]. . . ." Had he taken the trouble to drive by himself (I have confirmed that McDonald's has outlets in his area), the author might have discovered that nowadays many of the signs merely read, "Billions and billions served." With even less effort, he could have telephoned McDonald's headquarters. When I did so, a company spokesperson cheerfully provided the burger count, which was 80 billion at the time.

Elsewhere in *Beating the Dow*, the author repeats the entertaining tale that the now-defunct retailer E.J. Korvette derived its name from "eight Jewish Korean War veterans." In reality, the company was founded prior to the Korean conflict and was named after a type of World War II military vessel.

The author's easygoing approach to verification, it turns out, extends to his investment results. He bypasses even the most rudimentary tests that serious researchers apply to trading rules. At a minimum, a simple analysis of the wide year-to-year variance in his returns would be in order. Investors can chuckle when an author misses key data on Big Macs, but it's no laughing matter to risk hard-earned money on thinly supported strategies.

Many investment professionals will no doubt regard my comments as carping. They may argue that real-world money managers, writing for popular audiences, should not be held to the same nitpicking standards as ivory tower academics. However, no sane person would consult a health book that was edited on the same theory. An author's stylistic decision to use nontechnical language, rather than equations and Greek letters, cannot justify giving out unfounded investment advice. On similar grounds, publishers of investment books ought to demand a reasonable degree of rigor. They should be conscious of accuracy, regardless of whether the audience is general or academic.

Apparently, looseness regarding facts is not unique to the investment field. Journalist John Brodie, writing about nonfiction books on espionage in *The New Republic*, has this to say about publishers' commitment to quality: "Publishing houses do not employ fact-checkers as magazines like *Time* do. Accuracy is not a financial concern for a publishing house; libel is. A libel judgment can cost a publisher millions of dollars; an inaccuracy only detracts from a house's reputation. So books are subjected to a legal read, but not a factual review."

Notwithstanding such economic considerations, I can personally attest to the feasibility of conscientious editing. The copy editors who worked on a previous book of mine added up every column of figures in my manuscript. This procedure uncovered an arithmetic error that I had unwittingly reproduced from the annual report of the Niagara Mohawk Power Corporation. The publisher in question has been around for nearly 200 years, which suggests that financial success and editorial integrity are not necessarily incompatible.

Unfortunately, not every publishing house insists that its authors carefully substantiate their facts. It's therefore up to you to pick up where the publishers' quality control leaves off. If you happen to lack an advanced degree in finance, you can nevertheless protect yourself by considering a book's internal evidence. Does the author repeatedly make unsupported statements? Is there any evidence that investment recommendations have been statistically verified?

It's okay if the author relegates the proofs to an appendix. Detailed quantitative analysis may be expendable in a book intended for lay readers. If the author appears to be guided solely by instinct, however, keep your money in the bank. Otherwise, you may end up aping some investor who got rich simply by taking greater risks than you can tolerate and then decided to write a book. As I've already pointed out, you don't need an expert's assistance to widen your range of potential losses.

——— 25 ———

The Art of Plain Talk

Company Management Is the Most Direct Source, but Not Necessarily the Most Reliable

Seqouia Systems Inc. had "all the elements in place to be the next big computer company." So said chairman Gabriel P. Fusco on May 1, 1992. For the first nine months of fiscal 1992, revenues were up 40%. Fusco backed analysts' projections of $85 million for the full fiscal year. Within five years, he added, Sequoia might be a $300 to $400 million company.

Two months later, fiscal 1992 ended. After initially delaying the report of its results, Sequoia disclosed that revenues had come in at only $71 million. On October 1 the company revised that figure to $66 million. Revenue was restated once again, to $63 million, in December.

In May, with only about eight weeks remaining in the fiscal year, chairman Fusco had endorsed forecasts that Sequoia would earn $1.02 per share. After three revisions, the number was down to a 48-cents-a-share loss.

Other major developments at Sequoia during the period constituted a checklist of corporate distress signals. The Securities and Exchange Commission launched an informal inquiry into the company's accounting practices. Chief financial officer Kent R. Allen resigned "to pursue other interests." The company slashed its workforce and announced that it was in violation of certain bank loan covenants. Hewlett-Packard Company, Sequoia's 10% equity owner, declined to provide new financing. The SEC's informal inquiry turned into a formal investigation. One customer said that it had decided against buying a computer and had never received it, but Sequoia had nevertheless recorded a sale. When the company received a qualified opinion from its auditors, soon-to-be-ex-chairman Fusco declared, "We are convinced that we have the resources and ability to return the company to profitability."

The saddest thing about the episode is its familiarity. Why are comments that come directly from corporate executives so frequently unreliable? Sometimes, events truly take management by surprise. In other cases, the most plausible explanation is intentional deceit. There are still other instances in which executives refuse to face the facts. They continue to see signs of an upturn right until the day the company turns belly up.

All of this suggests a sensational profit-making opportunity. Suppose you could monitor management comments and somehow separate the accurate assessments from the bum steers. You'd then be able to identify out-of-favor companies that were poised to rebound, while selling short the hot names that were about to turn sour.

Unfortunately, it's impossible to develop ironclad rules. "Reading" management requires a lot of inference and gut feel, not to mention guesswork. Along with the subjective assessment, however, you can apply at least one constant. It's the principle that corporate executives don't obtain credibility simply by stating their positions emphatically.

In 1990, Paul Reichmann, of Olympia & York Development (O&Y) scoffed at rumors of financial difficulties at the company's ambitious Canary Wharf commercial real estate project in London. According to Reichmann, the negative comments were coming from "children who don't know what they're talking about." Michael Dennis, the head of the Canary Wharf undertaking, asked, "How can there be an issue, with a project that is 54 percent committed in the first phase, which is 70 percent completed, as to whether or not it is viable?"

In fact, skeptics found plenty to worry about. For one thing, they feared that Olympia & York was filling up the new office space by entering into money-losing leases. And only American and Canadian companies seemed interested in the bargain rents. British companies preferred, by and large, to remain in London's traditional financial district. As one English property agent put it, "The English attitude is, 'We've been in the City for 500 years; it is smelly, awful, noisy and there is no light, but we'd never leave it.' I am afraid it is the typical British mentality. Perhaps that is why we lost the empire."

As late as March 1992, O&Y's public relations firm was dismissing speculation of a bankruptcy filing as "completely without foundation." Dominion Bond Rating Service's recent downgrade of the developer's commercial paper, suggested the PR folks, was no sign of distress. "Olympia & York is current on all its obligations and expects to remain so," said the spokesperson.

The following month, O&Y failed to make a $62 million interest payment due on an $800 million Eurobond. In April, an O&Y representative reported that Canary Wharf was only about 60% occupied. Later, it would come out that the project was bringing in less than half the rental income that analysts had supposed.

Olympia & York filed for bankruptcy in Canada in May 1992. At that point, the company's $8\frac{1}{4}$% bonds due in 1996 were offered at 40 cents on the dollar. Commented the company's president, "We are making good progress. We believe we are on course."

Perpetual optimism was also a trait of the late press magnate Robert Maxwell. "He was a great positive thinker," observed his long-time secretary and office director. "He didn't have the words 'impossible' or 'can't' in his vocabulary." One word that was not missing from Maxwell's lexicon was "lawsuit." As he told an interviewer for *The Economist* in 1991, "I shall not answer your scurrilous and ignorant questions about the indebtedness of my private interests. If you print such things, I shall sue. My private affairs are no one's business but my own."

The board of one company Maxwell headed, the Mirror Group Newspapers, thought otherwise. In November 1991, the directors were anxious to know how £47 million had found its way from the company's coffers to U.S. banks and one of Maxwell's private companies. Maxwell broke a date scheduled to explain the transfer, saying he was ill, and went sailing. A short while later, he plunged from the deck of his yacht. His death was officially attributed to both drowning and heart trouble.

Maxwell's media empire quickly came unwound. His largest company, Maxwell Communication Corp., filed for bankruptcy on December 16, 1991. Just five weeks earlier, Maxwell's son Kevin had displayed the characteristic family optimism by saying, "There's been a lot of speculation about crisis meetings with bankers and I would like to, for the record, assure our employees and our shareholders that there have been no such meetings and bank arrangements for [Mirror Group and Maxwell Communication] are robust. . . . "

Little in statements from any of the Maxwells had suggested a looming disaster, even though the problems were a long time in the making. When Robert Maxwell began selling off chunks of his holdings, he pooh-poohed the plausible inference that he was in financial straits. The Mirror Group was so strong, he proclaimed, that even "a one-eyed Albanian" could see the attractions of buying shares in the company's public offering.

The Maxwell family's perennially upbeat comments were hardly unique in the realm of corporate communications. Robert Maxwell's penchant for stifling dissenting opinions, however, was exceptional. As already noted, one of his favorite techniques was aggressive use of the libel laws.

When free-lance author Tom Bower wrote an unflattering biography in 1988, Maxwell filed 11 separate lawsuits. Although the press baron failed to block the book's publication, he enjoyed considerable success in intimidating magazines that later commissioned articles by the offending biographer. During 1990–1991, five different periodicals jettisoned stories by Bower, preferring to pay "kill fees" for unused material rather than face lawsuits by Maxwell. Many booksellers likewise concluded that it wouldn't be prudent to carry a critical biography of someone known as "the most litigious man in Great Britain."

Litigation was not the only tool that Robert Maxwell employed in ensuring that discouraging words would seldom be heard. He also offered editorial suggestions on research that, in his not-so-humble opinion, conveyed the wrong message. In 1990, securities analyst Brian Sturgess had the temerity to recommend a "cautious stance" on Maxwell Communication. Sturgess, a media specialist for the British brokerage firm of Barclays de Zoete Wedd, wrote of "juggling" of assets between Maxwell's public and private companies. Predictably, Maxwell threatened to sue. More to the point, he contacted Barclays de Zoete Wedd's parent company, which also happened to be one of his major lenders.

Soon, Barclays de Zoete Wedd published a new research report on Maxwell Communication. It contained three corrections, all of which Sturgess objected to. A month later the brokerage firm fired Sturgess, while being careful to point out that there was "no connection" with the Maxwell incident. Subsequent investigations suggested that the raiding of public companies by private Maxwell entities escalated after that point.

The Maxwell example shows how companies can squelch discord while simultaneously offering excessively rosy pronouncements. What you don't hear, in short, may be as important as what you do hear. This rule applies not only to companies' informal public statements, but also to their official disclosures.

Caterpillar's 1989 annual report didn't mention that nearly a fourth of the company's net income for the year came from operations in Brazil. Few outsiders would have suspected such a large earnings contribution from that country, since it accounted for only about 5% of revenues. The Brazilian unit's outsized profits derived largely from currency translation gains and other effects of hyperinflation. By their nature, such economic conditions don't tend to continue indefinitely. Investors who based their 1990 earnings expectations on 1989 results may have been counting on profits that were unlikely to recur.

Brazil's new president announced major changes in economic policies in April 1990. In June, Caterpillar announced that earnings would be substantially lower than expected. That day, the company's stock fell by 16%. Analysts learned for the first time about the Brazilian unit's large impact on the previous year's total earnings.

Caterpillar's earlier uncommunicativeness precipitated a Securities and Exchange Commission charge of disclosure violations. According to the SEC, the machinery maker's board of directors was told early in 1990 that Brazilian earnings were "volatile." By then, the company knew of impending economic policy revisions, said officials of the agency. On that basis, the SEC argued that the "Management's Discussion and Analysis" section of Caterpillar's 1989 annual report should have warned investors about dependence on Brazilian earnings. The company settled the case without admitting or denying wrongdoing.

A final twist on the theme of corporate communications involves messages aimed at different audiences. Poormouthing is a tactic frequently adopted by companies in negotiations with labor unions and ratemaking bodies. Unfortunate consequences can arise when investors take a company's plea of poverty at face value.

Navistar International demonstrated the dilemma in a new context in July 1992. Like many other companies at the time, the truck manufacturer was attempting to rein in employee health care costs. As part of that effort, Navistar asked a U.S. District Court to confirm its right to revise benefits previously granted to retired workers. "[U]nless definite action is taken to permanently reduce retiree health costs," said Chairman James C. Cotting, "Navistar's continued solvency will be threatened." The cost savings were needed, he went on to say, in order for the company "to remain a viable operation."

To the court, this language may have sounded like a reasonable argument in favor of validating Navistar's proposed benefit reductions. Investors, however, interpreted the talk of solvency and viability as a signal that the company might fail to pay an upcoming dividend on its Series G convertible preferred stock. In early August, the shares slid from 38 to $27\frac{1}{2}$ before the New York Stock Exchange halted trading in response to an order imbalance.

Carmen Corbett, an assistant to Navistar's treasurer, suggested that investors' anxiety was unwarranted. She pointed out that Chairman Cotting's earlier statement had emphasized the company's ability, for the time being, to meet its obligations as they came due. Viability was a longer-term concern only.

Jumpy investors were unwilling or unable to make such distinctions, however. "The stock is for sale," said a managing director in one brokerage firm's convertible securities department. "Obviously, people think the company's not going to pay the dividend."

Navistar's mixed message illustrates yet one more way in which company comments can trip you up. In this case, the unfortunate consequences were apparently inadvertent. Frequently, however, incomplete or cryptic communications result in shocks to investors that are almost certainly foreseeable by the corporations.

Why don't companies head off this sort of nasty surprise? You'd think they would want to prevent doubt from being cast on their credibility. Many corporations in fact disclose bad news promptly, precisely because it's in their interest to preserve the trust of securities analysts and investors. Other companies, unfortunately, are quite willing to pump up investors' expectations to obtain short-term benefits. They evidence little fear of damage to their reputations.

An obvious reason for such seemingly short-sighted behavior is to boost the stock price. The company's executives may be unwise, however, to sell shares as a means of profiting from an artificial and unsustainable runup. For one thing, they might be accused of illegally manipulating the stock. Additionally, insiders' transactions are widely reported in the financial press nowadays. Large sales by senior managers could be interpreted as a sign of trouble, resulting in a drop in the value of their unsold shares.

Still, certain subtler strategies might prompt disclosure policies that would otherwise appear contrary to management's interest. Senior executives' compensation, for example, may be linked to the company's stock price as of a specified date. Withholding damaging information until after that date could ensure a maximum payout for management.

Alternatively, suppose that a corporation is planning to pay for a pending acquisition with its own stock. The higher the stock trades at the time that the deal is consummated, the fewer shares will be issued to the sellers. Once again, it may make sense to hold off on revelations that would hurt the stock price.

These shenanigans don't always result in convictions under the securities laws. But that's cold comfort to shareholders who later see a quarter or a third of their market value decimated in a day.

To an extent, investors have themselves to blame for such debacles. They're surprisingly eager to let bygones be bygones. A company can often wipe the slate clean merely by unveiling a new product or providing some other reason to be excited about its stock. Management has little incentive to be candid about future problems if past offenses are forgiven too quickly.

Unfortunately, there's not much you can do about the reluctance of the crowd to bear grudges. You can, however, unilaterally resolve not to trust executives who have burned you once before. Furthermore, when you're evaluating a company that you haven't previously invested in, you can investigate the past reliability of its public statements. The evidence you turn up may refute claims that the company's securities are undervalued. If a corporation has blindsided the market on many previous occasions, investors may have finally wised up. It's likely in that case that the market is placing an exceptionally low multiple on the company's earnings. A stock that's "cheap" on this basis will probably remain "underpriced" for the foreseeable future.

Above all, it's essential to maintain a skeptical attitude when companies discuss their prospects. This doesn't come naturally to most of us, since we like to believe that people are generally trustworthy. Remember that managers can be honest but deluded. Don't get caught up in their wishful thinking, just because you'll make money if they turn out to be right. Often, the correct answer to the question "Have I ever steered you wrong?" is a resounding "Yes!"

Part Five

DEFICIENT
MARKET
HYPOTHESES

26

Is Perfection Relative?

Some Funny Things Happen on the Way from the Textbooks to the Marketplace

On June 24, 1992, the United States Supreme Court opened a new avenue of litigation against tobacco companies. The justices ruled that smokers could file lawsuits alleging conspiracies to conceal or distort the health hazards posed by cigarettes. Previously, the manufacturers had successfully deflected such claims.

The high court's ruling was more than a boon to the plaintiffs' bar. To financial scholars, it provided an excellent opportunity to study the impact of new information on securities prices. For one thing, the information in question appeared to be genuinely new. Paul Barrett, writing in *The Wall Street Journal* (June 25, 1992), labeled the justices' decision "surprising." Accordingly, it seemed fair to characterize the news as unanticipated, in line with the academic definition of "new information."

Equally important, the cigarette ruling was reported to have material implications for the value of tobacco stocks. According to the *Journal*, the justices' vote "changed the law dramatically." The revised ground rules, the article went on to say, "could force cigarette makers to begin offering sizable settlements of the sort they previously sniffed at."

Consistent with academic models of the financial markets, stock prices swiftly incorporated the news of the court's decision. RJR Nabisco, for instance, promptly fell to 8, representing a 16% drop from its opening price of $9\frac{1}{2}$.

Before the day was over, though, RJR's stock was confounding financial theory. Without any additional news of consequence crossing the tape, RJR reversed direction. The shares closed at $9\frac{3}{8}$, down a slim 1.3% on the day.

As it turned out, there were two schools of thought about the high court's ruling. In direct contradiction to *The Wall Street Journal*'s interpretation, the *Bloomberg Business News* financial wire on June 24, 1992, headlined its account, "No Surprise Seen in Court's Split Decision on Tobacco Suits." Far from regarding the news as a negative, Fitch Investors Service, on the same day, saw "neutral, if not positive, implications for tobacco industry ratings." Philip Morris Companies was even more upbeat, labeling the decision "a significant victory." R.J. Reynolds Tobacco Company professed to be "very pleased."

Were these optimists allowing smoke to get in their eyes? Probably not. The tobacco ruling left plenty of room for debate about the impact on securities prices. For example, Michael Graham and Lisa Tesoriero, of Standard & Poor's, had this to say:

> Although the decision could result in a greater number of liability filings against cigarette manufacturers and an increase in legal expenses, S&P believes it will take a considerable amount of time before the court decision would affect creditor protection, if at all. This is due to the time and expense of litigating, the lengthy appeals process, the industry's track record of successfully defending its products and practices, and the difficulty of aggregating cases into class actions.

As Fitch noted, "The court largely affirmed the tobacco industry's most important defense of preemption of state law-based injury claims." Furthermore, the justices had ruled that smokers could not claim to have been inadequately warned of the risks in the period after 1969. That was the point at which cigarette companies had begun to place health warnings in their advertising.

It's no wonder investors had trouble determining how to incorporate the Supreme Court's ruling into the price of RJR's stock. Unlike the information described in finance textbooks, the tobacco decision had ambiguous implications. The cross-currents were so complex, apparently, that the market could not initially decide whether the news was good or bad.

Some rigid theorists would consider a statement of this nature heretical. Purists insist that the financial markets are perfectly efficient. By this they mean that new information is invariably digested swiftly and accurately. If that's literally true, however, the defenders of the thesis must solve a difficult riddle: Was the market perfect when RJR traded at 8 or when it traded at $9\frac{3}{8}$ on the same information?

The market's temporary befuddlement in the tobacco affair is hardly a unique occurrence. On October 9, 1990, for example, Carter Hawley Hale Stores announced an agreement to sell its Thalhimers chain to May Department Stores. Certain Carter Hawley bonds jumped by as much as 10 points on the news, before closing up 5 to 6 points. Despite that resounding vote of confidence, not everybody agreed that unloading Thalhimers for $325 million was a good deal. Constance Mitchell and Sam Alcorn reported in *The Wall Street Journal* that:

> "Although many Wall Street analysts hailed the asset sale as a positive move for the company, Moody's Investors Service Inc. late in the day downgraded its ratings on the company's senior debt to single-B-3 from single-B-2."

It's not solely Wall Street analysts with whom the rating agencies disagree in interpreting certain events. Occasionally, they disagree with one another. A case in point was the January 24, 1991, merger pact between Harcourt Brace Jovanovich and General Cinema. Standard & Poor's promptly watchlisted Harcourt for possible upgrading, based on an expectation that the publisher's competitive position would improve. On the same day, Moody's downgraded Harcourt's senior debt to the highly speculative rating of Caa.

Plainly, the news is not always subject to instantaneous, straightforward interpretation. While the theoreticians wrestle with the implications of complex information, they might also ponder the following items. All are culled from *The Wall Street Journal*'s "Abreast of the Market" and "OTC Focus" columns:

- "Nike added 2 to $76\frac{3}{4}$. Shearson Lehman Brothers repeated its buy rating on the stock." (January 16, 1992, C2)
- "Schlumberger rose $2\frac{1}{8}$ to 57. Goldman Sachs repeated a "buy" rating on it." (March 13, 1992, C2)
- "Armstrong World Industries rose $1\frac{5}{8}$ to $34\frac{3}{8}$. Smith Barney Harris Upham repeated its buy rating on the stock." (April 17, 1992, C2)
- "Software Etc. gained $\frac{3}{4}$ to $10\frac{3}{4}$. Robertson Stephens & Co. analyst Janet Joseph Kloppenburg repeated a "strong buy" recommendation on the Edina, Minn. software retailer's shares." (June 3, 1992, C6)

Here, apparently, are stocks moving up on no information. All that happened in each case was that the analyst repeated a previous recommendation.

It's reasonable, perhaps, to argue that the mere expression of an opinion by a securities analyst represents new information about a stock. However, is it not stretching a point to claim that an analyst can make a material difference by saying the same thing for a second or third time? Reiteration may render a statement more emphatic and therefore more persuasive, but it hardly fits a strict definition of new information.

To be fair about it, the repeated recommendations may not have been the only developments that affected the four stocks mentioned. In other instances during the same period, repeating of recommendations coincided with other potentially material developments. Sometimes analysts raised their already bullish earnings estimates. On one occasion, the "Heard on the Street" report included the pivotal news that a company was about to present a paper to the American Society of Hematology.

But even if the press sometimes omits pertinent details, I have doubts about the notion of a perfect market. In that Newtonian view of the world, all securities trade at their rationally correct levels. They remain at rest until acted upon by new information. Material developments move the stocks to their revised correct prices, where they remain until additional news appears. Although Newton's laws of motion work satisfactorily at the level of colliding billiard balls, physicists have had to devise additional theories to deal with the behavior of subatomic particles. Similarly, the securities markets appear less than perfectly rational when viewed in extreme close-up.

Sometimes new information does not create impact in a single, clear direction. The Supreme Court's June 1992 ruling on tobacco litigation is a case in point. In other instances, securities move on noninformation, such as repetitions of previously stated research opinions. Once in a while, an investor or market-maker simply makes a mistake.

An outstanding example of the last type of event occurred on March 25, 1992. Just minutes before the session's close, an order to sell several hundred million dollars worth of stock knocked the Dow Jones Industrial Average down by nearly 12 points. Salomon Brothers subsequently acknowledged that it had made an error in executing the order. According to press reports, a clerk had mistakenly instructed a computer to sell 11 million *shares*, rather than 11 million *dollars* worth of stock, as Salomon's customer had requested. Perhaps it would be possible to reconcile this incident with a model in which prices move exclusively in response to new information. Doing so would require grotesquely convoluted logic, however.

That's not to say that the concept of a perfectly efficient market is useless as a way of looking at investments. The assumption that prices are invariably accurate won't cause you to lose money through reckless speculation. You can't say the same for the model of a conspicuously *inefficient* market, which certain hucksters promote. In that view of reality, blatant mispricings are commonplace. Just by using a little common sense, say these securities floggers, you can profit at the expense of the slow-witted herd.

If you adopt this reasoning, you'll probably find in the end that other investors aren't so stupid after all. As you'll discover, it's no great trick to characterize a security as undervalued, based on five separate points of analysis. The problem is the sixth point, which demonstrates that the price is right where it ought to be.

Market perfection is clearly the more conservative assumption. You won't get into much trouble if you operate on the premise that genuine mispricings are rare occurrences. In fact, there's nothing wrong with acting as if the market priced every security correctly at every instant in time. Your logical course would then be to own a widely diversified portfolio, such as an index fund. Ferreting out elusive bargains would cease to be your objective. Instead, you'd simply seek to capture the predictable long-term returns arising from general economic growth.

Every so often, however, securities prices respond in a quirky manner to economic events. Momentary bargains may result. You'll forgo such opportunities for profits if you interpret the notion of efficient markets too literally.

27

Unlovely But Not Unloved

It's By No Means Clear That the Bankruptcy Stigma Creates Bargains

Stocks and bonds of bankrupt companies, as described by their boosters, are the contrarian's ultimate thrill. Scorned by conventional investors, they can be had at prices cheap out of all proportion to the securities' true risk.

After all, big, public companies that go bankrupt do not generally cease operations. They merely enjoy temporary respites from the inconvenience of having to pay their creditors. Eventually, they settle their claims and emerge from reorganization proceedings, possibly stronger than ever.

The misperceptions of conventional investors are dramatized by the Phoenix-like rise of Toys 'R' Us out of the ashes of Interstate Stores. Courageous, patient investors can exploit the obtuseness of the majority by reaping predictably spectacular returns in the securities of bankrupt corporations.

This tale is congenial to the American traditions of rugged individualism and rooting for the underdog. Even more important, it appeals to our egos, since we all imagine ourselves to be more astute than our fellows. If you leave aside investment considerations, it's a great story, regardless of whether it's true. It's another matter, though, if you consider the bankruptcy pitch as a money-making proposition. Now you must examine the evidence. Do securities of failed companies provide superior returns in fact, as well as in fiction?

As it happens, the preponderance of serious research indicates that investors in bankrupt companies earn rewards commensurate with the price swings they sustain—no more, no less. Employing standard risk-measuring analysis in a 1969 study, Edward I. Altman turned up no stronger argument for purchasing bankrupt equities than to say that their returns appeared to be "at least as attractive as average returns on listed securities." Even that tepid endorsement was qualified by Altman's warning of a possible upward bias in his calculations.

As for defaulted bonds, Dale Morse and Wayne Shaw found in their 1988 study, "Investing in Bankrupt Firms," that in the 36 months following default, "half the securities had price increases and half the securities had price decreases." Publicly available accounting data, added Morse and Shaw, seemed to provide no help in predicting which bonds would do well.

Finally, in 1991, Allan Eberhart, William T. Moore, and Rodney Roenfeldt reported that the pricing of failed companies' bonds, as of their bankruptcy filing dates, accurately anticipated the amounts subsequently received by creditors in satisfaction of their claims. As a result, no "free" gains over and above returns appropriate to the observed risks accrued to fearless investors who bought when (in Baron Nathan Rothschild's immortal, albeit morbid, phrase) "blood was running in the streets."

It would be an overstatement to say that there is no evidence whatsoever that a bargain has ever existed in failed companies' securities. Jerold Warner determined in a 1977 study that the bonds of bankrupt railroads may have been collectively undervalued during the period 1940–1942. The apparent cause was investors' failure to appreciate the significance of certain U.S. Supreme Court decisions. Aside from the windfall produced by that single episode, however, Warner confirmed the general conclusion of unexceptional returns in bankruptcy securities, once risk is taken into account.

Promoters of defaulted bonds have made much of W. Braddock Hickman's discovery of a 20% average annual return on defaulted bonds over the period 1900–1943. Many investors would no doubt consider that rate attractive at almost any risk level. Irwin T. Vanderhoof has pointed out, however, that Hickman found a rather ordinary 6% return on bonds that defaulted prior to 1930. A sensational 26% return was observed during the 1930s only because bankrupt companies' bonds—like most other types of assets—fell to extraordinarily low levels during the Great Depression. An averaging of the pre-Depression and Depression-era returns produces the previously mentioned 20% figure. Barring another economic calamity on the scale last seen in the 1930s, investors cannot count on achieving similar results with a market basket of defaulted bonds.

Neither is a diversified portfolio of Chapter 11 securities likely to produce results anything like the 75% compounded annual return earned by Interstate Stores/Toys 'R' Us common stock in the 10 years following the company's bankruptcy and suspension from trading on the New York Stock Exchange. Every sample has its outliers; in 1990 the New York Stock Exchange Index fell by 7.5%, while over the same period Cabletron Systems rose by 204%. Talking up such an extreme performer as though it were typical is misleading, to put it mildly. Despite its irrelevance to the question of what sorts of returns one might realistically expect to earn in bankruptcy investing, however, the Interstate Stores bonanza is almost invariably cited by promoters of the concept.

Equally prominent in distressed investing lore is the spectacular profit earned by holders of Penn Central Transportation Company's obligations following that corporation's 1970 bankruptcy. Aside from the usual cheap-because-shunned angle, astute purchasers of the bonds are said to have benefited from a general unawareness of valuable real estate that lay amidst the failed railroad operator's wreckage. Here, it might seem, is a clue to identifying in advance the spectacular winners within the universe of defaulted securities.

Unfortunately, Penn Central Transportation is another example of a legend that outstrips the facts. It's true that a representative PCTC subsidiary issue, the New York Central $4\frac{1}{2}$% refunding and improvement bonds of 2013, posted a 19.35% total return from bankruptcy through distribution of proceeds to creditors, which occurred in several stages. Before that happened, however, bondholders suffered through nearly a decade with no cash flow. They also sustained a 45% decline in value during the first six months of the bankruptcy. That ordeal was followed by a 30% price decline in 1972 and another 74% reduction in remaining value in 1974.

(The standard advice offered by advocates of bankruptcy investing is to wait for completion of the initial disgorging by nervous holders, then to jump in at the presumed bottom. In Penn Central Transportation's case, that strategy was not very rewarding for the first five years.)

On the whole, the high return that Penn Central Transportation holders ultimately realized can scarcely be described as a windfall. They earned every cent of it through severe mental anguish.

Some may argue that the wild price swings in the defaulted PCTC bonds are merely further evidence that conventional investors begin to behave irrationally as soon as the phrase "Chapter 11" is whispered. Indeed, it's difficult to prove beyond any reasonable doubt that each successive price plunge by the New York Central $4\frac{1}{2}\%$ bonds was a rational response to changes in expected recoveries by creditors. By the same token, Penn Central Transportation's decade-long reorganization proceedings were punctuated by several events that created considerable uncertainty about the amounts that would ultimately be recovered by bondholders.

For one thing, the bottom fell out of the New York City real estate market, where much of the company's vaunted hidden asset value lay. (In reality Penn Central Transportation's ownership of the Waldorf-Astoria and Biltmore hotels was far from a secret. A front-page article in *The Wall Street Journal* laid out the story of the real estate play in PCTC bonds one week after the company's bankruptcy filing.

A further risk was that the proceeds to be realized by bondholders were highly dependent on the courts. At issue was the value to be assigned to rail assets carved out of PCTC to establish the government-sponsored Conrail system in 1973. As an indication of the huge uncertainty inherent in the evaluation process, the estimates of the value of the Conrail assets at one point ranged from $13.6 billion (by the trustees representing the creditors) to $471 million (by the United States Railway Association).

Investors might have felt safe in betting on the judicial system to give bondholders a fair shake. Even so, the Supreme Court's ruling prompted dissenting Justice William O. Douglas to grouse that a comparable action by a private party would have been denounced as a fraudulent conveyance.

To sum up, the "cheap-because-shunned" thesis stands up better as an inspirational story than as a key to exceptional investment returns. As a group, defaulted securities offer ordinary returns (adjusted for risk), except under extraordinary circumstances. The illusion that sensational gains are regular occurrences is maintained by the perpetual recycling of a few showcase examples. Furthermore, it's only in retrospect that the occasionally lofty returns look like rewards for seizing obvious opportunities. Along the way, holders faced genuine risks that could have made the stories end quite differently than they did. Then, as now, investors were right to be skeptical of any story reducible, in essence, to "Dare to be great! Take advantage of those other investors who follow the herd and lack your boldness and vision."

28

Slow But Not So Steady

Bond Salesmen Who Like Predictability Follow This Rule: *"If It Ain't Fixed, Don't Broker It"*

Whatever the "fixed" in "fixed-income" means, it isn't a conventional definition. According to the dictionaries I've consulted, an item that is fixed is "constant," "set," and "not subject to change or variation." Yet many so-called fixed-income investments bear interest rates that vary, adjust, float, reset, or step up.

Some varieties of "fixed" obligations shift to higher rates when certain benchmark yields rise. Other types begin to pay *lower* rates under the same circumstances. A few issues have interest payments that fluctuate with movements in commodity prices. Distributions on mortgage-backed securities, on the other hand, vary according to how swiftly homeowners prepay their loans. In yet another variant, the cash payout remains steady, but the amount of a holder's taxable income changes from year to year. The determining factor is the proportion of the disbursement that the authorities deem to be return of capital.

All of this leaves aside the fact that a debt obligation can go into default. The good news is that while the issuer is bankrupt, payments to holders are fixed. The bad news is that the level at which payments are fixed is zero. Defaults drive home the point that "fixed-income" is largely a misnomer.

Life was far simpler for investors in a bygone era, when brokerage firms had bond desks. Nowadays, the units have been glorified into fixed-income departments. One reason for the re-christening is that the purveyors of debt-like securities traffic in a variety of obligations. Their wares include such instruments as certificates of deposit (CDs) and preferred stocks, which are not bonds. On the other hand, convertible debentures, which *are* bonds, are typically traded in the equity department.

Financial services companies might prevent some confusion if they were to replace the term "fixed-income" with "contractual-income." As we have seen, a bond's coupon can vary, just as a stock's dividend can. What truly differentiates the two forms of invest-ment income is the contractual nature of the coupon.

As a rule, the payment of a dividend in any given quarter is subject to approval by the board of directors. There's no such discretion in the case of coupons. The interest has to be paid, lest the corporation violate a contract with the owners of its bonds. Unlike stockholders, bondholders can enforce certain rights if their checks stop coming.

Under my proposed new terminology, by the way, it would be appropriate to continue trading preferred stocks alongside bonds. The dividends on preferreds are quasi-contractual, in that they're generally cumulative. This means that if a company omits its preferred dividend, it must make up the arrearage at a later date. In contrast, a company is under no obligation ever to repay the cash conserved by a temporary suspension of its common stock dividend. Switching to "contractual income" could accomplish much more than the elimination of semantic problems. It might also ease the distress that fluctuating interest payments cause for investors.

Most folks get upset when their ostensibly fixed income de-clines. The name leads them to expect that nothing will change. On the other hand, no one in this day and age supposes that contracts are sacrosanct. Boxing promoters, for example, regard them as nothing more than feints. Any correspondence between promot-ers' written promises and future events is purely coincidental.

As a result of such battering, the word "contract" no longer connotes "unwavering," as "fixed" does. Bondholders who squawk when their *fixed* income adjusts downward would probably take it in stride if their *contractual* income fell.

Nomenclature aside, however, the indisputable fact is that the income on a bond is subject to variation. The same is true for a mutual bond fund. Granted, investing in a fund eliminates, for all intents and purposes, the risk that your income will be cut off entirely. By owning a piece of a widely diversified portfolio, you will be affected only minimally by the default of an individual issue. Diversification does not guarantee you a specified income level, however. In fact, you may be surprised to learn just how unpredictable a bond fund can be.

Consider Table 28.1. It ranks 21 general corporate bond funds according to their estimated 30-day annualized yields as of the end of 1990. This is the sort of information you would have available if you comparison shopped for a fund based on advertised yields. (Naturally, you would also have the names of the funds. I've withheld them on the grounds that my object isn't to comment on their individual merits.)

By way of definition, the 30-day annualized rate is a standardized measure of bond fund yields. According to regulations of the Securities and Exchange Commission, funds must use this common yardstick if they choose to advertise their yields. In essence, the annualized yield is the ratio of income paid in the past 30 days to current net asset value, multiplied by 12. Recognized in the calculation is the accrual resulting from purchases of bonds at discounts or premiums to face value.

The SEC promulgated its 30-day standard in 1988. Prior to that time, a bond fund could advertise a yield based on whichever period made it look most competitive. The timespans selected by various funds ranged from one day to one year. *Business Week* (September 5, 1988) hailed the SEC's reform with the words, "What you see now is closer to what you get."

As the table shows, "closer to" can be quite a distance from "exactly." Actual yields generated during 1991 varied considerably from the 30-day rates indicated at the end of 1990. The 10 top-ranked funds wound up yielding less than their 30-day yields by an average of 62 basis points (hundredths of a percent). Meanwhile, the 10 funds initially ranked lowest produced yields that were 30 basis points higher, on average, than their 30-day rates.

TABLE 28.1
Indicated and Actual Yields of Selected General
Corporate Bond Funds

Fund	30-Day Annualized Yield December 31, 1990	Actual Yield 1991	Difference
1	12.35	10.16	−2.19
2	10.83	8.40	−2.43
3	10.45	9.83	−0.62
4	10.29	9.88	−0.41
5	10.01	9.78	−0.23
6	9.30	9.11	−0.19
7	9.15	9.11	−0.04
8	9.06	8.95	−0.11
9	8.99	8.87	−0.12
10	8.95	9.11	+0.16
11	8.85	8.32	−0.53
12	8.83	8.71	−0.12
13	8.61	9.03	+0.42
14	8.57	8.22	−0.35
15	8.51	8.20	−0.31
16	8.39	8.74	+0.35
17	8.13	8.28	+0.15
18	7.79	7.77	−0.02
19	7.07	7.35	+0.28
20	7.05	7.98	+0.93
21	7.02	8.68	+1.66

Note: All yields are percentages.
Source: Data extracted from *Barron's*, December 31, 1990, and December 30, 1991.

At the extremes, the deviations from the 30-day rates were substantially greater. The funds that were ranked number one and number two fell short of their prior-year-end yields by 219 and 243 basis points, respectively. As for the funds ranked last and second to last, the actual yields exceeded 1990 end-of-year levels by 166 and 93 basis points, respectively.

The divergences of funds from their 30-day yields is not surprising, considering that their portfolios are forever shifting. Some of the bonds held by the funds are retired through sinking funds. Others are called for redemption prior to maturity.

Portfolio composition also changes as a result of trading. Some of the swaps represent attempts to profit from shifts in interest rates or from temporary mispricings. Additionally, the manager may buy and sell bonds in order to maintain desired averages for maturity and credit rating. Suppose, for example, that a fund acquires a number of new seven-year notes. Three years later, the remaining lives of those securities will have shrunk to four years. This aging can reduce the fund's average maturity to less than the range specified in its investment policy. To offset such effects, the manager may liquidate the seasoned issues and replace them with newly floated seven-year paper.

Alternatively, a bond's credit rating may be reduced by Moody's or Standard & Poor's subsequent to its purchase by the fund. To stem deterioration in the portfolio's average quality, the manager might replace the downgraded issue with a higher-rated obligation.

Unfortunately, the need to reinvest the proceeds of bond retirements and liquidations can arise at an inopportune time. Prevailing yields may be less generous than the rates available formerly. In that case, the new mix of bonds will have a lower yield than the portfolio that generated the most recently posted 30-day rate.

A yield shortfall, incidentally, is just one of the ways in which the return on a bond fund can deviate from your expectations. Capital gains and losses also affect your results. Fluctuations in principal may not greatly trouble you if you truly intend to hold onto the fund indefinitely, but it's a different story if you ever need to raise cash by redeeming shares. In that situation, changes in the fund's net asset value can dramatically affect the success of your investment.

Whatever the source, the variability in bond fund returns underscores the potentially misleading nature of the phrase "fixed-income." Before leaving the subject, let's explore one final sense in which bond returns are highly susceptible to change. Suppose that instead of spending your coupons you reinvest them. This can be a wise strategy, given the well-documented power of compound interest. The "Rule of 72" states that a sum invested at 6%, compounded, will double in about 12 years. At a 9% rate, the doubling will occur in approximately eight years. Plowing back your profits is an effective means of building wealth over an extended period. There's a catch, however. Like the manager of a bond fund beset by premature redemptions, you may discover that rates have fallen when the time comes to reinvest.

The impact of reduced reinvestment rates can be substantial. Suppose, for example, that you buy a 30-year, 9% bond and reinvest all of the coupons until maturity. In the unlikely event that interest rates remain stable over the entire period, you will actually earn a 9% compounded return. If you're forced to reinvest your coupons at 8%, however, your actual return will be 8.37%. A 7% reinvestment rate will knock your return down to 7.77%.

You can eliminate the risk of a decline in reinvestment rates by purchasing a zero-coupon bond. Unfortunately, by doing so you'll forfeit the potential benefit of a rise in reinvestment rates. An additional disadvantage of zeros (unless you buy them in a tax-favored setting) is that they generate annual tax liabilities, payable in cash, even though they provide you no cash prior to maturity.

In concluding this discussion of fixed income, I urge you not to take too gloomy a view. True to their reputation, bonds provide steadier (although lower) returns than common stocks over long periods. In the process, they also provide a few surprises. But you'll get through them in satisfactory shape, as long as you don't count on your fixed income remaining fixed forever.

29

Foreign Matter

International Diversification Faces
Significant Regulatory and
Accounting Hurdles

"The internationalization of markets has a dark side." So said Philip A. Feigin, State Securities Commissioner of Colorado, early in 1992. He was speaking of the boiler room operators who were beginning to venture into foreign securities. It was a logical development for shady brokerage firms to latch onto the growing popularity of global investing. Offshore issues had a better chance of escaping regulatory scrutiny than the home-grown penny stocks in which fast-buck artists had customarily trafficked. As Commissioner Feigin put it, "How do we check out Indonesian companies with a $3 million float [the aggregate market value of all outstanding shares]?"

Happily, shell games are not the whole story of internationalization. There's also a legitimate (and much larger) side to it. As national economies become increasingly integrated with one another, financial markets are likewise breaking down national boundaries. Advances in communications are making it more and more difficult for securities exchanges to maintain isolationist policies.

Worldwide economic growth and efficiency are bound to benefit from these trends. More to the point, the expanded opportunities to diversify across continents can put money in your pocket. If you remain totally concentrated in the United States, most of your holdings will tend to go down together when the U.S. market slumps. Certain overseas markets, however, may be rallying at that time. By having some of your eggs in foreign baskets, you can potentially reduce the fluctuations in your overall portfolio. Global investing, in short, represents a genuine chance to reduce your risk of fluctuations without being forced to accept a lower rate of return.

International diversification will gain you nothing, however, if it merely enables you to make bad investments in several different countries at the same time. And it's not only the shifty brokers peddling obscure stocks who can saddle you with losses. It's quite possible to drop a bundle in eminently respectable circles.

For one thing, safeguards for investors aren't as well developed in most other countries as they are in the United States. This is not to say that the little guy always gets a fair shake in our markets. Still, I take some comfort from the nature of the debate in the United States. Here, the courts and regulators are tussling over such issues as whether it's illegal for acquaintances of relatives of corporate directors to trade on nonpublic information that they acquire inadvertently. In some other parts of the world, governments have only recently gotten around to prohibiting directors from blatantly capitalizing on undisclosed information.

Similarly, small investors should have felt grateful to be operating under U.S. rules in 1991, when major Japanese brokerage houses were found to be reimbursing their large customers for losses. The authorities couldn't charge the firms with anything worse than bad form. Under Japanese law at the time, it was only forbidden to promise customers in advance to cover their losses. The Ministry of Finance had condemned reimbursements in 1989, yet the practice was not unlawful. (Some prominent brokerage firm officials were nevertheless obliged to resign.)

When you wander to foreign realms, you're also likely to encounter strange happenings on the financial reporting front. Again, I would hardly claim the U.S. system is perfect, but the U.S. government does seem committed in principle to fair and honest disclosure, consistently applied.

Swedish authorities adopted a somewhat different approach a few years back, when Uddeholm AB was faced with potential insolvency. Wracked by losses, the steel and forest products manufacturer ended 1977 with its equity severely depleted. As a consequence, Uddeholm was in default on its debt and under obligation to repay its outstanding loans. To do so, however, would have wrecked the company.

The obvious first thought, an outright government bailout, was barred by international steel trade agreements. So instead of pumping in equity, the lawmakers provided Uddeholm with a line of credit. Then, in a splendid Orwellian touch, the solons passed legislation requiring the company to account for the new debt as equity. That piece of accounting gimmickry relieved Uddeholm's default.

Sweden's ad hoc rulemaking achieved its custom-tailored purpose of preventing the bankruptcy of that single company. In 1983, with Uddeholm safely out of the woods, the special legislation was repealed.

Certainly, the Uddeholm case is exceptional. Even so, it underscores the important point that the accounting environment changes dramatically when you go abroad. Quality of earnings is not regulated as closely overseas as it is by our Financial Accounting Standards Board. With less of a history of well-developed equity markets than the United States has, most other nations have yet to crack down on corporations' techniques for artificially smoothing out annual fluctuations in income.

By "other nations," incidentally, I don't mean Third World countries that are just beginning to industrialize. In a survey by New York University's Frederick D. S. Choi and Richard M. Levich, institutional investors listed Germany, Japan, and Switzerland as the countries that presented the greatest difficulties with respect to accounting practices. Even Great Britain, an industrial power since the 18th century, lags the United States in certain respects. As of 1991, according to the *Economist*, about half of all large British companies were reporting "extraordinary items" in their income statements. Relegating gains or (more likely) losses to that category is a classic device for expunging undesired volatility from an earnings record. Because the gambit is prone to abuse, U.S. accounting rules define "extraordinary items" much more tightly than the British standards do. Consequently, they appear on only about 5% of major U.S. companies' profit and loss statements.

The same *Economist* article describes another clever British method for smoothing earnings. Under British accounting rules, companies can revalue their assets upward to reflect changes in economic worth. The permitted writeups affect only the corporations' balance sheets, though. Companies can't pump up their reported profits by recognizing rises in asset values unless they sell the items in question. A popular way to take advantage of the rules is to sell an appreciated asset at a time when earnings need a boost. The company can book a profit on the transaction, even if it has already recognized the gain on its balance sheet. To put it mildly, the timing of such earnings may be quite arbitrary.

But let's not single out Great Britain among the highly developed nations for having underdeveloped financial reporting rules. Consider these observations by the brokerage firm of UBS Phillips & Drew. They appear in the 1992 book, *Global Investing: A Handbook for Sophisticated Investors*, edited by Sumner N. Levine:

> There is no requirement in Switzerland to disclose earnings per share. Further, any meaningful calculation of EPS is extremely difficult because of the notorious unreliability of published earnings figures.

> Published accounts in Germany tend to be guided more by compliance with legal requirements and by fiscal considerations than by the desire to present a true and fair view of the company's earnings, as understood by the accountancy profession in Great Britain and the United States.

While the advanced countries are less advanced than they might be in their financial reporting practices, they are ahead of certain other parts of the world. As you might guess, many of the biggest hazards are in regions where the hype about investment opportunities is most intense. In the former Soviet Union and satellite nations, it's premature even to speak of world-class accounting rules. Much of the requisite infrastructure is lacking. To begin with, there aren't yet enough locals with the requisite skills to perform satisfactory audits on all of the newly privatized companies. Furthermore, the previous lack of profit orientation has left behind systems that crank out voluminous statistics, yet give no indication of the enterprises' financial condition.

Western accounting firms are striving to inject some rigor into the process. In many instances, they've had to settle for "financial investigations" in lieu of full-blown audits. One auditor conducted a lengthy investigation of a Polish company and only afterwards discovered, by chance, its extensive holdings of lakeside property.

The Choi-Levich survey, cited earlier, reveals that some institutional investors are unable to cope with the vagaries of non-U.S. accounting. Their solution is to avoid investments in foreign corporate securities altogether. The others, say Choi and Levich, must become familiar with the accounting practices of each country in which they choose to invest.

Following that helpful recommendation may be an impractical solution for you. If so, relying on outside expertise is a realistic alternative. Make sure, however, that you investigate your expert's qualifications thoroughly. Your adviser may be an analyst who is attempting to transfer U.S. industry knowledge to foreign shores without a solid understanding of the accounting nuances.

If that sort of due diligence isn't feasible, you might consider participating in overseas economies through country funds. Owning a basket of companies should enable you to capture a nation's growth potential without unduly exposing yourself to any single corporation's financial reporting ruses. As with other categories of mutual funds, you have to be wary of following the crowd. Once a country gets hot, its securities can get bid up to excessive levels. This is particularly true when there are comparatively few issues available for gaining exposure to the currently voguish nation. There is also a danger that trading in country funds will be dominated by U.S. investors. Cross-border diversification benefits may be sacrificed as a result.

In time, many of the pitfalls of international diversification should become less severe. The long-term trend, in both market regulation and financial reporting rules, appears to be toward global standardization. I'm optimistic that the tendency will be to universalize the best practices, rather than to give way to Gresham's Law. Meanwhile, *caveat emptor* is the safest rule to follow. With global investing becoming increasingly popular, the con artists are sure to cut themselves in. And in the overseas market, even legitimate investment strategies can be perilous.

Never lose sight of the basic rationale for diversifying internationally. The idea is to moderate the swings in your net worth, not to accentuate them by being uninformed.

30

Muni Madness

Don't Let the Lure of Tax Savings Blind You to the Importance of Other Investment Considerations

"**H**ello, Mr. and Mrs. Prospect. You've never heard of me. Nor have you heard of my company. I'm selling bonds issued by a special governmental body of a type you're unfamiliar with. I have no financial data to present to you.

"The project backing these bonds is new and untested. I've identified you as suitable buyers of these obligations by picking your name from the telephone directory.

"My recommendation is that you invest a substantial portion of your life savings in these bonds. The income that you will receive is *tax-free.*"

* * *

If unscrupulous salesmen of municipal bonds were this candid, their siren's song would ensnare fewer investors. But even if purveyors of worthless munis were forced to operate on the basis of brutally full disclosure, they would still live comfortably. They'd simply focus their efforts on the portion of the public that is determined to avoid taxes, regardless of the cost. Rather than let a single dollar of their net worth pass into Uncle Sam's coffers, these uncompromising tax resisters would gladly set a match to it. Dealing with the less reputable denizens of the muni market achieves the same effect.

The first mistake to avoid in municipal bonds, then, is falling in with the wrong crowd. There are plenty of trustworthy tax-exempt bond specialists working for legitimate firms. Consequently, you never need to respond impulsively to a surprise telephone call from a fly-by-night muni peddler.

Considering the cost of falling prey to a dishonest broker, there are undeniable advantages to dealing with the noncriminal variety. Concern for your welfare and a solid reputation do not guarantee that you will escape financial embarrassment, however. A salesperson might sincerely try to maximize your after-tax income, yet inadvertently cause you to lose a big chunk of your principal. The hazard that remains, even when you deal with reputable brokers, involves municipal bond defaults. Financial failures by municipalities have a long history in the United States and, no doubt, a prolific future. If you hope to avoid them, you probably ought to study the characteristics of past debacles. Educating yourself will afford you better protection than the good intentions of a broker who has little sophistication in public finance.

Several themes recur repeatedly in municipal defaults going back to the early 19th century. Natalie R. Cohen, of the bond guarantor Enhance Reinsurance Co., lists, among others:

- Regional land development cycles.
- Commodity booms and busts.
- Financial mismanagement.
- Urban fiscal crises.

She also notes that, historically, municipal bond failures followed the nation's expansion across the continent. Defaults were typically concentrated near the westernmost areas of settlement.

Cohen's first theme, land development cycles, was prominent as far back as the Panic of 1837. The ensuing depression triggered defaults on one-half of all outstanding debt. Much of the ill-fated debt had been incurred for the purpose of chartering banks that in turn lent to real estate developers. Another cycle of soaring land prices, followed by collapse, precipitated the default of over 80% of all Florida taxing units in the eight years ending 1933. (Helping to touch off the downslide in land values was an invasion of Mediterranean fruit flies, which devastated the state's citrus crop.)

Notwithstanding numerous opportunities to learn from history, municipal bond buyers were devastated by yet another land development cycle beginning in the mid-1980s. Colorado land prices had boomed in the preceding years, creating unbridled optimism about the prospects for new construction. Capitalizing on the enthusiasm, developers bought parcels of land, which they turned into special taxing districts. To pay for sewers and roads, the developers sold tax-exempt bonds, figuring they would eventually cover the interest through taxes on the residents of their communities. Pending arrival of the proud new homeowners, the real estate operators floated additional bonds to cover debt service.

Unfortunately, some of the developments were simply too speculative, too remote from the settled areas and their conveniences. Fewer houses were built than the plans had called for, meaning that tax revenues were too low to cover interest costs on the bonds. As a result, the welcome wagon was often followed by a massive hike in property tax rates. Many taxing districts resorted to the unpleasant alternative—filing for bankruptcy.

Ironically, the residents had initially been lured by the prospect of unusually low property taxes. That marketing ploy, in the end, worsened the revenue shortfall and forced a huge burden to fall on the shoulders of the few.

As investment horror stories go, this one is no worse than many others in common stocks, corporate bonds, real estate, or commodities. Nevertheless, the municipal market does have a few distinctive, if not necessarily unique, wrinkles. For one thing, the quality of management in local governments covers a wide spectrum. The field of municipal administrators includes many capable and dedicated professionals. Also in the ranks are a lot of well-meaning but undertrained and overworked individuals.

In the latter category, it appears, were a number of the local finance officials who put their cash management programs into the hands of investment adviser Steven D. Wymer during the late 1980s. More sophisticated investment specialists might have questioned the Californian's claims about producing substantially better-than-average returns in the intensely competitive U.S. Treasury note market. Many small-town treasurers, however, are part-timers with a lot of other things to worry about. In the words of

Connie Jamieson, president in 1992 of the California Municipal Treasurers Association, "Some hire cops and firefighters and people to pick up the trash. And they're also given the responsibility of investing millions of dollars."

According to federal charges, the secret of Wymer's success was "a massive fraud scheme." By shuffling funds from one account to another, the government alleged, he swindled 14 cities and investment trusts out of more than $113 million. When federal agents searched Wymer's home for evidence, they found on a bedroom nightstand a book entitled *How to Launder Money*.

Reflecting the wide range of financial skills among municipal administrators, Wymer got on better in some towns than in others. One part-time city treasurer dismissed him after he failed to produce a single documented example of a successful trade. Others, however, were evidently impressed by the team of local politicians that Wymer recruited to aid in his marketing. (The president of Iowa's state senate signed on as a commissioned salesperson, for example.)

"Every time I asked for a withdrawal, I got my money that same day," said one local director of administrative services. "And we were getting returns of two or three percentage points over the CD rate. I didn't see how we could lose." Wymer seemingly found a way, however. The municipality's account, which the city fathers had thought to be worth over $500,000, actually had a value of less than $25,000, according to the Securities and Exchange Commission.

Assuming you can sidestep fraud-related disasters, there is still the problem of limited availability of information. Outstanding municipal obligations in the United States number approximately 1.5 million, according to the Public Securities Association. The tiny scale of many of the 50,000-plus issuers precludes dissemination of detailed financial reports. It can be difficult to keep up with even such basic developments as the fact that your bonds have been redeemed prior to maturity and have therefore ceased accruing interest.

When municipalities do report financial data, they present it in an unusual format. (Or, more precisely, in unusual formats. Standardization of their accounting practices is less advanced than in the private sector.) Most professional securities analysts, who are accustomed to studying the balance sheets and income statements of corporations, would have difficulty interpreting local governments' annual reports.

There are other investment professionals who understand municipal credit extremely well, however. Some of them work for organizations that manage tax-exempt bond funds and unit trusts. To obtain the benefit of these analysts' expertise, you must sacrifice a small portion of your yield to cover management fees. But when you also consider the benefits of holding a diversified portfolio, thereby spreading your credit risk across many different issuers, the tradeoff is likely to look attractive.

Another way to gain peace of mind, albeit at the cost of some return, is to buy insured municipal bonds. To maintain top credit ratings on their claims-paying ability, bond insurers have to perform meticulous financial analyses of the issues they guarantee.

Perhaps you're determined to grab as much tax-free yield as you possibly can. In that case, you'll opt for buying uninsured issues directly, rather than through a fund. If you go that route, be sure to do some comparison shopping. Munis trade over the counter, rather than on a centralized exchange. Prices can vary widely from dealer to dealer, depending on the firms' knowledge of the issuer and ability to place the paper. Remember, too, that it's not considered bad form to haggle.

Above all, don't let tax-free income blind you to standard investment considerations. Depending on your tax bracket and prevailing market conditions, you may be able to net more dollars by buying taxable bonds. And as with other fixed-income obligations, the highest yielding munis are generally the riskiest. There's no percentage in maximizing your income (even if it's shielded from the IRS) only to lose your principal.

31

I've Got the Horse Right Here

If Even the Sports Betting Markets Are Highly Efficient, How Valuable Is That Stock Tip from Your Brother-in-Law?

The next time you read about a reliable system for beating the stock market, ask yourself a simple question: "Is it reasonable to suppose that an infallible method can remain effective for any length of time?"

Logically, any published set of mechanical trading rules that produces extraordinary returns should attract legions of adherents. Eventually, thousands of investors will be poised to act the instant the miraculous system flashes a "Buy" or "Sell" signal. It will then become impossible to execute the system's recommended trades, except at prices that already have the profit potential wrung out of them.

To those who dream of finding shortcuts to success, however, it does not seem implausible that even a perfect system could be overlooked. After all, hundreds of different ideas are competing for investors' attention at any time. Unless every single strategy receives intensive scrutiny, some genuine money-makers may get lost in the shuffle.

To develop a feel for just how carefully investors pick over the endless supply of trading systems, consider some evidence from another sort of market—the market for wagers on sporting events. For the vast majority of participants, sports betting is strictly a pastime. Football pools and parimutuel windows might therefore seem likely settings for winning systems to go unnoticed. The professionally dominated securities market, by comparison, ought to be a tough place to gain an edge.

As it turns out, a number of high-powered thinkers have expended considerable energy in trying to identify superior strategies in sports betting. Over the years, numerous articles on the subject have appeared in academic journals. A frequently examined question in this research is the degree to which the pricing of bets on a game (i.e., the odds offered by bookmakers) accurately reflects all facts that might affect the outcome. (In studies of securities prices, closely analogous problems are addressed under the rubric of "market efficiency.") The intensity with which professors of finance have studied the unacademic-seeming world of longshots and tipsters is dramatically illustrated by the debate surrounding National Football League betting.

In 1985, a trio of scholars claimed to have found a method for profiting from the Las Vegas NFL point spreads. The researchers' data suggested that bettors could beat the odds by properly factoring in the competing teams' previous performance in such areas as rushing yardage, lost fumbles, interceptions, and penalties. These findings prompted a response by four other academics, who disputed the statistical analysis performed by the first group. In addition, the new study found that the initial researchers' formula was effective only during the test period, which was the 1983 season. Applying the same "winning strategy" to the 1984 season, the second set of authors found that only 39 of its 101 recommended bets were money-makers.

Such evidence of the accuracy of NFL point spreads has not discouraged other scholars from trying to devise winning systems. In 1990, for example, a University of Massachusetts professor tested no fewer than 15 different betting strategies. All were based on the outcomes of past games—precisely the sort of information that ought to provide no edge if pro football betting constitutes an efficient market.

The researcher concluded that certain strategies produced winning bets more than 50% of the time. Success ratios for some betting rules more than covered the bookmakers' "vigorish," or built-in profit margin. Making money on the winning strategies required steel nerves and hefty bankrolls, however. As an example, the professor found that 57.5% of the time, teams that failed to cover the spread in two consecutive weeks also failed to cover in the following week. He outlined a "doubling" strategy to exploit this apparent tendency of bettors to overestimate the prowess of habitual noncoverers, as follows:

1. In Week 2 of the NFL season, bet $100 on each of the 14 (out of 28) teams that failed to cover the point spread in Week 1.

2. In Week 3, bet $200 on the teams that failed to cover for the second week in a row. (Collect your winnings on the teams that covered in the second week and cease betting on them.)

3. In each subsequent week, double the bets on teams that continue to fail to cover. Stop wagering on each team as soon as it produces a winning bet by covering.

Eventually, the professor reasoned, the bettor who adhered to this strategy was virtually assured of winning. The probability that any team would fail to cover the spread at least once during the season, he found, was less than 0.02%. Subject to that small risk, the doubling strategy seemed to guarantee a profit. For example, if the bettor were to lose a $100 bet in Week 2, then win a $200 bet on the same team in Week 3, the winnings ($400) would exceed the cumulative amount wagered ($100 + $200 = $300) by $100.

During the 1985 and 1986 NFL seasons, the doubling strategy worked admirably. Never in these two years was the bettor forced to double up to the point of risking more than $1,600 at a time. In both 1985 and 1986, all of the original 14 teams initially bet upon managed to cover the spread at least once by the Week 6. The strategy terminated at that point with a $1,040 profit, net of book-makers' vigorish.

Following the identical plan led to disaster in 1984, however. That year, the Houston Oilers failed to cover the point spread in any of their first 10 games. Forced to keep doubling, the bettor saw transaction costs cutting deeper and deeper into potential profits each week. Worse yet, the doubling strategy snowballed into a bet of $51,200 in Week 11. At that point, the bettor was $55,450 in the hole. This meant that anyone who adopted the system but started out with a stake of less than $106,650 was forced to drop out at a huge loss before the hapless Oilers finally covered. Undoubtedly, many followers of the doubling strategy would have lost their nerve much earlier, perhaps cutting their losses at $13,210 after Week 9. Furthermore, the eleventh-hour rebound to a loss of only $4,250 was dependent on finding a bookmaker willing to accept a bet as large as $51,200.

In practical terms, then, if there is truly some marginal inaccuracy in NFL point spreads, it represents an opportunity that relatively few can exploit. Moreover, football wagering is not unique in terms of its merciless efficiency. Another sizable body of research confirms that horseracing odds leave little room for profiting on information that is available to all.

Researchers at the University of British Columbia found that the odds at Exhibition Park in Vancouver completely adjusted for the slight advantage enjoyed by horses with inside track positions. (A horse posted closer to the outside of the track must run a greater distance to reach the finish line.) Similarly, a team from Australian National University concluded that gamblers could gain no edge by analyzing shifts in the odds prior to post time or by following the advice of newspaper tipsters.

The hopes of those who play the ponies are not entirely in vain, however. A University of Alberta research team tentatively concluded that it was possible to beat the odds with a handicapping model involving readily available data. Among the predictive factors were the horse's past percentage of winning races; the disadvantage it would suffer when running a new, unfamiliar distance; and the jockey's past success rate in booting home winners.

In a similar vein, various studies have found that North American bettors tend to bet too heavily on longshots and not heavily enough on favorites. Smart players can lay their bets so as to take advantage of this bias. Unfortunately, the edge derived thereby is less than the percentage that the track extracts from winning bets.

* * *

This brief sampling of the voluminous research on sports wagering demonstrates one simple fact: The bettors you compete against are not leaving easy profits on the table.

Some 500 U.S. companies are solely engaged in the business of selling predictions to sports bettors. Finance professors regularly toss off 20-page articles brimming with terms such as "multinomial logit model" and "semistrong efficiency" to ascertain whether bettors can gain slight advantages by detecting minor flaws in the odds. Often, the answer turns out to be "yes" in theory, but at best "maybe" after taking into account the practical difficulties.

If the ostensibly recreational market for sports bets is as unforgiving as all that, imagine how much more merciless the securities markets must be. More than 5,000 member firms of the National Association of Securities Dealers employ over 400,000 registered representatives. Among their tasks is pouncing upon bargains that appear for fleeting moments. Furthermore, millions of investors around the world comb U.S. stocks hour by hour, scavenging for mispricings of any magnitude.

On the whole, it is a far different picture from the one favored by some stockbrokers and investment gurus. In their depiction of reality, ridiculously easy gains are available to anybody with common sense and a little time to kill. Would that it were that easy.

32

Begin by Collecting Your Thoughts

Collectibles Are Full of Fun and Nostalgia, But Should Not Be the Cornerstone of Your Financial Security

*A*ctor Charlie Sheen portrayed an inside trading conspirator in the film *Wall Street*. In *Eight Men Out*, he was cast as a member of the infamous Chicago "Black Sox," who threw the 1919 World Series. Later on, in real life, the worlds of investments and baseball converged for Sheen. The outcome was no less harrowing than in the movies.

In August 1992, Sheen made the winning bid for the "Mookie Ball" in the Leland's Hall of Fame Live Auction in New York. The thespian shelled out $85,000, plus a 10% commission, for the baseball that Mookie Wilson of the New York Mets hit through the legs of Bill Buckner. Buckner's error cost the Boston Red Sox the pivotal sixth game of the 1986 World Series.

Prior to the auction, the ball had been expected to fetch no more than $8,000 to $10,000. Judging by the prices paid for certain other items the same night, however, Sheen might have gotten a bargain. Detroit Tiger great Ty Cobb's 1924 uniform went for $160,000. (This was in turn small change next to the $451,000 that hockey star Wayne Gretzky and his team's owner, Bruce McNall, shelled out in 1991 for a circa-1910 baseball card. It depicted the immortal Pittsburgh Pirates shortstop, Honus Wagner.)

Perhaps a more suitable benchmark from the Leland auction would be the $10,000 paid for a jacket worn by Tom Seaver of the

Mets from 1967 to 1969. On the other hand, an astute collector managed to snag a toothpick from the same jacket for just $400. Depending on which of these "comparables" you select, Sheen may have made a shrewd purchase or he may have paid full value. Either conclusion, naturally, assumes that the ball he bought was actually the one that Buckner bobbled.

Joshua Leland Evans, founder of the auction house that collected the $8,500 commission from collector Sheen, expressed little doubt on this point. When questioned about the item's authenticity, Evans declared, "Anyone who looks at the ball can tell that it's genuine—that it's no ordinary thing."

For skeptics who mistrusted their ability to distinguish the $85,000 collectible from any other used baseball, there was the testimony of Mookie himself. Wilson confirmed that it was the real McCoy, based on a chewing tobacco stain that he recognized. Reportedly, Wilson had been asked to autograph the ball, shortly after the conclusion of the fateful game, by Mets official Arthur Richman. Richman said that he had obtained the celebrated spheroid from the right-field umpire. Auctioneer Evans theorized that Mets center fielder Lenny Dykstra slobbered the tobacco juice during the postvictory celebration.

Notwithstanding these persuasive details, Buckner also claimed to own the Mookie Ball. According to his recollection, he had picked up the memento immediately following his error. Buckner's account did not negate the authentication of the ball. It was only his word against Richman's. Still, the dispute must have taken some of the joy out of being the winning bidder at $85,000.

Poor Charlie Sheen. His character in *Wall Street* only had to worry about apprehension by the law enforcement agencies. Nowadays, clearinghouse arrangements allow brokerage houses to dispense with the exchange of physical stock certificates. Consequently, Sheen's character did not have to fear that he was buying bogus shares. Furthermore, unless he got involved in fairly esoteric securities, the movie stockbroker could count on a reasonably liquid market. Granted, if he received a quote of $10,000 for a chunk of stock, the actual price that he'd pay an hour or two later might be slightly higher. It would not be $85,000, however, unless something truly monumental had happened in the interim.

Sheen's sorrows are far from unique in the world of collectibles. The market for sports memorabilia, for instance, is rife with forgery. At least four different criminal operations have reportedly counterfeited the 1986 Fleer basketball card of Michael Jordan. Another popular scam is shaving the frayed edges of cards to restore them (seemingly) to mint condition. More brazen crooks have peddled cleats that were supposedly worn in competition by Stan Musial, yet bore a manufacturer's date six years later than the slugger's retirement. Babe Ruth's autograph mysteriously appeared on a ball produced forty years after his death.

Sports memorabilia account for only a small portion of total collectibles. Therefore, they presumably generate only a minor fraction of the field's total chicanery.

In June 1992, the Federal Trade Commission brought its first case of postage stamp fraud. The defendant was accused of routinely marking up stamps to twice, or as much as 10 times, the going market rates. Additionally, the FTC charged the dealer with overstating the investment potential of postage stamps. For example, the firm had allegedly reported a 37.7% average annual appreciation on its index of 36 stamps. Other dealers put the true rate of price gains at 5% a year.

As the FTC's director of consumer protection was quick to point out, there was not yet any evidence of widespread fraud in the stamp business. The regulators just wanted to head off the sort of deceptive tactics that had previously arisen in the marketing of rare coins.

In fine art, there seems to be no sense of urgency about eliminating tricky practices. A common ploy of auctioneers is to move the price higher by acknowledging a bid that nobody has actually made. One industry leader has defended the practice on the grounds that auction houses have operated that way for hundreds of years.

Art lovers call the fabrication of price signals "chandelier bidding." The securities market also has a name for it—in fact, a name with artistic associations. It's called "painting the tape," and it's against the law. But even though stocks and bonds offer a relative advantage in the form of regulatory oversight, many people find them prosaic. Collectibles offer a lot of sexy alternatives.

A few years back, Turkoman camel trappings were very hot in the rug trade. They were designed to be worn on the side of a camel during a wedding procession and featured ivory backgrounds. Small ones went for $45,000 to $50,000. How about memorabilia of the 1970s? Platform shoes that originally sold for $60 to $80 a pair shot up to as much as $500 in the early 1990s. Boxes of General Mills Mr. Wonderfull's Surprize cereal, empty or full, traded as high as $100 each.

Earlier periods of American history yield even more valuable treasures. A doll modeled after Samantha of the *Bewitched* television series, which retailed for $3.98 in 1965, rose to $600 in 1992. The nurse doll that was marketed as a companion to the G.I. Joe figure during the 1950s was valued at around $1,200 in 1991. That same year, a 1933 *King Kong* movie poster sold for $57,200.

And by the way, if you like cards but don't care for sports, you can collect the historical variety. There's the 1951 "Fight the Red Menace" series, for example. (Mao Tse-tung has been quoted at $20.) The Persian Gulf War spawned a "Desert Storm Series," as well as 36 "Damn Saddam, the Wacky Iraqi" cards, produced by Pot-Shot Productions. Also in the nonsports category are cards glorifying science fiction, cheesecake photography, famous American Indian chiefs, and the immortal *Hogan's Heroes* TV program. No fewer than four sets of Elvis cards have been produced since 1956. There's even a 1988 series that celebrates illustrious 20th-century rabbis.

Collecting this stuff sounds like a lot of fun. But somehow, it doesn't sound like investing. Just what is it that strikes the wrong chord? Frivolity is not the problem. The fine art segment of the collectibles market includes many works of great solemnity. Conversely, the securities market has its share of whimsy, despite indisputably qualifying as an area of investment. Nude Beer was the subject of a 1984 initial public offering, to cite one example. (The bottles featured female models with tear-away adhesive bikinis.)

Nor are most of the other pitfalls cited above unknown in other, better-established sectors of the investment world. Excessive markups in penny stocks require constant policing by securities regulators. Liquidity may not be great in collectibles, but it's not exactly superb in real estate. Bid/asked spreads can be fairly wide in many over-the-counter securities. And fraud, in one form or another, crops up occasionally in just about every market.

Rather than any of these traits, the distinguishing characteristic of collectibles is their nonfinancial appeal. Collectibles don't simply represent streams of future dividends or coupons. They engender emotional attachments that can cloud investors' perceptions of value.

Certainly, collectibles aren't unique in this respect. Real estate has a sentimental pull that induces many individuals to overinvest in it. Gold is likewise difficult to contemplate in totally dispassionate terms. Noneconomic considerations seem to reach an entirely different level in the collectibles sector, however. Even as unusual a taste in collecting as slavery-related items can generate powerful emotions. Says one fancier of shackles and slave inventories, regarding his hobby, "It's like the woman you're in love with telling you everything you want to hear. Your heart just flutters."

This is precisely the attitude that wise securities investors endeavor to avoid. Seasoned investment counselors caution their clients against "falling in love" with a stock. Never refuse to dump a holding, they say, merely because it performed superbly in the past. This message was reinforced by the collapse of the "glamour" stocks of the 1960s. In hindsight, they turned out to have been loved not wisely but too well. Emotional attachments have no place in a serious investor's plans.

In the securities markets, total hardheadedness is a plausible objective. When it comes to more tangible items, though, complete objectivity is just not feasible for most people. Financial considerations are paramount when you're choosing a house, but you can't forget that you also have to live in it. And I sincerely doubt that anybody really bought the quintessentially 1980s concept of "investment clothing." As much as people may have cared about how their "shirtings" and "suitings" would hold their value, they also cared about how they would hold a press.

It's best to acknowledge openly the nonfinancial dimension of collectibles. Don't deceive yourself that you're investing when you're really collecting. The professionals generally agree, even though they would stand to gain by encouraging expectations of handsome profits in collectibles:

- "[T]here is a limit to which the art market can become a financial market, because at heart it is really an intellectual activity." (Jeffrey Deitch, a specialist in art finance)

- "Sotheby's doesn't really encourage the concept of investing in art. . . ." (David Redden, auction house director)

- "People should buy wine as an investment in pleasure, not as a financial investment." (Michael Aaron, chairman of New York wine merchant Sherry-Lehmann)

The last-mentioned category offers a benefit that no conventional investment can match. It enables you to find solace, if you lose money, by drinking an asset or two. Likewise, if your one-of-a-kind baseball turns out to be something other than you thought, you can still play catch with it.

These forms of recourse are far more appealing than papering your walls with stock certificates of bankrupt companies, as the cliché goes. But as investments, securities have it over collectibles in just about every way. Classic automobiles and antique furniture simply won't cut it as cornerstones of your financial empire.

Bibliography

Whooaa! What's a bibliography doing here? This isn't a scholarly treatise. (You can tell, because it contains no footnotes.)

Nevertheless, I've endeavored to be correct in my facts and precise in my supporting arguments. You ought to have the opportunity to check me for accuracy, whether or not you want to undertake the effort.

A second reason for listing my sources is related to an essential point of *Investment Illusions:* It pays to study the propositions that get repeated frequently, but often uncritically. To help you dig deeper into the concepts and canards that I've discussed, I've included selected books and articles beyond my direct references.

If you find these topics as fascinating as I do, one source will lead you to another. You'll discover that when it comes to setting the record straight about the securities markets, there's no end to the work that remains to be done.

Chapter 1   On the Contrary

De Bondt, Werner F.M., "What Do Economists Know About the Stock Market?" *The Journal of Portfolio Management* (Winter 1991): 84–91.

De Bondt, Werner F.M., and Richard H. Thaler. "Do Security Analysts Overreact?" *The American Economic Review* (May 1990): 53–57.

Garber, Peter M. "Who Put the Mania in Tulipmania?" In *Crashes and Panics: The Lessons from History,* edited by Eugene N. White, 3–32. Homewood, Illinois: Dow Jones-Irwin, 1990.

Guenther, Robert. "Indiscriminate Run on Bank Stocks Means Some Investing Bargains May Be Available." (Heard on the Street column) *The Wall Street Journal* (April 9, 1990).

Renshaw, Edward. "Some Evidence in Support of Stock Market Bubbles." *Financial Analysts Journal* (March/April 1990): 71–73.

Todd, Richard Cecil. *Confederate Finance*. Athens, Georgia: The University of Georgia Press, 1954.

Chapter 2 Who's Hot, Who's Not

Cohen, Jerome B., Edward D. Zinbarg, and Arthur Zeikel, "Common Stock Valuation" and "Company Analysis." Chapters 10 and 12 in *Investment Analysis and Portfolio Management*, Fifth Edition. Homewood, Illinois: Richard D. Irwin, 1987.

Reilly, Frank K. "Introduction to Security Valuation." Chapter 8 in *Investments*, Third Edition. Fort Worth, Texas: The Dryden Press, 1992.

Chapter 3 Sounds Fine in Concept

Banks, Howard. "Now Everybody's Doing It." *Forbes* (May 6, 1985): 32–33.

Banks, Howard. "People Power." (Faces Behind the Figures column) *Forbes* (April 25, 1983): 170.

Byrne, John A. "Up, Up and Away? Expansion Is Threatening the 'Humane' Culture at People Express." *Business Week* (November 25, 1985): 80 ff.

Donlan, Thomas G. "Flying High: Can People Express Continue Its Heady Growth?" *Barron's* (July 2, 1984): 30–31.

Donlan, Thomas G. "More Dead Than Alive? People Express: Where It's At and What It's Worth." *Barron's* (June 30, 1986): 13, 26.

Dubin, Reggi Ann. "Growing Pains at People Express." (Transportation column) *Business Week* (January 28, 1985): 90–91.

Ehrlich, Elizabeth, and Michael A. Pollock. "A Fight at United May Seal People's Fate." (Airlines column) *Business Week* (August 25, 1986): 40–41.

Garrett, Echo M. "The Troops Are Restless at People Express." (Managing Ventures column) *Venture* (April 1986): 102, 104.

Hawkins, Chuck. "People Express Wants All the Frills It Can Get." (Aviation column) *Business Week* (May 12, 1986): 31–32.

Hawkins, Chuck. "People Is Plunging, but Burr Is Staying Cool." (Airlines column) *Business Week* (July 7, 1986): 31–32.

Ivey, Mark. "People Express Wins the Duel for Frontier Air." (Aviation column) *Business Week* (October 21, 1985): 42.

Norman, James R., with John A. Byrne. "Nice Going, Frank, but Will It Fly? Lorenzo's Gutsiest Move Yet Is Adding People to His Texas Air

Empire." (Airlines column) *Business Week* (September 29, 1992): 34–35.

Palmer, Barbara. "Flying on Empty at People Express." (Financing Profile) *Institutional Investor* (December 1983): 79, 82.

Chapter 4   It's Lonely at the Top

Allen, Michael. "Posner Pleads No Contest to Charges of Tax Evasion, Ending Lengthy Fight." *The Wall Street Journal* (September 30, 1987).

Allen, Michael. "Troubled Raider: Victor Posner Battles a Variety of Financial and Legal Difficulties." *The Wall Street Journal* (July 14, 1987).

Bloomberg Business News. "DWG Chairman Posner Agrees to Divest Stake, Resign." (September 3, 1992).

Bloomberg Business News. "DWG Corp.'s New Owners Say They Don't Plan to Sell Operations." (September 7, 1992).

Bloomberg Business News. "DWG to Save Tens of Millions of Dollars in Debt and Legal Fees." (September 4, 1992).

Bloomberg Business News. "DWG's Shares Are Undervalued, Analyst Tells Dorfman." (September 3, 1992).

Bloomberg Business News. "Earl Scheib Inc. Names Late Founder's Son as President, CEO." (March 9, 1992).

Bloomberg Business News. "Junk Bonds End Lower, but Macy Bonds Rise as Chairman Retires." (April 27, 1992).

Bloomberg Business News. "Wang Labs Files for Chapter 11 Bankruptcy Protection." (August 18, 1992).

Bryant, Adam. "Wang Files for Bankruptcy; 5,000 Jobs to Be Cut." (August 19, 1992).

Bulkeley, William M., and John R. Wilke. "Steep Slide: Filing in Chapter 11, Wang Sends Warning to High-Tech Circles." *The Wall Street Journal* (August 19, 1992).

Cohn, Gary. "Jury Convicts Victor Posner of Tax Evasion." *The Wall Street Journal* (July 21, 1986).

Cooper, Helen. "DWG's Posner Will Sell His Holdings, Quit as Chairman, Chief and Director." *The Wall Street Journal* (September 4, 1992).

Davis, T. "Put the Principal on Detention." *Beverage World* (October 1991): 44, 46.

DeGeorge, Gail. "Is Victor Posner Off His Leash?" *Business Week (Industrial/Technology Issue)* (December 30, 1991/January 6, 1992): 39.

DeGeorge, Gail. "Victor Posner May Soon Taste His Own Medicine." *Business Week* (April 10, 1989): 34, 36.

Economist. "Martyrs to Their Share Price." (March 24, 1990): 70.

Gallese, Liz Roman. "Wang Laboratories Stock Plunges as Earnings Report Delayed." *Bloomberg Business News* (August 14, 1992).

McWilliams, Gary. "Did DEC Move Too Late? The Comeback Costs Are Staggering." *Business Week* (August 3, 1992): 62–64.

Myerson, Allen M. "Dow Off 29.99 as I.B.M. Is Pummeled." *New York Times* (July 18, 1992). Reference to resignation of Kenneth H. Olsen.

Nazario, Sonia L. "Earl Scheib Inc. Stock Soars After Founder Death; Change Seen." *Dow Jones Newswire* (March 2, 1992).

New York Times. "Co-Founder of Digital Plans to Leave Board." (September 15, 1992).

New York Times. "DWG Investor Group Sees No Sale of Assets." (September 8, 1992).

New York Times. "Posner Set to Reduce DWG Stake." (September 4, 1992).

Pauly, David, MaryAnn Stokolosa, and Louise Witt. "Finkelstein Loses Macy's After All." *Bloomberg Business News* (April 27, 1992).

Public Relations Newswire. "DWG Announces Results." (July 29, 1992).

Public Relations Newswire. "DWG Corporation Signs Letter of Intent on Behalf of Trian Group." (September 3, 1992).

Public Relations Newswire. "Wang Laboratories Files under Chapter 11; Reports Fourth Fiscal Year [sic] Results; Noon News Conference in Cambridge, Mass." (August 18, 1992).

Public Relations Newswire. "Wang Laboratories Reports Third-Quarter Results." (April 23, 1992).

Rifkin, Glenn. "Digital Leaders: Varied Style, Similar Histories." *New York Times* (July 18, 1992): 9.

Rose, Frederick. "Occidental's Hammer Gets Pacemaker, Is Expected Back at Office Tomorrow." *The Wall Street Journal* (November 13, 1989).

Rose, Frederick, and Roger Lowenstein. "A New Era: How Will Occidental Fare After Hammer? Traders Bet Both Ways." *The Wall Street Journal* (December 12, 1990).

Stevens, Amy. "Occidental Petroleum Aides Draw Fire by Allegedly Raiding Hammer Home." *The Wall Street Journal* (December 14, 1990).

Trachtenberg, Jeffrey A. "Macy Officials Preview Plan for Longer Than Expected Bankruptcy Protection." *The Wall Street Journal* (August 31, 1992).

The Wall Street Journal. "Occidental Petroleum Chief Denies Takeover Rumors." (November 15, 1989).

Wilke, John R. "Digital Equipment Gives Palmer Jobs of President, Chief." *The Wall Street Journal* (July 23, 1992).

Wilke, John R. "Digital's President Is Said to Claim He Was Forced Out." *The Wall Street Journal* (July 22, 1992).

Wilke, John R. "Palmer Faces Big Challenge at Digital." (Computers column) *The Wall Street Journal* (July 20, 1992).

Wilke, John R. "Wang Founder Apparently Forces His Son to Step Down as President." *The Wall Street Journal* (August 9, 1989).

Wilke, John R., and William M. Bulkeley. "DEC's Olsen Stuns Industry by Resigning." *The Wall Street Journal* (July 17, 1992).

Winski, Joseph M. "The Man Who Stood Up to Victor Posner." *Advertising Age* (November 27, 1989): 1 ff.

Chapter 5 Technical Difficulties

Black, Fischer. "Yes, Virginia, There Is Hope: Tests of the *Value Line* Ranking System." Paper presented at a seminar of the Center for Research in Security Prices, Graduate School of Business, University of Chicago, 1971.

Cassidy, Donald L. *It's Not What Stocks You Buy, It's When You Sell that Counts: Understanding and Overcoming Your Self-Imposed Barriers to Investment Success.* Chicago: Probus, 1991.

Cohen, Jerome B., Edward D. Zinbarg, and Arthur Zeikel. *Investment Analysis and Portfolio Management,* Fifth Edition. Homewood, Illinois: Richard D. Irwin, 1987, p. 298.

Dorfman, John R. "Is There Safety in Numbers? Technical Analysts Say So." *The Wall Street Journal* (May 1, 1992).

Hendrick, Bill. "Guru: Folks All over the World Seek Georgia Financial Seer's Advice." *The Atlanta Journal/The Atlanta Constitution* (March 4, 1990).

Mamis, Justin. *The Nature of Risk: Stock Market Survival & the Meaning of Life.* Reading, Massachusetts: Addison-Wesley, 1991, p. 137.

O'Higgins, Michael, and John Downes. *Beating the Dow.* New York: HarperCollins, 1991.

Peters, Edgar F., *Chaos and Order in the Financial Markets: A New View of Cycles, Prices and Market Volatility.* New York: John Wiley & Sons, 1991, p. 133.

Seiver, Daniel Alan. *Outperforming Wall Street*. Englewood Cliffs, New Jersey: Prentice Hall, 1991.

Sheimo, Michael D. *Dow Theory Redux: The Classic Investment Theory Revised & Updated for the 1990's*. Chicago: Probus, 1989, pp. 10, 69.

Technical Analysis: A Personal Seminar. New York: New York Institute of Finance, 1989, p. 7.

Chapter 6   Take Me Out of the Ballgame

Dorfman, John R. "Lady Luck for Third Month Sticks Pins Into the Pros." (Your Money Matters column) *The Wall Street Journal* (September 6, 1991): C1.

Dorfman, John R. "Once Again, Pros Beat Darts in Stock-Picking Contest." (Your Money Matters column) *The Wall Street Journal* (April 5, 1991).

Dorfman, John R. "Small-Stock Fan Picks Another Winner." (Your Money Matters column) *The Wall Street Journal* (March 5, 1992): C1.

Dorfman, John R. "Stock-Picking Pros Trounce Industrials." (Your Money Matters column) *The Wall Street Journal* (March 5, 1991): C1.

Huntley, Helen. "Ready—Set—Invest! The *Times'* Annual Off-Wall Street Stock Challenge Starts This Week." *St. Petersburg Times* (February 17, 1992): 12–15.

Scholl, Jaye. "Ms. Midas: Meet Lori Tanner, Stockpicker With a Golden Touch." *Barron's* (March 9, 1992): 14–15, 64.

Steinberg, Jonathan. Advertisement for "Special Situations Report." *Barron's* (March 23, 1992): 40.

Chapter 7   It's an Ill Wind

Bloomberg Business News. "Insurance Industry Losses from Andrew Top Stormy Period." (August 24, 1992).

Bloomberg Business News. "Insurance Rate Increases Expected to Trail Hurricane Iniki." (September 14, 1992).

Bloomberg Business News. "Insurer Called Storm Rate-Hike 'Opportunity.'" (September 5, 1992).

Bloomberg Business News. "Insurers' Response to Hurricane Andrew Could Bring Regulations." (September 2, 1992).

Bloomberg Business News. "Lennar Sued by Owners of Homes Damaged by Storm." (September 2, 1992).

Bibliography

Bloomberg Business News. "Motor Club Sees $21 Million Charge from Hurricane; Cancels Spinoff." (September 15, 1992).

Bloomberg Business News. "Muni Bonds Fall 1 Point as Insurance Companies Liquidate Bonds." (September 15, 1992).

Bloomberg Business News. "Natural Gas Futures Contract Sets New Volume Record." (August 25, 1992).

Bloomberg Business News. "U.S. Property Casualty Industry Increases First-Half Income 22%." (September 7, 1992).

Blumenthal, Robin Goldwyn. "Motor Club Unit Takes Heavy Blow from Storm Claims." *The Wall Street Journal* (September 16, 1992).

Calian, Sara. "Composite Index Falls 1.1% as Investors Turn Cautious in Wake of Monday Rally." (OTC Focus column) *The Wall Street Journal* (September 16, 1992). Comment on Motor Club of America.

Cooper, Helene. "Suit Against Lennar May Portend Flood of Hurricane Andrew Cases." (Law column) *The Wall Street Journal* (September 3, 1992).

Dow Jones Broadtape. "S&P Sees Few Insurance Downgrades from Andrew." (September 15, 1992).

Dow Jones Newswire. "Building Concerns See Silver Lining in Florida's Gloom." (August 31, 1992).

Dow Jones Newswire. "Homeowners File Suit Against Lennar for Hurricane Damage." (September 2, 1992).

Fitch Financial Wire. "Hurricane Won't Sink Insurers, Cutthroat Pricing Might, Fitch Says." (August 27, 1992).

Goldman, Kevin, and Patrick M. Reilly. "Untold Story: Media's Slow Grasp of Hurricane's Impact Helped Delay Response." *The Wall Street Journal* (September 10, 1992).

Grossman, Laurie M. "Florida Builders Face Complaints of Shoddy Work." *The Wall Street Journal* (September 14, 1992).

Hicks, Jonathan. "Rebuilding of South Florida Aids Mobile-Home Orders." *New York Times* (September 14, 1992).

Levingston, Steven E. "Stocks Rebound 9.18 to 3287.87 as Insurance Companies Rally." (Abreast of the Market column) *The Wall Street Journal* (September 25, 1992). Comment on Continental Corp.

McCorry, John, et al. "Ways of Wall Street: Andrew Hits Some Markets, Avoids Others." *Bloomberg Business News* (August 24, 1992).

McCorry, John, and Mani Sandhu. "South Florida Bonds Unaffected by Hurricane Andrew." *Bloomberg Business News* (August 24, 1992).

Meuchner, Gerard. "Insurers Aren't Selling U.S. Bonds to Pay Hurricane Claims." *Bloomberg Business News* (September 2, 1992).

Moody's Investors Service. "Moody's Downgrades Ratings of Continental Corp. and Subsidiaries (Senior to Baa1)." (September 25, 1992).

Myerson, Allen R. "Investing Into the Wind: An Odd, Volatile Game." *The Wall Street Journal* (September 3, 1992).

New York Times. "Limits Are Urged on Insurers After Storm." (September 8, 1992).

Patterson, Gregory A. "Moody's Places Debt of Sears under Review; Rating Agency Cites Impact of Hurricane Claims on Allstate's Earnings." *The Wall Street Journal* (September 14, 1992).

Pearl, Daniel. "Rebuilding Trust: Big Florida Developer Faces Tough Questions in Wake of Hurricane." *The Wall Street Journal* (September 14, 1992).

Pearl, Daniel, and Martha Brannigan. "Building Concerns See Silver Lining in Florida's Gloom." *Dow Jones Newswire* (August 31, 1992).

Public Relations Newswire. "American International Group Responds to Order and Press Release Issued by Florida Department of Insurance." (September 9, 1992).

Public Relations Newswire. "Class Action Lawsuit Filed Against Lennar for Damages Resulting from Hurricane Andrew." (September 10, 1992).

Public Relations Newswire. "Kendall Homeowners File Lawsuit Against Lennar Homes for Damages from Hurricane Andrew." (September 2, 1992).

Smith, Craig S. "Stocks Fall 10.26 in Quiet Trading, but Pre-Holiday Gains Expected." (Abreast of the Market column) *The Wall Street Journal* (September 1, 1992). Comment on railroad play in Hurricane Andrew's aftermath.

Standard & Poor's CreditWire. "Continental Corp., Units Placed on S&P Watch; Negative." (September 25, 1992).

Steinmetz, Greg. "Continental Cuts Dividend, Sets Big Charge; Insurer's Stock Falls $6.125 on Hurricanes' Losses, but Industry Issues Soar." *The Wall Street Journal* (September 25, 1992).

Steinmetz, Greg. "Prudential Lifts Loss Estimate from Hurricane; Andrew's Toll Is Quadrupled to More Than $1 Billion; S&P to Review Rating." *The Wall Street Journal* (September 24, 1992).

Steinmetz, Greg. "Sears Rating Cut; Prudential Put on Review; Actions of Moody's Investors Are the Result of Impact of Hurricane Losses." *The Wall Street Journal* (September 28, 1992).

The Wall Street Journal. "Lennar Corp." (September 11, 1992). Company response to lawsuit.

Williams, Christopher C. "Hurricane Andrew Boosting Lennar, Housing Stocks." *Dow Jones Newswire* (August 27, 1992).

Wyatt, Edward A. "Ill Wind." (Noteworthy: Items of Investment Interest column) *Barron's* (September 7, 1992): 16.

Chapter 8 Gambler's Blues

Breo, Dennis L. "In Treating the Pathological Gambler, MDs Must Overcome the Attitude, 'Why Bother?'" (At Large column) *Journal of the American Medical Association* (November 10, 1989): 2599–2606.

Cordtz, Dan. "Betting the Country." *Financial World* (February 20, 1990): 23–26.

Finch, Peter. "Confessions of a Compulsive High-Roller." *Business Week* (July 29, 1991): 78–79.

O'Connor, John J. "The Urge to Gamble, and How to Fight It." (TV Weekend column) *New York Times* (June 29, 1990).

Vatz, Richard E. "'Compulsive Gambling' Is a Phony Excuse." *The Wall Street Journal* (July 3, 1991).

Chapter 9 Out of the Blue

Carroll, Paul B. "Big Blues: IBM Earnings Shock Raises New Concern on Economic Rebound." *The Wall Street Journal* (March 20, 1991).

Institutional Brokers Estimate System. (March 14, 1991).

Laderman, Jeffrey M., and John W. Verity. "Red-Faced Over Big Blue: Why the Analysts Blew It." *Business Week* (April 8, 1991): 77–78.

Markoff, John. "I.B.M. Faces a Harsher World in the 90s." *New York Times* (March 21, 1991).

Markoff, John. "I.B.M. Sees Sharp Drop in Earnings." *New York Times* (March 20, 1991).

Sease, Douglas R., and Michael R. Sesit. "Markets Are Pummeled by IBM and Inflation." *The Wall Street Journal* (March 20, 1991).

Standard Periodical Directory. New York: Oxbridge Communications (1991).

The Wall Street Journal. "Tsongas Proposes Ending Quarterly Earnings Reports." (May 23, 1991).

Chapter 10 Fundamental Assumptions

Azarchs, Tanya. "Citicorp Ratings Affirmed, But Outlook Is Negative." *Standard & Poor's CreditWeek International* (September 2, 1991): 20.

Azarchs, Tanya. "Citicorp Ratings Downgraded." *Standard & Poor's CreditWeek International* (November 4, 1991): 26.

Bartlett, Sarah. "Citicorp's Incredible Shrinking Debt: Has It Really Cut Its Foreign Risk?" (Banking column) *Business Week* (February 8, 1988): 23.

Bartlett, Sarah. "The Citi Squeezes Its Lemons: Moving to Clean Up LDC Losses." (Banking column) *Business Week* (June 15, 1987): 31.

Bleakley, Fred. "S&P Lowers Debt Ratings for Citicorp." *The Wall Street Journal* (November 6, 1990).

Fridson, Martin S. *Financial Statement Analysis: A Practitioner's Guide.* New York: John Wiley & Sons, 1991.

Guenther, Robert. "Citicorp Debt and Preferred Downgraded: S&P Move Hits $30 Billion of Securities; Rating on Paper Is Affirmed." *The Wall Street Journal* (April 7, 1990).

Guenther, Robert. "Citicorp Expects Profit to Triple by Late 1990s." *The Wall Street Journal* (March 21, 1990).

Guenther, Robert. "Citicorp Profit Drops 56%; NCNB Net Rises 85%; Hibernia Corp. Reports Loss." *The Wall Street Journal* (April 18, 1990).

Guenther, Robert. "Moody's Lowers Citicorp Debt Ratings; Low Reserves, Capital Levels Are Cited." *The Wall Street Journal* (April 20, 1990).

Guenther, Robert. "Moody's Weighs Downgrading Citicorp Debt: Long, Short Terms Studied; Move Could Shake Up Nation's Bank System." *The Wall Street Journal* (April 20, 1990).

Guenther, Robert, and Richard E. Rustin. "Citicorp Lifts Reserves $1 Billion for Quarterly Loss, Picks President." *The Wall Street Journal* (January 17, 1990).

Hilder, David B. "Citicorp to Post 4th-Quarter Loss of Over $300 Million, Cut Payout: Firm Wants to Slash Dividend 44%, Shrink Payroll by 8,000 Jobs." *The Wall Street Journal* (December 19, 1990).

Lipin, Steven. "Citicorp Posts Big Loss, Suspends Payout; Other Banks' Stocks Rally on Wall Street." *The Wall Street Journal* (October 16, 1991).

Mayer, Jane. "Krim's Tales. Hollywood Mystery: Woes at Orion Stayed Invisible for Years." *The Wall Street Journal* (October 16, 1991): A1.

Public Relations Newswire. "Orion Pictures Reports Results." (November 14, 1991).

Standard & Poor's CreditWeek International. "Citicorp and Related Entities." (December 3, 1991): 70–71.

Standard & Poor's Standard NYSE Stock Reports. Report on Citicorp, April 8, 1991.

The Wall Street Journal. "S&P Ratings Outlook on Citicorp Is 'Negative.'" (August 5, 1991).

Chapter 11 Droll Models

Schnader, M.H., and H.O. Stekler. "Evaluating Predictions of Change." *The Journal of Business* (January 1990): 99–107.

Spiro, Peter. *Real Interest Rates and Investment and Borrowing Strategy.* New York: Quorum Books, 1989.

Chapter 12 Improbable Though It Seems

Barksdale, Edgar W., and William L. Green. "Performance Is Useless in Selecting Managers." *Pensions and Investments* (September 17, 1990): 16.

Gilovich, Thomas. *How We Know What Isn't So: The Fallibility of Human Reason in Everyday Life.* New York: The Free Press, 1991.

Lemaire, Jean. "When You're Hot, Maybe You're Not." *New York Times* (April 9, 1990).

New York Times. " 'Hot Hands' Phenomenon: A Myth?" (April 19, 1988). Report of Tversky's study of Phildelphia 76ers.

Chapter 13 Beware the Bond Rating Bashers

Business Wire. "Calmar 'CCC+' Subordinated Notes Still on S&P Watch; Now Negative." (November 27, 1991).

Fons, Jerome S., Andrew E. Kimball, and Denis Girault. "Corporate Bond Defaults and Default Rates, 1970–1991." *Moody's Special Report* (January 1992).

Moody's Bond Record. Moody's Investors Service (Monthly).

Moody's Investors Service. "Calmar Inc. Assigned Ba3 to Senior Debt; Subordinated Debt Raised to B2." (November 25, 1991).

Standard & Poor's Bond Guide. Standard & Poor's Corporation (Monthly).

Weiss, Robert A. "Texaco Debt Ratings Lowered to 'D.'" *Standard & Poor's CreditWeek* (April 20, 1987): 8.

Chapter 14   The Missing Link

Bernstein, Peter L., and Theodore H. Silbert. "Are Economic Forecasters Worth Listening To?" *Harvard Business Review* (September/October 1984): 32 ff.

Belongia, Michael T. "Predicting Interest Rates: A Comparison of Professional and Market-Based Forecasts." *Federal Reserve Bank of St. Louis Review* (March 1987): 9–15.

McNees, Stephen K., and John Ries. "The Track Record of Macroeconomic Forecasts." *New England Economic Review* (November/December 1983): 5–18.

Zarnowitz, Victor. "The Accuracy of Individual and Group Forecasts from Business Outlook Surveys." *Journal of Forecasting* (January–March 1984): 11–26.

Chapter 15   How to Run a Boiler Room

Barker, Robert. "In Trouble Again: Delaware Indicts First Jersey Securities." *Barron's* (October 20, 1986): 51, 67.

Cecere, Linda. "Let the Seller Beware." (On the Docket column) *Forbes* (September 22, 1986): 96.

Hyatt, James C. "SEC Says Stratton Oakmont Manipulates Stock Prices, Uses 'Boiler Room' Tactics." *The Wall Street Journal* (March 23, 1992).

Landler, Mark, and Julia Flynn. "The Penny-Stock Boys Are Back." *Business Week* (July 20, 1992): 76–78.

McMurray, Scott. "First Jersey and Chairman Brennan Again Sued by SEC on Fraud Charges." *The Wall Street Journal* (November 1, 1985).

McMurray, Scott. "First Jersey Securities, SEC Settle Feud; Charges Dismissed After 10-Year Inquiry." *The Wall Street Journal* (November 21, 1984).

McMurray, Scott. "NASD Reactivates Charges Against Firm, President." *The Wall Street Journal* (March 26, 1985).

Newman, Anne. "NASD Bars 2 Arizona Brokers for Selling Worthless Stock." *The Wall Street Journal* (August 28, 1992).

Norris, Floyd. "Oklahoma Twister: The Crash of a Small Stock Levels Brokers and Customers." *Barron's* (March 11, 1985): 15 ff.

Odean, Kathleen. *High Steppers, Fallen Angels and Lollipops: A Word Book.* New York: Henry Holt and Company, 1988.

Pasztor, Andy, and Bruce Ingersoll. "First Jersey Securities, Chairman Probed in Case of Alleged Illegal Contributions." *The Wall Street Journal* (April 17, 1986).

Penn, Stanley. "Some Disappearing Documents Stir a Fight Between SEC, First Jersey." *The Wall Street Journal* (February 7, 1983).

Poole, Claire. "Hello, Sucker." *Forbes* (March 30, 1992): 58–60.

Power, William. "Robert Brennan, Firm He Controls Are Sued by Holder." *The Wall Street Journal* (August 19, 1986).

Salwen, Kevin G. "Penny-Stock Swindlers Are Using Higher-Priced Bait." *The Wall Street Journal* (August 26, 1992).

Scholl, Jaye. "Off to the Races? Further Adventures of Robert Brennan and First Jersey Securities." *Barron's* (March 28, 1983): 8 ff.

Scholl, Jaye, and Lawrence J. Tell. "Not So Fond Farewell? First Jersey's Robert Brennan Exits, Unsmiling." *Barron's* (August 11, 1986): 11 ff.

Smith, Randall. "First Jersey Securities Gets More Pressure from U.S. as Employees Are Indicted." *The Wall Street Journal* (December 3, 1985).

Stewart, James B. "First Jersey Securities' Brennan Resigns Two Top Positions at Fast-Growing Firm." *The Wall Street Journal* (August 7, 1986).

Swartz, Steve, and Priscilla Ann Smith. "First Jersey Securities to Sell Its Retail Lines." *The Wall Street Journal* (December 24, 1986).

Tell, Lawrence J. " 'Good Luck, Heroes': SEC Lowers the Boom on Multi-Vest." *Barron's* (February 27, 1984): 60.

Totty, Michael. "Claim to Make Gold from Sand Brings Lawsuit." *The Wall Street Journal* (November 1, 1988).

The Wall Street Journal. "First Jersey Securities Aide Is Found Guilty of Obstructing Probe." (October 10, 1986).

The Wall Street Journal. "First Jersey Securities and President Accused of Stock Fraud by SEC." (January 17, 1983).

The Wall Street Journal. "First Jersey Securities Had Oversight Gaps, A Consultant Finds." (June 18, 1985).

The Wall Street Journal. "First Jersey Securities' Legal Adviser Resigns over Conflict Issue." (February 9, 1983).

The Wall Street Journal. "First Jersey Securities' Trading in 4 Stocks Questioned in Report." (December 19, 1986).

The Wall Street Journal. "Murlas Commodities Inc. Found Guilty of Churning." (November 22, 1988).

The Wall Street Journal. "New Jersey Brokerage Is Fined by NASD, Barred From Industry." (April 28, 1988).

The Wall Street Journal. "Regulators' Data on First Jersey Again Are Missing." (November 21, 1985).

The Wall Street Journal. "SEC Accuses Stuart-James of Breaking Securities Law." (April 11, 1989).

Weiss, Gary. "J. David's Legacy: Investors Sue Wall Street Firms." *Barron's* (May 21, 1984): 28.

Weiss, Gary. "Rematch: The SEC and First Jersey Clash Again." *Barron's* (November 4, 1985): 79.

Wyatt, Edward A. "The Comeback Kid: Bob Brennan Is Once Again Wheeling and Dealing." *Barron's* (July 20, 1992): 14, 15–57.

Chapter 16 Two-Timers and Second Chances

Dunn, Henry W. "A Persistent Delusion." In *Classics: An Investor's Anthology,* edited by Charles D. Ellis with James R. Vertin, 25–32. Homewood, Illinois: Business One Irwin, 1989.

Hulbert, Mark. "Buy-and-Hold." *Forbes* (July 20, 1992): 339.

Paulos, John Allen. *Innumeracy: Mathematical Illiteracy and Its Consequences.* New York: Hill and Wang, 1988.

Chapter 17 When Audits Win No Plaudits

Bailey, Jeff. "Waste Management Plans Public Offer of 20% Stake in Its Foreign Operations." *The Wall Street Journal* (March 20, 1992).

Berton, Lee, and Stephen J. Adler. "CPA's Nightmare: How Audit of a Bank Cost Price Waterhouse $338 Million Judgment." *The Wall Street Journal* (August 14, 1992).

Bloomberg Business News. "Chambers Took the Initiative in Accounting Change, Auditor Says." (March 18, 1992).

Bloomberg Business News. "SEC, Amex, CBOE Investigating Put Activity in Chambers Stock." (March 19, 1992).

Bryant, Adam. "Tracing the Twisted Trail of Cascade International." *New York Times* (March 12, 1992).

Cascade International. *Annual Report 1990.*

Dow Jones Newswire. "Cascade International Files for Chapter 11 Protection." (December 16, 1991).

Dow Jones Newswire. "Cascade International Internal Review Near Completion." (December 2, 1991).

Dow Jones Newswire. "Cascade International Plans To File for Chapter 11." (December 13, 1991).

Dow Jones Newswire. "Cascade International Says Ex-Chairman Issued Large Amounts of Stock." (January 7, 1992).

Dow Jones Newswire. "Cascade International Stock Down 22%; Cites Newsletter Recommendation." (October 2, 1991).

Dow Jones Newswire. "Cascade International Sues Newsletter for Alleged Trade Defamation." (October 30, 1991).

Dow Jones Newswire. "Coniston Corp. Files For Chapter 11 Protection." (February 24, 1992).

Feder, Barnaby J. "After Abrupt Exit, Groping for Clues." *New York Times* (November 22, 1991).

Feder, Barnaby J. "Cascade International Chain Plans to File for Bankruptcy." *New York Times* (December 14, 1991).

Henriques, Diana B. "A Hot Stock Crashes and the Chief Vanishes." *New York Times* (November 21, 1991).

Marcial, Gene G. "A Retailing Match Made in Chapter 11." (Inside Wall Street column) *Business Week* (June 3, 1991): 120.

New York Times. "Illegal Sales of Cascade Stock." (January 8, 1992).

Pearl, Daniel. "Cascade International Pursues Claims Against Incendy's Ex-Wife." *The Wall Street Journal* (January 27, 1992).

Pearl, Daniel. "Cascade to File Chapter 11 Petition; Possible Stock Manipulation Is Cited." *The Wall Street Journal* (December 16, 1991).

Pearl, Daniel. "Court Examiner Finds Deltec Securities Transactions With Cascade 'Suspicious.'" *The Wall Street Journal* (March 27, 1992).

Pearl, Daniel. "Highflier's Plunge: Cascade International, Its Chairman Missing, Reviews Its Finances." *The Wall Street Journal* (November 21, 1991).

Pearl, Daniel. "Troubled Cascade Has Been Cutting Its Work Force." *The Wall Street Journal* (November 26, 1991).

Poppe, David. "Cascade Comes Down Hard." *Miami Review* (November 21, 1991).

Poppe, David. "Cascade Report Implicates Director." *Miami Review* (January 15, 1992).

Poppe, David. "Dragged Down by the Tale." *Miami Review* (November 8, 1991).

Poppe, David. "Fingers Point to One Man: Cascade's Future Awaits Assessment of Harm." *Miami Review* (November 26, 1991).

Poppe, David. "Insiders Disagree About What's Left of Cascade." *Miami Review* (December 18, 1991).

Poppe, David. "Is Apparel Retailer Paying Price for Deception?" *Miami Review* (October 14, 1991): Sec. 1, p. 1. Reference to Overpriced Stock Service newsletter.

Poppe, David. "Regulators Probe Cascade's Huge Trading Volume." *Miami Review* (December 27, 1991).

Poppe, David. "Trading Halted in Cascade Stock." *Miami Review* (November 20, 1991).

Poppe, David, and Robert Sherefkin. "Cascade Free Fall Leaves Trail of Sinners, Winners and Losers." *Miami Review* (November 27, 1991).

Public Relations Newswire. "Chambers Announces Changes in Accounting Method and Revisions to 1991 Earnings." (March 17, 1992).

Spiro, Leah Nathans. "Small Is Beautiful—Small Caps, That Is." (Mutual Funds, Midyear Investment Outlook) *Business Week* (June 24, 1991): 90–91.

Stern, Gabriella. "Chambers Again Will Lower '91 Profit, Plans to Dismiss Outside Auditing Firm." *The Wall Street Journal* (April 14, 1992).

Stern, Gabriella. "Chambers Development Co. May Face Further Write-Offs Over Accounting." *The Wall Street Journal* (April 10, 1992).

Stern, Gabriella. "Chambers Says Ex-Accountant Raised Query." *The Wall Street Journal* (April 24, 1992).

Stern, Gabriella, and Laurie P. Cohen. "Chambers Development Switches Accounting Plan." *The Wall Street Journal* (March 19, 1992).

The Wall Street Journal. "Cascade International Reviews Its Finances; Chairman Missing." (November 21, 1991).

Weiss, Gary, and David Greising. "The Best of 1991 So Far." (The Best, Midyear Investment Outlook) *Business Week* (June 24, 1991): 98–99.

Chapter 18 Pass the Trash

Code of Federal Regulations. "Banks and Banking: Part 300 to End, Revised as of January 1, 1980." Office of the Federal Register, National Archives and Records Service, General Services Administration.

Cohen, Jerome B., Edward D. Zinbarg, and Arthur Zeikel. "Beyond Securities—Additional Investment Choices." Chapter 16 in *Investment Analysis and Portfolio Management*, Fifth Edition. Homewood, Illinois: Richard D. Irwin, 1987.

Cohen, Norma. "Investors Query the Rewards of Risk." *Financial Times* (September 22, 1992).

Fabritius, M. Manfred, and William Borges. *Saving the Savings and Loan: The U.S. Thrift Industry and the Texas Experience, 1950–1988.* New York: Praeger, 1989.

Chapter 19   Buzzwords and BOMFOG

Bohle, Bruce, ed. *The Home Book of American Quotations.* New York: Dodd, Mead, 1967. Entry on page 69 on origins of "BOMFOG."

Davidson, Joe. "U.S. Plans Freeze on Medicare Payments to Hospitals Without Action by Congress." *The Wall Street Journal* (June 12, 1985).

Hull, Jennifer Bingham. "Medical Turmoil: Four Hospital Chains, Facing Lower Profits, Adopt New Strategies." *The Wall Street Journal* (October 10, 1985).

Putka, Gary. "Big Hospital Chains Continue Healthy Showing Even as Limit on Medicare Costs Appears Certain." (Heard on the Street column) *New York Times* (March 11, 1983).

Schorr, Burt. "Hospitals Scramble to Track Costs as Insurers Limit Reimbursements." *The Wall Street Journal* (December 2, 1983).

Smith, Timothy K., and Jennifer Bingham Hull. "Market Batters Hospital Industry Stocks as 2 Firms Signal Disappointing Results." *The Wall Street Journal* (October 3, 1985).

Waldholz, Michael. "Discount Medicine: To Attract Patients, Doctors and Hospitals Cut Prices to Groups." *The Wall Street Journal* (November 22, 1983).

The Wall Street Journal. (Business Bulletin column) "Hospitals Struggle as New Medicare Payment Formulas Shrink Revenues." (October 13, 1983).

The Wall Street Journal. "U.S. to Set Rates for Hospice Care below Earlier Plan." (December 15, 1983).

Welling, Kathryn M. "Negative Prognosis: Why Analyst Michael Gray Is Bearish on HMOs." *Barron's* (August 19, 1985):13 ff. Interview with O. Michael Gray.

Chapter 20   Incentive-Debased Pay

Antilla, Susan. "With No Fees, a Fund Shrinks." (Market Place column) *New York Times* (August 4, 1992).

Ricks, Thomas R. "SEC Cites Financial Planner for Failing to Disclose Conflict of Interest as Broker." *The Wall Street Journal* (May 24, 1988).

Chapter 21 All the News That's Fit—And Then Some

New York Times. "Roy Rogers Rides Again." (April 20, 1992).

Nutile, Tom. "Footwear Co. Ready for Next Step; Ryka CEO Helps Fund Market Push." *Boston Herald* (April 21, 1992).

Pensions & Investments. "And the Next Nobel Winner Is . . ." (January 21, 1991): 10.

Pensions & Investments. "Corrections & Clarifications." (February 4, 1991): 4.

Suriano, Rosanna. "Ryka Says Misquote in Boston Herald Caused Stock Price Drop." *Bloomberg Business News* (April 27, 1992).

The Wall Street Journal. "Imasco's Hardee's Unit Restores Roy Rogers Menu." (March 3, 1992).

Chapter 22 Missing Records

Barron's. "Granville's Stock Picks Missed Bull Market." (Up & Down Wall Street column) (January 12, 1981): 1.

Barron's. "Joe Granville Is Alive, Well and Is No. 1." (May 11, 1987): 13.

Brammer, Rhonda. "Fallen Prophet: 10 Years After He Peaked, Will Joe Granville Rise Again?" *Barron's* (August 24, 1992): 10 ff.

Business Week. "Book Briefs" review of *The Book of Granville: Reflections of a Stock Market Prophet*, by Joseph E. Granville. (April 15, 1985): 22.

Business Week. "Granville's Road Shows: A Broker Backlash." (January 26, 1981): 108.

Business Week. "Joe Granville's Balloon Comes Back to Earth." (February 14, 1983): 116.

Business Week. "Why Granville Can't Be Ignored." (October 12, 1981): 134.

Hulbert, Mark. "Half the Picture." (Wall Street Irregular column) *Forbes* (December 28, 1987): 140.

Katz, Donald R. "The Comeback Kid: Meet the New Joe Granville." *Ingram's* (April 1990): 21 ff.

Marcial, Gene G. "Granville Sees Pow in the Dow." *Business Week* (February 15, 1988): 91.

Newsweek. "Granville Rises Again." (May 25, 1981): 67.

Newsweek. "When Granville Speaks . . . " (January 19, 1981): 75.

Time. "Granville Stuns the Market; A 'Hole in One' for a Flamboyant Wall Street Tipster." (January 19, 1981): 68.

U.S. News & World Report. "Market Forecaster Granville: It's a Hit and Miss Business." (September 28, 1987): 84.

Wermiel, Stephen. "High Court Rules Certain Newsletters Are Exempt From Regulation by SEC." *The Wall Street Journal* (June 11, 1985): 3.

Chapter 23 Everyone's a Winner

Barron's. "*Barron's*/Lipper Gauge: Debt and Equity Funds." (February 11, 1991): 1924–1927.

Edgerton, Jerry and Prashanta Misra. "The Good, the Bad and the Mediocre." (The *Money* Rankings special section) *Money* (February 1991): 118–152.

Forbes. "Annual Fund Survey" (September 2, 1991): 157–320.

Laderman, Jeffrey M. "Steady Hands for Unsteady Times: Our Mutual Fund Scoreboard Tracks the Best Bets in a Volatile Market." *Business Week* (February 18, 1991): 76–108.

Chapter 24 Going By the Book Can Be Hazardous

Brodie, John. "Brought to Book." *The New Republic* (March 16, 1992): 19–23.

Galloway, Paul. "Researcher Finds His Findings Under Siege." *Chicago Tribune* (July 26, 1987).

Gruber, William. "O'H~re Van Service off to a Flying Start." *Chicago Tribune* (July 22, 198?). "Columnist's Credibility" brief refers to Srully Blotnick.

New York Times. "Columnist Investigated by New York Officials." (July 24, 1987).

New York Times. "Forbes Column Ended as Research Is Doubted." (July 21, 1987).

New York Times. "Secret of a Success." (August 3, 1987).

O'Higgins, Michael, with John Downes. *Beating the Dow: A High-Return, Low-Risk Method for Investing in the Dow Jones Industrial Stocks with as Little as $5,000.* New York: HarperCollins, 1991, p. 106

Rosenstiel, Thomas B. "Srully Blotnick Drops Column in Forbes Magazine; Business Psychologist's Credentials Questioned." *Los Angeles Times* (July 22, 1987).

Scherer, Ron. "Popular Forbes Columnist Departs Amid Charges of Faked Research." *Christian Science Monitor* (July 22, 1987).

Chapter 25   *The Art of Plain Talk*

Bloomberg Business News. "American Express Said to Consider Breaking Canary Wharf Lease." (May 29, 1992).

Bloomberg Business News. "London's Canary Wharf 60% Occupied, Olympia & York Says." (April 22, 1992).

Bloomberg Business News. "O&Y Canary Wharf Rental Income Less Than 10 Million Pounds a Year." (June 5, 1992).

Bloomberg Business News. "O&Y Says British Filing Won't Affect Canadian Restructuring." (May 28, 1992).

Bloomberg Business News. "O&Y's Canary Wharf Contractor Halt [sic] Work." (June 17, 1992).

Bloomberg Business News. "Olympia & York Files for Canadian Bankruptcy Protection." (May 15, 1992).

Bloomberg Business News. "Olympia & York Ratings Cut by DBRS." (February 13, 1992).

Business Wire. "O&Y Water Street Finance, O&Y Maiden Lane Finance on S&P Watch; Negative." (March 26, 1992).

Business Wire. "Sequoia Systems Announces Final 1992 Results and Expense Control Measures." (October 14, 1992).

Dow Jones News Service. "Navistar Preferred G Halted Amid Dividend Payment Concerns." (August 13, 1992).

Dow Jones News Service. "Sequoia Backs View of FY92 Revenues of $85 Million, Net $1.02-Shr." (May 1, 1992).

Dow Jones News Service. "Sequoia Says SEC Formally Probing Revenue Recognition System." (October 5, 1992).

Dow Jones News Service. "Sequoia Systems Remains Haunted by Phantom Sales." (October 30, 1992).

Dow Jones News Service. "Sequoia Systems Revises 1992 Revenue Down to $65.7 Million." (October 1, 1992).

Gallese, Liz Roman. "Sequoia Systems Stock Down 15% After Release of Results Delayed." *Bloomberg Business News* (July 30, 1992).

Economist. "The Shadow Maxwell Leaves." (November 9, 1991): 79–80.

Gilbert, Mark. "O&Y Says 'No Assurance' Canary Wharf Will Find Equity Investors." *Bloomberg Business News* (May 28, 1992).

Ipsen, Erik. "Call It Albatross Wharf." *Institutional Investor* (November 1990): 106–109.

Kohn, Ken. "Olympia & York Investors Say They're Holding onto Bonds." *Bloomberg Business News* (May 15, 1992).

Leefeldt, Ed, and David Zielengier. "Sequoia Officials Unavailable on SEC Inquiry Report." *Bloomberg Business News* (June 17, 1992).

Lyons, James. "Crusade for Candor." *Forbes* (May 25, 1992): 74.

Milligan, John W. "Blind Faith." *Institutional Investor* (September 1992): 27–33.

Moore, Timothy. "Olympia & York Sees Successful Restructuring." (May 15, 1992).

Moore, Timothy. "Olympia & York's Financial Health Intact, Spokesman Says." *Bloomberg Business News* (March 5, 1992).

New York Times. "Sequoia Stock Slides After Financing Refusal." (December 5, 1992).

Pauly, David, Ken Kohn, and Mark Gilbert. "Restructuring, the Olympia & York Way." *Bloomberg Business News* (April 16, 1992).

Pereira, Joseph. "Sequoia Again Cuts Its Work Force, Restates Results." *The Wall Street Journal* (December 14, 1992).

Pereira, Joseph. "Sequoia Chairman Resigns; Firm Sees Operating Losses." *The Wall Street Journal* (November 9, 1992).

Public Relations Newswire. "Navistar Seeks Declaration of Its Right to Change Retiree Medical Benefits." (July 28, 1992).

Salwen, Kevin G. "SEC Charges Caterpillar Failed to Warn Holders of Earnings Risk Posed by Unit." *The Wall Street Journal* (April 2, 1992).

Wells, Ken, and Tony Horwitz. "Drowning Man: Frantic Last Months Show Robert Maxwell Knew End Was Near." *The Wall Street Journal* (December 19, 1991).

Zweig, Jason, and John Chamberlain. "Windbag Theory." *Forbes* (August 3, 1992): 43–44.

Chapter 26   Is Perfection Relative?

Barrett, Paul M. "New Liability: Tobacco Industry Faces Fresh Legal Danger After Justices' Ruling." *The Wall Street Journal* (June 25, 1992): A1 ff.

Bloomberg Business News. "No Surprise Seen in Court's Split Decision on Tobacco Suits." (June 24, 1992).

Business Wire. "Philip Morris Considers Today's Supreme Court Decision as a Significant Victory." (June 24, 1992).

Carranza, Paul. "Top Court Says Tobacco Firms Can Be Sued for Conspiracy." *Bloomberg Business News* (June 24, 1992).

Crawford, William C. "Advice Every Investor Should Ignore." *New York Times* (February 10, 1991).

Crehan, Michael J., and Lisa M. Tesoriero. "S & P Affirms U.S. Tobacco Firms After Supreme Court Ruling." *Standard & Poor's Credit Wire* (June 24, 1992).

Fitch Financial Wire. "Tobacco Ratings Off FitchAlert After Supreme Court Decision." (June 24, 1992).

Keane, Simon M. "Paradox in the Current Crisis in Efficient Market Theory." *The Journal of Portfolio Management* (Winter 1991): 30–34.

Harverson, Patrick. "Salomon Blunder Fuels Trading Row." *Financial Times* (March 27, 1992).

Mankowski, Cal. "Salomon Stock Error Reopens Debate on Computer Trades." *The Reuter Business Report* (March 26, 1992).

Mitchell, Constance, and Sam Alcorn. "Bond Prices Plunge Sharply to News about Oil, the Middle East and the Budget Plan." (Credit Markets column) *The Wall Street Journal* (October 30, 1990): C17. Comment on Carter Hawley Hale Stores.

Moody's Investors Service. "Moody's Downgrades Credit Ratings of Harcourt Brace Jovanovich Inc. (Senior to Caa, Preferred to 'ca')." (January 24, 1991).

Morgan, David. "Stocks Rise Again as Fallout from Salomon Mistake Clears." *The Reuter Business Report* (March 26, 1992).

Pauly, David, with Ed Leefeldt and Paul Carranza. "Ways of Wall Street: The Cigarette Companies' Winning Hand." *Bloomberg Business News* (June 24, 1992).

Pettit, Dave. "Index Edges Up for Fifth Gain in Row, but Traders Call the Advance Spotty." (OTC Focus column) *The Wall Street Journal* (June 3, 1992): C6. Comment on Software Etc.

Pettit, Dave. "Stock Prices Finish Session Mixed Despite Negative Economic News." (Abreast of the Market column) *The Wall Street Journal* (June 25, 1992). Comment on tobacco stocks.

Power, William, and Craig Torres. "Stocks Drop as Salomon Clerk Errs; Bungle Spurs Selling, Turning Dow's Gain into 1.57-Point Loss." *The Wall Street Journal* (March 26, 1992).

Radwell, Steven. "Stocks Weaken on Economic News, Salomon Gaffe." *The Reuter Business Report* (March 27, 1992).

R.J. Reynolds Tobacco Company. Statement on Supreme Court Ruling, June 24, 1992.

Smith, Craig. "Stock Averages Set More Records Amid Massive Rotational Buying." (Abreast of the Market column) *The Wall Street Journal* (January 16, 1992): C2. Comment on Nike.

Smith, Craig. "Stocks Finish Mixed as Rate News Offsets Sizable Gain in Retail Sales." (Abreast of the Market column) *The Wall Street Journal* (March 13, 1992): C2. Comment on Schlumberger.

Smith, Craig. "Industrial Gain 12.74 to a Record, but Broader Indexes End Lower." (Abreast of the Market column) *The Wall Street Journal* (April 17, 1992): C2. Comment on Armstrong World Industries.

Smith, Craig. "Industrials Lose 17.89 as Reports on Economy Still Show Softness." (Abreast of the Market column) *The Wall Street Journal* (December 15, 1991). Comment on U.S. Bioscience.

Toh-Patin, Christina. "Salomon Bros. Embarrassed by Huge Stock Miscue." *The Reuter Business Report* (March 26, 1992).

Chapter 27   Unlovely But Not Unloved

Altman, Edward I. "Bankrupt Firms' Equity Securities as an Alternative Investment." *Financial Analysts Journal* (July/August 1969): 129–133.

Anderson, Harry B. "Long, Long Trail: Penn Central Settlement Will Take Years Even If Accord Is Reached Fairly Quickly." *The Wall Street Journal* (June 3, 1976).

Doughen, Joseph R., and Peter Binzen. *The Wreck of the Penn Central.* Boston: Little, Brown, 1971.

Eberhart, Allan C., William T. Moore, and Rodney Roenfeldt. "Security Pricing and Deviations from the Absolute Priority Rule in Bankruptcy Proceedings." *The Journal of Finance* (December 1990): 1457–1469.

Fridson, Martin S., and Michael A. Cherry. "Penn Central Transportation Rides Again." *Extra Credit: The Journal of High Yield Bond Research* (March 1991): 4–19.

Hickman, W. Braddock. *Corporate Bond Quality and Investor Experience.* Princeton: Princeton University Press, 1958.

Hickman, W. Braddock. *Statistical Measures of Corporate Bond Financing since 1900.* Princeton: Princeton University Press, 1960.

Madrick, Jeffrey. "Uncovering the Wealth at Penn Central." *Inside Wall Street* (September 6, 1976): 60.

Moody's Transportation Manual. New York: Moody's Investors Service, 1979; 322 ff.

Morse, Dale and Wayne Shaw. "Investing in Bankrupt Firms." *The Journal of Finance* (December 1988): 1193–1206.

Paul, Bill. "Supreme Court's Upholding of Rail Act Far from Solves Penn Central's Woes." *The Wall Street Journal* (December 24, 1974).

Pinkerton, W. Stewart, J. "Long Haul Ahead: Penn Central Faces Lengthy Legal Snarls Under Bankruptcy Laws." *The Wall Street Journal* (June 30, 1970).

Putnam, George, III. *The Ten Largest Bankruptcies—And Their Lessons for Investors.* Boston: New Generation Investments, 1987.

Standard & Poor's Bond Guide. New York: Standard & Poor's, 1970–1981 editions.

Vanderhoof, Irwin T. "Hickman's Other Shoe." *Extra Credit: The Journal of High Yield Bond Research* (May 1991): 7.

The Wall Street Journal. "Northeast Roads' Creditors Can Only Get Liquidation Value of Assets, Court Rules." (October 13, 1977).

The Wall Street Journal. "Penn Central Scores U.S. Take-Over Plan for Ailing Roads, Especially Valuation." (September 16, 1975).

The Wall Street Journal. "Penn Central Unit's Trustees to Sue U.S. for Line's Alleged Value Loss Since 1970." (September 17, 1975).

The Wall Street Journal. "Top Court Backs Plan to Revamp Northeast Rails." (December 17, 1974).

Warner, Jerold B. "Bankruptcy, Absolute Priority, and the Pricing of Risky Debt Claims. " *Journal of Financial Economics* 4 (1977): 239–276.

Chapter 28 Slow But Not So Steady

Donnelly, Barbara, and Robert McGough. "Sometimes Individual Bonds Are Better." (Your Money Matters column) *The Wall Street Journal* (July 7, 1992).

Fried, Carla. "How the SEC Would Make It Easier for You to Shop for Government Bond Funds." (Fund Watch column) *Money* (November 1986): 43 ff.

Gillis, John G. "The Self-Regulation Movement." (Securities Law & Regulation column) *Financial Analysts Journal* (May/June 1986): 16–18.

Weiss, Gary. "Flashy Ads Could Lead to Crackdown by SEC." *Barron's* (February 17, 1986): 60.

Yang, Catherine. "Now There's One Yardstick for Mutual Funds." (Personal Business/Smart Money column) *Business Week* (September 5, 1988): 110.

Chapter 29 Foreign Matter

Bailey, Warren, and Joseph Lim. "Evaluating the Diversification Benefits of the New Country Funds." *The Journal of Portfolio Management* (Spring 1992): 74–80.

Blake, John. "Problems in International Accounting Harmonization." *Management Accounting* (February 1990): 28 ff.

Brauchli, Marcus W. "Japan's 4 Big Securities Firms Must Pay Taxes on Compensation Given to Clients." *The Wall Street Journal* (July 8, 1991).

Chandler, Clay. "Nomura's President Resigns Amid Scandal." *The Wall Street Journal* (June 24, 1991).

Chandler, Clay. "Nomura's Two Top Officers Will Resign." *The Wall Street Journal* (July 23, 1991).

Chandler, Clay, and Masayoshi Kanabayashi. "Japan's Big Four Securities Firms Raided by Government Officials." *The Wall Street Journal* (July 19, 1991).

Chandler, Clay, and Masayoshi Kanabayashi. "Unfair Advantage: Japanese Stock Scandal Sends Strong Message: Small Investors Beware." *The Wall Street Journal* (June 25, 1991).

Chipello, Christopher J., and Masyoshi Kanabayashi. "Japanese Paper Lists Firms, Individuals as Recipients in Securities Controversy." *The Wall Street Journal* (July 29, 1991).

Choi, Frederick D.S. "Corporate Disclosure Policy in an Asymmetric World." Working paper, New York University Salomon Center, Leonard N. Stern School of Business, May 1, 1992.

Choi, Frederick D.S., and Richard M. Levich. "International Accounting Diversity: Does It Affect Market Participants?" *Financial Analysts Journal* (July/August 1991): 73–82.

Economist. "British Accounting Standards: Bean-Counters Fight Back." (December 14, 1991): 85–86.

Economist. "Japanese Financial Regulation: Who Watches the Watchdog?" (September 21, 1991): 94–96.

Foust, Dean. "The Penny-Stock Boys Are Back." *Business Week* (July 20, 1992).

Ipsen, Erik. "Eastern Bean Fields Lure Accountants." *International Herald Tribune* (June 12, 1992).

Levine, Sumner N., ed. *Global Investing: A Handbook for Sophisticated Investors.* New York: HarperBusiness, 1992, pp. 548–636.

Mitchener, Brandon. "Germany Lags on Insider Trading Curbs." *The Wall Street Journal* (August 17, 1992).

Chapter 30   Muni Madness

Asinof, Lyn, and Tom Herman. "Muni Investors Study Past Defaults to Assess the Risk in Today's Issues." (Your Money Matters column) *The Wall Street Journal* (February 7, 1991).

Barrett, William P. " 'I Guess We Look Stupid.' " *Forbes* (February 3, 1992): 64.

Charlier, Marj. "Junk Munis: Many Tax-Free Bonds Are Going Into Default in Colorado Land Bust." *The Wall Street Journal* (December 7, 1990).

Cohen, Natalie R. "Municipal Default Patterns: An Historical Study." *Public Budgeting & Finance* (Winter 1989): 55–65.

Fadem, Rod. "So You Want to Buy a Muni—Things You Should Know Before You Do." *Barron's* (March 4, 1991): 22–23.

Gottschalk, Earl C., Jr. "Smooth Operator: Small Town Treasurers Rue the Day They Met Steve Wymer." *The Wall Street Journal* (January 22, 1992).

Herman, Tom. "How to Get Best Price in Buying, Selling Municipals? Shopping Around Is a Must." (Your Money Matters column) *The Wall Street Journal* (May 8, 1992).

Hylton, Richard D. "The Coming Rebound—and Risk—in Municipal Bonds." *New York Times* (January 28, 1990). Inset: "Do Mutual Funds Really Serve as a Safety Net?"

Mitchell, Constance. "Defaults Are Seen in California; Trouble in Municipals Likely in Bonds Tied to Developments." (Credit Markets column) *The Wall Street Journal* (November 4, 1991).

New York Times. "Ex-Manager Plans a Plea." (September 2, 1992).

Chapter 31   I've Got the Horse Right Here

Banker, Lem, and Frederick C. Klein. *Sports Betting.* Toronto: Fitzhenry and Whiteside, 1986.

Bird, Ron, and Michael McCrae. "Tests of the Efficiency of Racetrack Betting Using Bookmaker Odds." *Management Science* (December 1987): 1552–1562.

Bolton, Ruth N., and Randall G. Chapman. "Searching for Positive Returns at the Track: A Multinomial Logit Model for Handicapping Horse Races." *Management Science* (August 1986): 1040–1060.

Canfield, Brian R., Bruce C. Fauman, and William T. Ziemba. "Efficient Market Adjustment of Odds Prices to Reflect Track Biases." *Management Science* (November 1987): 1428–1439.

Gabriel, Paul E., and James R. Marsden. "An Examination of Market Efficiency in British Racetrack Betting." *Journal of Political Economy* (August 1990): 874–885.

Gandar, John, Richard Zuber, Thomas O'Brien, and Ben Russo. "Testing Rationality in the Point Spread Betting Market." *Journal of Finance* (September 1988): 995–1008.

Hausch, Donald B., and William T. Ziemba. "Arbitrage Strategies for Cross-Track Betting on Major Horse Races." *Journal of Business* (January 1990): 61–78.

Lacey, Nelson J. "An Estimation of Market Efficiency in the NFL Point Spread Market." *Applied Economics* (January 1990): 117–129.

Sauer, Raymond D., Vic Brajer, Stephen P. Ferris, and M. Wayne Marr. "Hold Your Bets: Another Look at the Efficiency of the Gambling Market for National Football Games." *Journal of Political Economy* (February 1988): 206–213.

Silberstang, Edwin. *Losers, Weepers*. Garden City, New York: Doubleday, 1975.

Zuber, Richard A., John M. Gandar, and Benny D. Bowers. "Beating the Spread: Testing the Efficiency of the Gambling Market for National Football League Games." *Journal of Political Economy* (August 1985): 800–806.

Chapter 32   Begin by Collecting Your Thoughts

Belsky, Gary. "Trading Up: With 'Desert Storm' Cards Setting the Pace, Non-Sport Collectibles Are Joining Baseball in the Big Leagues." *Money* (May 1991): 156–160.

Brown, Christie. "Tides of Prints." (Personal Affairs: Collectors column) *Forbes* (February 17, 1992): 144–145.

Deutschman, Alan. "A Calculus of Collectibles." *Fortune* (1992 Investor's Guide): 115–120.

Dobrzynski, Judith. "Agony and Ecstasy in the Art Market." (The Arts Business column) *Business Week* (August 13, 1990): 110–111.

Dunn, Don. "See Those Mouse Ears? They're Worth a Mint." (The Investment Spectrum column) *Business Week* (December 30, 1991): 157.

Grimes, William. "Who Painted This Picture?" *New York Times* (August 9, 1992).

Hernandez, Carol. "Black Memorabilia Find Big Demand." (Collectibles column) *The Wall Street Journal* (August 10, 1992).

Liscio, John. "Say It Ain't So: Fraud Threatens the Baseball-Card Boom." *Barron's* (March 19, 1990): 14, 63.

Madden, Stephen. "A Rare Seminar on Collectibles." *Fortune* (1989 Investor's Guide): 67 ff.

Meier, Barry. "In Trading Cards, a New Ball Game." *New York Times* (September 19, 1992).

Moore, Lisa J. "Gems from the Disco Decade." (Money Guide special section) *U.S. News & World Report* (August 10, 1992): 55.

New York Times. "$85,000 Paid for 'Mookie Ball.' " (August 5, 1992).

New York Times. " 'I'll Swap You 2 'Hound Dogs' for . . . ': Elvis Trading Cards Fuel His Fans' 'Burning Love.' " (August 28, 1992).

New York Times. "Moet in Suit on Fake Wine." (September 1, 1992).

New Yorker. "Missing the Ball." (The Talk of the Town column) (August 24, 1992): 22–23.

Newman, Anne. "Connecticut Treats Rare Coin Portfolio as Securities, Sets Charges Against Firm." *The Wall Street Journal* (September 11, 1992).

Peers, Alexandra. "Forgeries Are Coming to Bat More Often as Sports Memorabilia Prices Hit Homer." (Your Money Matters column) *The Wall Street Journal* (August 14, 1992).

Queenan, Joe. "Other People's (Very, Very Stupid People's) Money." *Spy* (December 1991): 54–58.

Raghavan, Anita, and Michael Siconolfi. "FTC Expanding Its Investigation into Stamp Firms." *The Wall Street Journal* (June 18, 1992).

Siconolfi, Michael. "FTC Accuses Stamp Dealer of Sales Fraud." *The Wall Street Journal* (June 10, 1992).

Walley, Wayne. "National Pastime—It's in the Cards." *Advertising Age* (August 29, 1988): S10–S11.

Zipkin, Amy. "Premiums from the Past Take on Classic Quality." *Advertising Age* (May 1988): S10.

Index

Aaron, Michael, 195
Abboud, Robert, 23
Accounting, 57–58
    accrual method, 56
    foreign practices, 175–178
    rules, 175–177
    U.S. practices, 175–177
Airlines, deregulation of, 14
Alcorn, Sam, 159
Allen, Kent R., 147
Allstate Insurance Group, 40
Altman, Edward I., 164
American Association for Public Opinion, 143–144
American International Group (AIG), 40
American Medical International (AMI), 111
Annual reports, 56, 59
Antitakeover provisions, 108
Arbitrage Pricing Theory, 126
Armstrong World Industries, 160
Art market, 192–193, 195
Auditors, independent, 96
Audits, 95–101

Balis & Zorn, Inc., 58
Bankruptcy, 163–167
Barclays de Zoete Wedd, 150–151
Barksdale, Edgar W., 69–70
Barrett, Paul, 157
Barron's, 26, 35, 70, 85, 131, 135, 139, 171
    top 10 mutual funds, 1991, 136t
    how competing surveys rank, 140t
Basic value investing, 33
Beating the Dow: A High-Return, Low-Risk Method for Investing in the Dow Jones Industrial Stocks with as Little as $5,000, 144–145
Berner, Roland, 21
A.M. Best, 72
Betting, 44–48
    horse, 188
    NFL, 186–188
    sports, 185–186

Big Blue. *See* International Business Machines
Bloomberg Business News, 126, 158
Blotnick, Srully, 142–144
Boiler rooms, 85–89
    getting started, 86
    landing on your feet, 89
    marketing techniques
        advanced, 87–88
        basic, 86–87
    public relations, 88–89
BOMFOG, 107, 109, 111
Bond funds, 170, 172
    general corporate, indicated and actual yields, 170, 171t
Bond ratings, 71–78, 172
Bond returns, 172–173
Bond salesmen, 168–173
Bondholders, 169
Bonds, 173
    confederate, 5
    corporate, 112
    municipal, 180–184
    U.S. Treasury, shorting, 38–39
    zero-coupon, 173
Boston Herald, 126
Bower, Tom, 150
Breo, Dennis, 45
Bribery, 114
Britt Airways, 17
Brodie, John, 145
Buchalter, Irwin, 21
Bucket shops, 85, 89
Buckner, Bill, 190–191
Burr, Donald, 14–17
Business Week, 99, 131, 134–135, 139, 170
    mutual fund ratings five-year risk-adjusted total returns vs. S&P's 500, 1991, 137t
    ranking of *Barron's* top 10 mutual funds, 1991, 140t
Buzzwords, 107–111

Note: Page numbers followed by t indicate tables.

Cabletron Systems, 165
California Municipal Treasurers
    Association, 183
Calmar Inc., 71–72
Campbell Soup, 21
Cards, 192–193
Carter Hawley Hale Stores, 159
Cascade International, 98–101
Cassini, Oleg, 99
Catchphrases, 107
Caterpillar, 151–152
CGMA Capital Development, 136t–137t,
    140t
Chambers Development, 96–98
Chandelier bidding, 192
*Chaos and Order in the Financial Markets: A
    New View of Cycles, Prices, and
    Market Volatility*, 28
Chaos theory, 27–28
Chartists, 26–31
Cheap-because-shunned thesis, 165, 167
Chief executive officers (CEOs),
    dislodgment and death of, 19–25
Choi, Frederick D. S., 176, 178
Churning, 113
Citicorp, 6, 57, 59
Clearly Canadian Beverage Corp., 35
Closet indexers, 116
Cohen, Jerome B., 27
Cohen, Natalie R., 181
Collectibles, 190–195
    cards, 192–193
    dolls, 193
    fine art, 192–193
    memorabilia, 192–193
    movie posters, 193
    platform shoes, 193
    postage stamps, 192
    slavery-related items, 194
    Turkoman camel trappings, 193
Commodity Futures Trading
    Commission, 86
Common stock(s), 34, 53
Communications, corporate, 148
Community Psychiatric Centers, 56, 58–59
Company management, 147–154
Compensation systems
    commissions, 113
    for financial advisers, 112–119
    flat-percentage arrangement, 114
    salary plus subjective bonus, 113
Concept stocks, 14, 18
Confederate bonds, 5
Conflicts of interest, 114–115
Conrail, 166
Consumer protection, 70

Continental Airlines, 17
Continental Corp., 40
Contracts, 169
Contractual income, 169
Contrarians, 3–7, 163
Corbett, Carmen, 152
Corporate bond funds, general, indicated
    and actual yields, 170, 171t
Corporate bonds, 112
Corporate communications, 148
*The Corporate Steeplechase: Predictable
    Crises in a Business Career*, 142–143
Cotting, James C., 152
Curtiss-Wright, 21
Custer, Robert, 44–45

Defaulted securities, 167
Deitch, Jeffrey, 195
Dell Computer Corp., 35
Deregulation, of U.S. airlines, 14
Digital Equipment Corp. (DEC), 19–20
Dominion Bond Rating Service, 149
Dorrance, John, 21
Douglas, William O., 166
Dow Jones Industrial Average, 129, 132,
    161
Dow Theory, 31
*Dow Theory Redux: The Classic Investment
    Theory Revised & Updated for the
    1990's*, 29–30
Duff & Phelps, 72
Dunn, Henry W., 93
DWG Corp., 24–25
Dycom Industries, 41–42

Earl Scheib Inc., 20–21
Earnings estimates, quarterly figures, 53
Earnings forecasts, short-run changes in,
    51–54
Earnings releases, 124
Eastman Kodak, 51
Eberhart, Allan, 164
Economic indicators, 79
Economist, 149, 176–177
E.J. Korvette, 145
Elcor, 41
Energy-related revenues, 107–108
Enhance Reinsurance Co., 181
Evans, Joshua Leland, 191
Evans Industries, 24
Extraordinary items, 176

Facts on File, 144
Fair price amendments, 108
Fashion Bug, 99
Fat tails problem, 27

Index

Federal Savings and Loan Insurance
    Corporation, 103
Federal securities regulations, 128
Federal Trade Commission (FTC), 192
Feigin, Philip A., 174
Fidelity Destiny, 136t–137t, 140t
Fidelity Magellan, 136t–137t, 140t
Financial Accounting Standards Board,
    55, 176
Financial advisers. *See also* investment
    advisers; money managers
    compensation systems for, 112–119
Financial Analysts Journal, 144
Financial investigations, 178
Financial journalists, 123–127
Financial News Network Inc., 35
*Financial Statement Analysis: A
    Practitioner's Guide*, 58
Financial statements, 13, 55–59
    certifying, 96
    independent validations of, 95–101
    quarterly, 96
Fine art, 192–193
Finkelstein, Edward, 20
First Financial Management, 96
Fitch Investors Service, 40, 72, 158
Fixed income, 168–169, 172–173
Fixed-income departments, 169
Fixed-income investments, 168
Florida
    Dade County, 42–43
    Hurricane Andrew, 38–43
    South, rebuilding of, 38–39
Florida Department of Insurance, 40
Forbes, 93, 129, 134–137, 139, 143–144
    ranking of *Barron's* top 10 mutual
        funds, 1991, 140t
Forecasting
    earnings, short-run changes in,
        51–54
    economic, 79–81
    GNP, 81
    methods of, 60–64
    models, 60–64
    single-point, 63
    value of, 63
Foreign markets, 174–179
Frontier Airlines, 16–17
Fundamental analysis, 55–56, 58
Fusco, Gabriel P., 147–148

Gabelli, Mario, 21
Gambling, 44–48. *See also* betting
Gaming the index, 116
Garber, Peter M., 4
General Cinema, 159

General corporate bond funds, indicated
    and actual yields, 170, 171t
Germany, accounting practices, 176–177
Getty Oil, 73
Glamour stocks, 194
Global investing, 174–179
*Global Investing: A Handbook for
    Sophisticated Investors*, 177
Gold, 194
Goldman Sachs, 160
Graham, Michael, 158
Grant Thornton, 97
Granville, Joseph E., 130–133
Granville Market Letter, 131–132
Great Britain, accounting practices,
    176–177
Green, William L., 69–70
Gross domestic product (GDP), 79, 81
Gross national product (GNP), 80
    forecasting, 81
    real, 79
Gulf Coast, 38
Gutek, Barbara, 143

Hammer, Armand, 22–23
Hampshire Homes, 43
Harcourt Brace Jovanovich, 159
Hardee's Food Systems Inc., 123
Harvard Business School, 15
    stock market games, 32–33
Hewlett-Packard Company, 147
Hickman, W. Braddock, 164
Holiday Inn, 17
Hospital Corp. of America (HCA),
    111
Hot hands, 68–70
Housing stock, turnover in, 62
How to Launder Money, 183
Hulbert, Mark, 93, 129
Hulbert Financial Digest, 93, 131–132
Hunter, J. Robert, 40
Hurricane Andrew, 38–40, 42–43
    related earnings impact of, 41
Hurricane Iniki, 40

Iacocca, Lee, 147
Incendy, Victor, 98–100
Independent auditors, 96
Industry statesmanship, 108
Ingram's, 132
*Innumeracy: Mathematical Illiteracy and Its
    Consequences*, 91
Institutional Brokers Estimate System
    (IBES), 51
Institutional investors, 47
Institutional Investor, 32

International Business Machines (IBM), 51–53
International diversification, 174–179
  basic rationale for, 179
Interstate Stores, 163, 165
Investment advisers, 128. *See also* money managers
Investment Advisers Act of 1940, 129–130, 133
Investment Analysis and Portfolio Management, 27
Iraq, takeover of Kuwait, 1990, 81

Jamieson, Connie, 183
Japan, accounting practices, 175–176
Japan Fund, 136t–137t, 139, 140t
Journal of the American Medical Association, 45
The Journal of Finance, 141
Journal of Financial and Quantitative Analysis, 141
Journalists, 123–127

Karp, Aaron, 100
Keating, Charles, 102
Kloppenburg, Janet Joseph, 160
Kuwait
  Iraqi takeover, 1990, 81
  rebuilding of, 37

Labor unions, 15–17
Lemaire, Jean, 69
Lennar, 42–43
Lesieur, Henry R., 45
Letter-writing scam, 90–91
Leveraged buyouts (LBOs), 20, 106
Levich, Richard M., 176, 178
Levine, Sumner N., 177
Levy, Bernard H., 98–100
Lincoln Savings, 102
Lindner Dividend, 136t–137t, 140t
Lockheed, 51
Lynch, Jones & Ryan, 51

R.H. Macy, 20
Macy's, 20
Magazine surveys. *See also specific publication*
  of mutual funds, 134–140, 136t–137t, 140t
Mamis, Justin, 31
Management Co. Entertainment Group, 35
Market efficiency, 157–162, 186
Market timing, 90–94
Maxwell Communication Corp., 150–151

Maxwell, Kevin, 150
Maxwell, Robert, 149–151
May Department Stores, 159
McDonald's, 17, 144
McDonnell Douglas, 9–10
McNall, Bruce, 190
Medicare, 110
Memorabilia, 192–193
Mental health care providers, 55
Merrill Pacific, 136t–137t, 140t
Miami Review, 98
Michaels Stores, 35
Miller, Leonard, 42
Miller, Richard, 24
Mirror Group Newspapers, 149–150
Mitchell, Constance, 159
Mitchell, Hutchins Inc., 32–33
Molybdenum, 108
Money, 134–135, 139
  ranking of *Barron's* top 10 mutual funds, 1991, 140t
  top 10 mutual funds five-year risk-adjusted returns, 1991, 137t
Money managers, 115–119
  compensation systems for, 114–115, 119
Moody's Investors Service, 40, 71–77, 159, 172
Mookie Ball, 190
Moore, William T., 164
Morse, Dale, 164
Mortgage-backed securities, 168
  value of, 61–62
Mortgage prepayment rates, underestimation of, 61–62
Motor Club of America (MCA), 41
Motor Club of America (MCA) Insurance, 41
Municipal bonds, 180–184
Municipal defaults, 181
Murdock, David, 22
Mutual funds, 65–66
  alternative measures of return for, 137–139, 138t
  Barron's top 10, 1991, 136t
  how competing surveys rank, 140t
  comparison of risk-adjusted return ratings, 1991, 137t
  objective rankings of, 134–140

Nader, Ralph, 40
National Association of Securities Dealers, 189
National Football League (NFL) betting, 186–188
National Insurance Consumer Organization, 40

Index

Natural disasters, 37–43
Navistar International, 152–153
The New Republic, 145
Newsletters, 26, 28–30, 128, 133
  writers of, 128–133
Newsweek, 131
New York Central, 165–166
New York Daily News, 143
The New York Institute of Finance, 31
New York Mercantile Exchange, 38
New York Society of Security Analysts, 23
New York Stock Exchange (NYSE), 111,
  132, 152
New York Stock Exchange Index, 165
New York Times, 123, 143
Niagara Mohawk Power Corporation, 145
Nike, 160
Nixon, Richard, 22
Noise (statistical), 53

Occidental Petroleum, 22–23
Olsen, Kenneth H., 19–20
Olympia & York Development (O&Y),
  148–149
Oppenheimer Target, 136t–137t, 140t
Options, 46–47
Orion Pictures, 57–59
*Otherwise Engaged: The Private Lives of
  Successful Career Women*, 143
Overpriced Stock Service, 98, 100
Overreaction thesis, 5–6

Painting the tape, 192
Panic of 1837, 181
A Passion for Excellence, 15
Patton, James, 97
Paulos, John Allen, 91
Pendulum metaphor, 5
Penn Central Transportation Company
  (PCTC), 165–166
Penny stocks, 87, 193
Pennzoil, 73
Pension plan sponsors, 117
Pensions & Investments, 125–126
People Express, 14–18
Persian Gulf War, 37, 193
Peters, Edgar F., 28
Peters, Tom, 15
Philip Morris Companies, 158
Phoenix, 136t–137t, 140t
Poe-Brieske, Sheri, 126
Poland, accounting practices, 178
Poppe, David, 98
Porter, Linsey, 147
Posner, Victor, 24–25
Postage stamps, 192

Pot-Shot Productions, 193
Prechter, Robert, 129
Preferred stocks, 169
Probability, basic laws of, 65–70
Progressive Corp., 17
Promoters, 105–106
Property and casualty (P&C) insurers, 39
Provincetown-Boston Airlines, 17
Prudential Insurance Co. of America, 40
Public Securities Association, 183
Publication standards, 141–146

Quality control, 144
Quarterly earnings figures, 53
Quarterly financial statements, 96
Quest for Value, 136t–137t, 140t

Random walk hypothesis, 27–28
RCB International, 69
Redden, David, 195
Reed, John S., 6
Regulations
  federal securities, 128
  SEC, 9, 129, 170
Reichmann, Paul, 148
Resistance, 28
Reverse stock splits, 87
Rich, Marc, 113
Richman, Arthur, 191
Risk sharing
  inequitable, 105
  unequal, 105
Risk transfer, involuntary, 102–106
R.J. Reynolds Tobacco Company, 158
RJR Nabisco, 157–159
Robertson Stephens & Co., 160
Rockefeller, Nelson, 107
Roenfeldt, Rodney, 164
Rogers, Roy, 123
Ross, Stephen A., 125–126
Ross, Steven, 125
Rothschild, Nathan, 164
Rule of 72, 173
Ryka Inc., 126

Salomon Brothers, 161
Savings and loan (S&L) crisis, 102–106
Scams
  boiler rooms and bucket shops, 85–89
  letter-writing, 90–91
Scheib, Donald R., 21
Scheib, Earl, 20–21
Schlumberger, 160
Score Board, 35
Scudder, Stevens & Clark, 93
Sears, Roebuck & Co., 40

Securities analysts, 8–12
    function of, 8
Securities and Exchange Commission
    (SEC), 24, 55, 58, 87, 98, 151–152, 183
    regulations, 9, 129, 170
Sequoia Fund, 136t–137t, 140t
Sequoia Systems Inc., 147–148
Service Merchandise, 17
Shareholder rights, 108
Sharon Steel, 24
Shaw, Wayne, 164
Shearson Lehman Brothers, 160
Sheen, Charlie, 190–191
Sheimo, Michael D., 29–30
Sherry-Lehmann, 195
Singer, Eleanor, 143–144
Smith Barney Harris Upham, 160
Software Etc., 160
Software Toolworks, 35
Sotheby's, 195
Soviet Union, accounting rules, 177
Special Situations Report, 35
Speculation, 44–48
Sports betting, 185–186
Sports memorabilia, 192
Standard Periodical Directory 1991, 51
Standard & Poor's (S&P), 40, 59, 71–77,
    80, 116, 158–159, 172
Stealth bomber, 9
Steinberg, Jonathan, 35–36
Stock market contests, 32–36
Stock tips, 185–189
Stocks
    common, 34, 53
    concept, 14, 18
    glamour, 194
    penny, 87, 193
    preferred, 169
    reverse splits, 87
Sturgess, Brian, 150–151
Sweden, accounting practices, 175–176
Switzerland, accounting practices,
    176–177

Tax savings, 180–184
Technical analysts, 26–31
Terminology, 107–111
Tesoriero, Lisa, 158
Texaco, 73, 77
Texas Air, 17–18

Texas International, 14
Thalhimers chain, 159
Thomson McKinnon Securities, 99
Time, 131–132, 145
Tinker, John, 58
Toys 'R' Us, 163, 165
Trading rules, 141–142
Trian Group L.P., 25
Tulipmania, 3–4
Tversky, Amos, 68

UBS Phillips & Drew, 177
Uddeholm AB, 175–176
Undervalued, definition of, 12
Union Carbide, 109
United Airlines, 17
United States accounting practices,
    175–177
United States Defense Department, 9–10
United States economy, predicting, 79–81
United States Railway Association, 166
United States savings rate, 61
United States Supreme Court, 129, 132,
    157–159, 161, 164, 166
United States Treasury bills, 34
United States Treasury bonds, shorting,
    38–39
United States Treasury yields, 10-year, 62
U.S. News & World Report, 132

Vanderhoof, Irwin T., 164
Viking Penguin, 144

The Wall Street Journal, 5–6, 19, 57–58, 81,
    97, 110–111, 123, 129, 157–160, 166
    Investment Dartboard, 34–35
Wang, An, 23–24
Wang, Frederick, 24
Wang Laboratories, 23–24
Warner, Jerold, 164
Wermail, Stephen, 129
Who Put the Mania in Tulipmania?, 4
Wilson, Mookie, 190–191
Wymer, Steven D., 182–183

Xerox, 51

Zeikel, Arthur, 27
Zero-coupon bonds, 173
Zinbarg, Edward D., 27